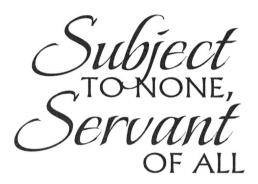

Subject TO NONE, Servant OF ALL

Essays in Christian Scholarship in Honor of Kurt Karl Hendel

Peter Vethanayagamony
and Kenneth Sawyer, editors

D1522271

Lutheran University Press
Minneapolis, Minnesota

Subject to None, Servant of All
Essays in Christian Scholarship in Honor of Kurt Karl Hendel

Peter Vethanayagamony and Kenneth Sawyer, editors

The chapter, "Theology of the Cross" by Kurt K. Hendel, is reprinted from *Currents in Theology and Mission* 24 no 3 (June 1997): 223-231.

ISBN 978-1-942304-15-9

Lutheran University Press, PO Box 390759, Minneapolis, MN 55439
www.lutheranupress.org
Manufactured in the United States of America

Table of Contents

Section Three: Concluding Essays

Dr. Kurt Karl Hendel

Introduction

Peter Vethanayagamony and Kenneth Sawyer

It is a true privilege to introduce this *Festschrift* in honor of our colleague Kurt Karl Hendel. While it is a commonplace, especially within seminary communities, to praise the ideal of the scholar–pastor, rarely has this ideal been embodied in such winning and winsome ways as in the life and work of Kurt Hendel. We have taken the title from Luther's *Von der Freiheit eines Christenmenschen* (1520), in which Luther summarizes the paradox of Christian freedom, noting a Christian is free and "subject to none," but that a Christian is also the dutiful servant, "subject to all." Kurt has shown his freedom and his service as a friend, a professor, a trusted mentor, a doctor father, a colleague, a churchman, a pastor, a husband, a father and grandfather, a respected scholar of the broad Reformation traditions, but especially of the life and times of Martin Luther and of the remarkable circle called to that mighty work. As a masterful teacher, Kurt has offered over thirty years of scholarly leadership at the Lutheran School of Theology at Chicago (LSTC) and ten prior years in service to the faithful community of Christ Seminary–Seminex, all while being closely attentive to the needs of parish and family. Kurt is an example to us all as he teaches by precept and example, by his quiet but joyful way of telling the story, by his dogged attention to detail, by his gentle and occasional satire, and by his earnest admonition and glad praise. This volume is a testament of thanks to and for a gifted teacher who has dedicated his life to the ongoing reformation of God's people through the power of the gospel.

Kurt has devoted himself to the service of God's "dear people," wherever they are to be found. As a child of the church and as one called to serve the church as a pastor and as a teacher, Kurt has lived in the parish and in close attention to the needs of congregations. In congregations Kurt encourages a bold scriptural life of biblical, sacramental, confessional, and historical literacy. With the church, Kurt teaches the deep promises of baptism which take a lifetime to understand and which are never completely fathomed by any Christian. With the church, Kurt recognizes Christ in the sacrament of the Eucharist where bread and wine truly bear divinity. With the church, Kurt confesses the freeing power of the God's gift in Christ—not based on our merit or standing or office, but on God's loving and gracious provision. This centering gospel truth has enabled Kurt to experience the liberties of Scripture study, the critical engagement with tradition, the freedom to recognize God's new work in the church, and the resulting freedom to resist false accusation, even in times of division.

Kurt has been attentive to the need to connect seminaries with congregations and with the broader world. He is a popular and admired teacher in continuing education programs throughout and beyond Chicago-area congregations, crossing confessional lines to connect a too-often fragmented church scene. He is known for the insights he brings to travel seminars to Lutherland and beyond. As a trusted colleague in the network of Lutheran seminaries and within the consortium of local seminaries, Kurt is respected and sought after because he brings his own hard-won wisdom to the service of current challenges. Kurt rolls up his sleeves to get to work, not to show the scars of past battles or the heightened privilege of exilic identity.

Throughout his scholarly career Kurt has also borne administrative duties, and he has done so with generosity, poise, and grace. In his written work he offers testimony to the examples of grace and courage he learned from his own seminary teachers and administrators in the 1960s and early 1970s. Now his students offer their own stories of his faithfulness, his gracious ways, and his courage. His life illustrates the quiet truth that grace can be found in the faithful enacting of policies and programs, ever open to sound reason, best practices, and especially to scriptural warrant. As an academic administrator, Kurt has shown both humane care and gospel charism.

But it is in the seminary classroom that he is best known, and it is from the classroom that his work will continue into future generations. For over forty years he has welcomed students into the robust and demanding discipleship of the seminary classroom. Of course the seminary classroom is a peculiar and particular space, neither church nor public square, neither family room nor private garret. Kurt has lived out his vocation in this peculiar and particular space, bringing generations of students to a deeper engagement with the living Word through the historical process of document, narrative, and testimony. Kurt's classroom is a welcoming place and a brave place where hard truths and tender mercies meet in the retelling of the old, old story of God's ways with crooked humanity. Kurt is an exacting scholar with a righteous impatience with all things inaccurate and imprecise. His students, and the church, and all of us, are the beneficiaries of this impatience. Anyone called to be an historian of the church must bear this blessed impatience.

It is fitting that this *Festschrift* be presented to Kurt on the eve of the 500th year since the academic quarrels which inaugurated a new stage of Reformation. Luther's insight into the gospel prompted an escalating quarrel with his Wittenberg colleagues and with the broader church he sought to render more faithful. Having come to know God's grace, Luther was intolerant of any church system or tradition or practice which hid or denied the grace God offers to all. Luther was unable to bend or dissemble or run when he was ordered to deny faith in this gracious God. The recovery of God's grace rendered Luther a foe of anyone or any tradition which might diminish or dilute or deny that grace. What happened in Wittenberg in 1517 was the culmination of years of yearning and preparation, of course, but Martin Luther is key to the changes by which what could have been just another local or passing reform instead became a movement which has changed the world. Kurt is a master in telling this story, and all who have traveled with him in these years have heard his masterful telling of this story of God's provision, God's Word proclaimed, and the Reformation which resulted from that proclaimed word.

Kurt is no stranger to conflict. His professorial life unfolded within a particularly startling and important chapter in American religious history. After graduating from Concordia Seminary, St. Louis, and beginning his doctoral work at Ohio State University, Kurt was asked to return to Concordia Seminary to teach. With his family he arrived on campus in the summer of 1973, and, as the school year proceeded, the continuing conflict within the Lutheran Church–Missouri Synod grew to crisis, culminating in a student-led moratorium and a board directive for the faculty to resume teaching. Kurt continues to be clear that his decisions and the decisions of his colleagues in those days were not perfect, but they were expressions of the freeing power of the gospel. These were, certainly, difficult days of costly discipleship, but also heady days of freedom. Kurt's career and his life display that costly discipleship. We are in his debt. We offer this volume as a small way of our thanks for God's grace in the continuing work and life of Kurt Karl Hendel.

Summary of the Volume

These essays were selected from among many offered by Kurt's students, friends, and colleagues. As arranged, the essays fall into three groups. Following this introduction and a brief biography of Kurt by his gracious spouse, Jobey Hendel, Section One offers five appreciative and personal essays presenting Kurt's ways as a mentor and teacher and pastor, whether in the classroom, in the parish, or while on a distant travel seminar in difficult times. Section Two gathers scholarly offerings spanning the history of Christianity, with each relating to broadly Lutheran themes. Section Three offers a reminder of the tasks to which Kurt was called as a church historian, a bibliography of Kurt's work, and an excellent sample of Kurt's life in scholarship as trustworthy guide to the life and work of Luther.

Chapter One, by Jobey Hendel, gives a brief but succinct biographical account of Kurt Hendel. Having lost his father even before his birth, Kurt was raised by his mother. His immigration to the United States at the tender age of twelve gave him the privilege of attending church school, and this facilitated his call to ministry. He began his teaching career at Concordia Seminary during the crucial 1973-74 academic year. Jobey Hendel sketches the broad outlines of a pastor–scholar serving in difficult days. This faith experiment has several key themes that have lasted for more than four decades. Kurt has remained a faithful expositor of the theology of Luther. And as an expression of his interest in Luther's circle of pastor theologians, Kurt has continued to study the life and work of Johannes Bugenhagen from his student days to the present. And Kurt has remained a lively and engaged scholar who loves the give-and-take of teaching.

Summary of Chapters

Section One: Personal Tributes

Chapter Two by Robert Shaner gives another account of the formation, preparation, participation, and fruition of the life of Kurt Hendel. Shaner argues that the formation of Kurt may not have happened the way it did had he not left his homeland. As it is customary in the Lutheran

Church–Missouri Synod, his preparation for ministry took place at Concordia Senior College, culminating in Concordia Seminary. His Fulbright year in Göttingen to do additional post-doctoral work further fortified his engagement with the works of Johannes Bugenhagen. Shaner notes that the defining moment in Hendel's professorial life came when he decided to join in the walkout of students and faculty at Concordia Seminary without security or a predictable future, but with the courage of his convictions and a firm belief in the centrality of the gospel. It is this kind of courage and commitment for Christ and the church that earned him the trust of students and colleagues, culminating in the honor of being named the Bernard, Fischer, Westberg Distinguished Ministry Professor of Reformation History, a position he has held till his retirement. Besides being a robust scholar and professor of church history, he always kept a central relationship with congregational ministries. Shaner argues this parish-shaped character is the best way of understanding Kurt Hendel. In this, he shows himself to be a true Lutheran pastor.

In the third chapter, Lu Bettisch pens a letter to Hendel expressing her gratitude to him for his guidance, compassion, and persuasive role in encouraging her to consider that God might be calling her to ordained pastoral ministry. As a woman coming from a conservative Lutheran tradition, Bettisch had never considered ordination as an option. Hendel's encouragement for her to begin to read the Bible differently changed her life, as it freed her to hear God's call and then to follow God's call. As she humorously ruminates, seminary didn't seem to be very relevant when it came to the daily challenges of pastoral life until she recalled Hendel's words of assurance of God's grace even when we think we do not deserve it.

In the fourth chapter, reflecting on Kurt Hendel's passionate, insightful, and occasionally tangential pedagogical style, Jonathan Wilson offers commendation and appreciation for Hendel's support throughout his studies at LSTC. Wilson notes that he is just one in a long line of people who benefited from Dr. Hendel's "hawk-like" support and inclusion as part of the "dear people." This reflection will remind anyone who has been Hendel's student and will serve as a window into his classroom for anyone who was not fortunate enough to learn from him in person.

The fifth chapter presents a personal reminiscence of an amazing travel seminar Kurt Hendel led through Lutherland in September 2001. Ruben Dominguez, one of the participants in the seminar, recalls that the trip turned out to be an unforgettable event because of the terrorist attacks of September 11. Besides the standard Luther sites, places related to the broader Lutheran heritage like the Halle Orphanage were crucial reminders of the rich and continuing legacy of German Lutheranism, now a global presence. The author reminds us about Francisco de Enci-nas, a Spanish reform-minded leader who sought the help and advice of Martin Luther.

In Chapter Six, Carrie L. Lewis La Plante, eliciting the famous phrase of Kurt Hendel, "dear people," reiterates the importance of including children and youth in worship and preaching. Evoking Hendel's sharing of a personal story, the author argues that "dear people" must be under-stood to include everyone, and that all, including children, are invited to worship together. La Plante notes that God often uses children to remind adults of the central teachings of the faith. Having been impacted by this thought of her teacher Kurt Hendel throughout her seminary days and later in ministry, La Plante now strives to include children and youth into the weekly worship life of the congregations, including sermons. The au-thor then outlines some of the ways in which inviting, connecting, and engaging children and youth have helped to include all of God's "dear people" in the peaching act.

Section Two: Engaging the Christian Tradition

Moving on to Section Two of the volume, in Chapter Seven, Dean M. Apel plumbs the depths of Luther's theology of marriage and fami-ly, suggesting that the ethical stance he took arose from a very specific historical context. Utilizing the works of several Lutheran scholars, both historical and contemporary, Apel examines Luther's ethics on marriage and relationships, focusing especially on how they relate to the rest of Luther's theological and ethical schema in macro, noting how the con-textual reality in which Luther lived inspired his reforms. Of particular interest is the idea that Luther brought the spiritual ideas of monasti-cism into the everyday lives of believers (and non-believers, too). For Luther, Christianity must also be considered an institution as well as a faith and a way of life: Everything for Luther, then, was directly under the control of God, who laid down secular law so that even non-believers could (or were obligated to) care for one another. Apel concludes his es-say by engaging several contemporary feminist scholars.

In Chapter Eight, Mark P. Bangert, one of Kurt's professors, discuss-es the changing role and identity of the church musician. He notes that different titles used for the church musicians indicate there is no single model prevalent in contemporary congregations. Bangert argues that leaders of church singing, commonly known in Lutheran circles as cantors, do not receive any of the forms of recognition they deserve. He argues that "one place to begin the process of rehabilitation is the proposed title of deacon." Bangert adds that "to see the benefits of re-thinking the church musical vocation as diaconal ministry it is necessary to clear a path back to the emergence of that ministry in the church." In surveying the role of music in the church, Bangert joins Kurt Hendel in praise of Johannes Bugenhagen's close attention to the role of music to provide excitement, cheer, joy, and delight in the lives of students.

In Chapter Nine, Ken Sawyer narrates the checkered career of Jerome Bolsec, whose biography of Calvin set the tone for much subsequent anti-Calvin rhetoric. Sawyer argues that the heated theological disagreements Bolsec had with Genevan reformers led to his profoundly negative portrait of Calvin, and that his *streitschrift* on Calvin was written to counter the unrelentingly positive portrayal by Theodore Beza. Drawing upon his direct experiences with Calvin, sources from Beza and others, as well as his own imaginings, Bolsec offered a portrait of Calvin as the "ambitious, cruel, arrogant, and vindictive chief of sinners." In addition, Bolsec also attempted to "destroy Beza's reputation and his (Beza's) authority as Calvin's interpreter, to present a counter narrative *streitschrift*, and to defend Bolsec's own reputation and theological views." Sawyer traces how the conflict between Bolsec and the Geneva reformers began in disagreement, moved through denunciation, and culminated in defamatory biography.

In Chapter Ten, David D. Daniels points out while the discipline of Renaissance studies had taken up the study of Africans in sixteenth-century Europe, Reformation studies has not yet taken up the study of Afro-Europeans and African Christians living in Europe. His essay considers some possible consequences of including the study of people of African descent to widen the scope of the study of the Reformation. He challenges the dominant historiography of the Reformations as the study of white Europeans while being silent on the presence and activities African Christians in Europe. He takes up the study of the life of Father Vicente Lusitano, an Afro-Portuguese Catholic priest who lived in Europe and converted to Protestantism. Lusitano presents an excellent opportunity to explore the presence of Africans in Europe and to explore the Reformations as an expression of World Christianity. He notes the sixteenth-century reception of Lusitano and other Afro-European and African Christians differs markedly from later constructs of "race."

In Chapter Eleven, Elizabeth L. Hiller bemoans the lack of biblical and theological literacy among contemporary Lutherans. Upon discovering a set of church council minutes among her grandmother's belongings, Hiller examines the ways in which untrained Norwegian, Swedish, and German immigrants pursued complex and sophisticated theological issues. Hiller's examination of these church minutes from the late 1800s, regarding a discussion on predestination, got her to thinking with dismay about how comparatively little contemporary Lutherans know about their own faith. The people of her grandmother's church were not trained, but they were baptized and were good theologians. They were not shy about speaking up about their faith. Consequently, Hiller suggests the need for reform among Lutheran congregations. Seldom, she says, do Lutherans speak out and proclaim the gospel boldly; it is time, she reasons, that Lutherans not only educate themselves about their traditions and faith but also learn to articulate not only what *church* does for them—or does for the good of the world—but also what God has done for them through Jesus Christ.

In Chapter Twelve, Keith Killinger provides a lively review of Luther's contributions to the debate about the nature of the Lord's Supper. The first half addresses specifically what Luther and his contemporaries considered a perversion of Jesus' Last Supper—the Roman Catholic theology surrounding Communion. Killinger details the ways Luther viewed adoration of the Eucharist in the Roman Catholic tradition and how the Catholic Mass had grown up around it. He also points out that Luther hearkened back to Scripture and claimed that Jesus' words to his disciples were immediate, as actions to be carried out in a particular place and time. After tracing the history of the Lord's Supper as it developed in the sixteenth century, Killenger, challenges Lutherans today to take a hard look at some of the modifications the modern-day church has made. Finally, Killenger points out the central truth: that for all of the church's goodwill, it is not the *church's* supper, nor should it be modified accordingly.

In Chapter Thirteen, Andrew F. Weisner examines the life and contributions of John Gerhard, the third in a trio of Lutheran theologians prominently engaged in Lutheran–Roman Catholic polemics during the first century after the Reformation. Weisner's essay presents Gerhard's formation and emergence as a prominent Lutheran theologian. A prolific writer and theologian, Gerhard devoted himself wholeheartedly to his work, sometimes at the expense of his health. He contributed heavily to political and state functions in advisory roles while also participating in convocations during theological disputes. Weisner's essay presents Gerhard's significant contributions and allows a renewed appreciation.

In Chapter Fourteen, Jonathan Wilson examines the career of Friedrich V. Melsheimer, a chaplain serving in a German auxiliary regiment aiding the royalists in the American Revolutionary War. He remained compliant even after his conscience troubled him concerning the gap between the commands of Jesus and the demands of military life. When his regiment was defeated he wanted to resign his call as a chaplain and join the Lutheran rostered ministry. Because his regiment considered him a deserter, it would not officially release him, and this became an impediment for his acceptance into the Pennsylvania Ministerium. Wilson recounts the complex circumstances that led to Melsheimer's decision to leave the regiment and the challenges he faced to be accepted into the Lutheran ministry. Wilson traces Lutheran intentions to be neutral in the Revolutionary War and the ways those intentions impeded Melsheimer at every turn.

In Chapter Fifteen, James A. Scherer invokes Bugenhagen as an exception to the noisy clamor of much of sixteenth-century Reformation polemics. Bugenhagen presented a friendlier face of Lutheranism with an emphasis on wholistic ministry with music, liturgy, and sound catechesis incorporated into worship. That tradition was continued and broadened in subsequent centuries in missions, voluntary societies, service groups, and rescue missions. Scherer argues the finest Lutheran hour came only in these later centuries and is illustrated in the inspirational but less well-known efforts of sacrifice and generosity by Lutherans during and after World War I when missions groups cooperated to continue the work of "Orphaned Missions."

In Chapter Sixteen, in appreciation of the spirit of the work of Kurt Hendel, colleague historian Mark Swanson approaches the paradox of incarnational theological language: the ways by which Christians have, throughout the centuries, made sense of the divine taking flesh in the person of Jesus. Of particular interest to Swanson is the language which Luther and later reformers used to frame the Incarnation and its implications. Throughout the essay Swanson arranges significant quotes from various contemporary poets and ancient theologians as one would encounter a printed poem on a page. This not only draws the reader to the dual nature of Jesus' divinity and humanity, but also underscores the power of language to stand for otherwise intangible or impossible theological concepts. Swanson also raises up a lesser-known Christian theologian, Eustathius, hoping that his scarcely-read writings might shed light on the discussion of Christ's dual nature and the mystery of the Incarnation which Hendel so lovingly passed on to his students.

In Chapter Seventeen, after tracing the history of his friendship with Kurt Hendel, which spans some sixty years of personal and professional practice, Roger E. Timm explores ways science and religion have related to each other. In discussing four models generally used to describe the ways in which the two disciplines can interact with each other—conflict, independence, dialogue, and integration—Timm then goes on to speculate which might best apply to Luther and his theology—with implications for theologians today. Of particular interest is Luther's open conflict with Copernicus and the heliocentric model of the universe. Timm examines each model of interaction in turn as it is evidenced in Luther's writings, pointing out that several blanket statements often applied to Luther (such as those gleaned from Luther's *Table Talk*) are often decontextualized. Given this, he also proposes a fifth model, in part drawn from H. Richard Niebuhr's work: faith and science in paradox. Finally, Timm suggests that this model is not only best for Lutheran theologians, but also for Christian scientists in general.

In Chapter Eighteen, acknowledging the role Kurt and Jobey Hendel played in helping watch and raise Timothy and Elizabeth Hiller's son, John, Timothy Hiller seeks to explore Luther's theological perspective on parenting. Although his reasons stem from personal experience, he notes the interesting dichotomy between conservative Christians and mainline (or "liberal") denominations and academia concerning parenting. While conservative Christians put parenting and family at the center of its focus, mainline groups scarcely address either. Hiller presents Luther's own reflections on the "gift and task" of parenting as helpful for contemporary discussions on family, as they provide an excellent counter to some conservative models. After considering major trends in modern parenting, Hiller delves into Luther's theology, wherein a child does not exist in the secular sphere but is a gift from God, freely given in God's grace and goodness.

In Chapter Nineteen, Ralph Klein emphasizes the unique perspective Lutherans should employ when reading the Bible. He does so by exploring the main keynotes for exegeting a biblical text, pursuing a truly Lutheran perspective of the basis of the Bible's authority, engaging the Bible critically, paying special attention to the differences in biblical and contemporary contexts, and inviting the exegete to wonder what a text might have meant and what it might mean today. Klein also notes his appreciation for Martin Luther's exegetical works as he challenges contemporary exegetes not only to take into consideration Luther's contributions but also to transcend the limits of Luther's exegetical biases, affirming God's righteousness and the central Christian ethic of life.

In Chapter Twenty, Vitor Westhelle recounts the sermon he was privileged to preach in the Wittenberg Castle Church at the eve of the 495th anniversary of Luther nailing his ninety-five theses to a Wittenberg church door. As a preamble to the homily he preached, Westhelle explores the crux of Kurt Hendel's theological work: what to do with some of the implications of Lutheran theology, particularly as expressed by Luther and Bugenhagen by way of the epistles of Paul, and what are the interrelationships between the theological-doctrinal and ethical-pastoral pursuits? What does love—specifically, love of the neighbor which Luther exalted—look like? Finally, Westhelle provides the text of the homily he preached on 1 Corinthians 7:29-31, which questions how one ought to live and love the world when one is merely a guest.

Section Three: Concluding Essays

In Chapter Twenty-one, after recording anguish over the lackadaisical attitude many seminarians bring to the study of church history, Kurt's colleague historian Peter Vethanayagamony seeks to reemphasize Luther's own emphasis on history and what the study of church history brings to a well-rounded seminary education as pertinent preparation for ministry. Furthermore, he hopes to reclaim the study of history as a theological discipline, not an empirical science—as some modern-day church historians are inclined to do. After surveying two major schools of thought regarding history—that it is what "really happened in the past," and that it is entirely relativistic—Vethanayagamony asserts that the study of church history is not only (nor should it limit itself to) the study of the church as an institution. Rather, the primary focus of scholarship should be on the communities within the church and how they sought and experienced the Kin(g)dom of God. Scholarship should not be wholly empirical, concerned merely with facts; rather, it would do well to consider the relationships among the communities of God and how those same paradigms can perhaps be applied or adapted to the modern church today.

A bibliography of Kurt Hendel's works, as well as the final representative essay of his excellent scholarship, "Theology of the Cross," reprinted from *Currents in Theology and Mission*, complete the volume.

Vethanayagamony wishes to acknowledge his gratitude to student research assistants, Dione Miller and Dylan Huntington, for the editorial support they provided.

CHAPTER ONE

A Brief Biography of Kurt Hendel

Jobey Hendel

Kurt Karl Hendel was born in Wolfsdorf, Germany, on May 27, 1944. His father, Karl Hendel, passed away even before Kurt's birth. His mother, Ottilie Hendel, brought him up along with his sisters Hermine and Hilde. When Kurt was eight months of age, the family fled from home and spent several months in a refugee camp. His family was eventually placed with a southern German farm family. Kurt was baptized on November 18, 1945. His baptism certificate has served as his birth certificate ever since.

Kurt lived in the small rural town of Kirchweidach in the foothills of the Alps until the age of twelve when he and his mother emigrated to the United States to join his sister Hilde, her husband Werner, and their daughter Carin in St. Joseph, Michigan. He was confirmed in May 1958 at Trinity Lutheran Church in Saint Joseph, Michigan. Among many milestones, May 19, 1966, is a memorable day in Kurt's life because on that day he was sworn in as a U.S. citizen.

His education continued at a local Lutheran school, then Concordia High School and Junior College in Milwaukee, Wisconsin, to prepare for ordained ministry. The first indication that God was calling Kurt to ministry may have come from a Roman Catholic priest in his German hometown of Kirchweidach. The priest there made several attempts to recruit Kurt into the priesthood. While the majority of his friends did not continue ministerial preparation, Kurt's strong commitment to faith, nurtured by his mother, led him to continue his studies at Concordia Senior College in Fort Wayne, Indiana. He graduated from Concordia Senior College in 1966. While studying there, he met his future wife at a Christmas party.

Ministerial training followed at Concordia Seminary in St. Louis, Missouri. He married Jobey in August of 1968 prior to an internship year in Connecticut. In 1970 he graduated with a Master of Divinity degree. Hoping to one day teach at a Lutheran college or seminary, he decided to attend graduate school. He received a full four-year scholarship to Ohio State University where he studied with prominent Reformation historian, Professor Harold Grimm. Kurt's doctoral dissertation, "Johannes Bugenhagen's Educational Contributions," was completed in 1974.

Prior to his final year of graduate school he was approached by one of his former seminary professors to join the faculty of Concordia Seminary as a visiting professor for the 1973-74 academic year. That year was a momentous one in the history of American theological education and in the history of American Lutheranism. After one semester of seminary teaching and while continuing to research and write his dissertation, seminary events forever changed Kurt's academic and personal life. Concordia Seminary students expressed support for faculty accused of false teaching by declaring a moratorium on attending classes. Kurt honored the student moratorium and, knowing that God has a sense of humor, thought that his teaching career would last only a few short months.

Through the efforts of God's people who were guided by the Spirit, Concordia Seminary-in-Exile (Seminex) and the Association of Evangelical Lutheran Churches came into existence in January 1974 to continue to prepare men and women for ministry. During the next ten years Kurt served in several capacities in addition to teaching and administration, becoming especially adept at admissions and financial aid. Kurt completed his dissertation while teaching and serving in several roles within the new seminary. Kurt was ordained in January 1976, just prior to the arrival of a second daughter, Elizabeth, who joined her sister Heidi. Two years later son Joshua arrived.

Kurt served as an assistant pastor at Bethel Lutheran Church in St. Louis along with his responsibilities at the seminary. When the Seminex faculty and staff deployed to other areas of the country, Kurt continued his calling to the teaching ministry at the Lutheran School of Theology at Chicago. His main focus has always been on preparing women and men for ministry as he taught Reformation History, Luther's Theology, Luther's Social Ethics, and The Lutheran Confessions, besides church history survey courses. He served as the director of the Masters of Arts program for the majority of his tenure at the seminary and was honored by appointment as the Bernard, Fischer, Westberg Distinguished Ministry Professor of Reformation History.

Kurt has a passionate and generous personality. First and foremost he is passionate about the gospel. All other passions are measured by, influenced by, and judged by this. He is also passionate about his family, matters of justice, those less fortunate (especially those who do not have enough to eat), the church, and teaching. Sports could also be added to that list with soccer at the top, which he insists is the "sport of choice in heaven."

His greatest gift to the leadership of the church is helping to prepare future leaders through his teaching ministry and sharing his passion for the gospel and the Lutheran Confessions with God's people through other teaching opportunities such as adult forums, preaching, conference presentations, travel seminars, and writings and translations of the founders of the Lutheran church.

He retired from full-time teaching ministry in May 2015. However, his passion for and love of working with students of all ages continues as he serves the church through adult forums, travel seminars, preaching, and teaching seminary classes. His many plans during retirement include traveling in the United States and Europe, writing projects, and enjoying family time, especially with his children and grandchildren.

SECTION ONE

Personal Tributes

CHAPTER TWO

Professor Hendel

Scholar, Theologian, Partner in Parish Ministry

Robert Shaner

A "Child of God"—The Journey—Leaving and Becoming

> The gifts he gave were that some would be apostles, some prophets, some evangelists, some pastors and teachers, to equip the saints for the work of ministry, for building up the body of Christ, until all of us come to the unity of the faith and of the knowledge of the Son of God, to maturity, to the measure of the full stature of Christ (Ephesians 4:11-13).

ACT I—Formation

"Kurt, child of God, you are sealed by the Holy Spirit and marked with the cross of Christ forever." Those words spoken at Kurt Hendel's baptism define his identity—always in relationship with God as a child and an heir. There was never any question of who Kurt was or to whom he belonged; however, what he would do, where he would apply his gifts and energies to make a contribution, and how he would spend his life represents an incredible journey, shaped at the beginning and throughout by the support and encouragement of the local parish. As a young nine-year-old lad from Germany arriving in western Michigan without English language skills, Kurt was "formed and informed" by the community of faith. His parish engendered in him an amazing hunger and thirst to discern what it means to be "a child of God," a member of the "body of

SUBJECT TO NONE, SERVANT OF ALL

Christ" and thus part of "the communion of saints." The parish stirred a life-long quest for living out that identity, which he has done as scholar, theologian, and partner in and with parish ministry. This journey to fulfill God's plan for life could not have been taken without the partnership of wife, Jobey, and their three children whose support, encouragement, and joy helped to keep Kurt grounded and grateful. This first act, "Formation," would not have happened without leaving his "homeland."

ACT II—Preparation and Participation

Concordia Senior College in Fort Wayne, Indiana, prepared him for Concordia Seminary in St. Louis, where he developed a deep desire to know more about church history and the Reformation in particular. So, when the opportunity came to study under the influential Reformation scholar Harold Grimm at Ohio State, Kurt blossomed. With a newly earned Ph.D. followed by a Fulbright year in Gottingen and additional post-doctoral work, Kurt was given a rare opportunity from his alma mater, Concordia Seminary, to teach—filling in for a professor on sabbatical. That venture would prove to be a tumultuous, pivotal, and life-changing experience, for in that year amid the theological and ecclesiastical power conflict within the Lutheran Church–Missouri Synod, faculty and students "walked out" of Concordia Seminary in protest and became the first ever seminary-in-exile, Seminex. Kurt, a relatively junior colleague with little ranking as a sabbatical fill-in, was nevertheless part of that teaching and learning community accused of false doctrinal teachings by its national leadership. Without tenure or security, but with the courage of his convictions and a firm belief in the centrality of the gospel, he would, like Luther, his faith hero, symbolically state: "Here I stand [or walk, as was the case], I can do no other." A venture into the unknown, a defining moment!

Seminex would be invited to become part of the Lutheran School of Theology at Chicago (LSTC) in 1983, and with other colleagues Kurt came to Chicago where he worked with Robert Fischer in church history. Upon Dr. Fischer's retirement Kurt became the seminary's "go-to" Reformation scholar. In 2002 when Grace Lutheran Church in LaGrange, Illinois, endowed a seminary chair to honor three of its member pastors (George Bernard, leader in parish ministry; Robert Fischer, esteemed seminary professor; and Granger Westberg, national pioneer in pastoral care), Dr. Jim Echols, then LSTC president, nominated Kurt Hendel to become the first occupant of the Bernard, Fischer, Westberg Distinguished Ministry Professor of Reformation History, a position he has honored and held for the past thirteen years. This second act, "Preparation and Participation," would not have developed without his leaving his alma mater which he loved, a leaving which led to formidable and respected teaching and scholarship.

ACT III—Fruition

A teacher of the church, mentor to students, friend of pastors, colleague of the faculty, and partner with parishes, Kurt's many roles stimulated and inspired life-long learning and scholarship. Seeking to shed new light on Luther's life, Kurt's on-going research and writing have made him one of the world's leading authorities on Johannes Bugenhagen (1485-1558), the pastor to Martin Luther. The historical significance of figures whose lives were spent behind the scenes in support and care for the leaders and/or luminaries of the day often have been overlooked. The pastoral care and influence of Bugenhagen on Luther cannot be dismissed or treated lightly. Kurt's two-volume work, recently published, on Bugenhagen will be received as "definitive and baseline."

As a scholar, Kurt encouraged the church community and students alike to treasure the genius and insights of the participants with the sixteenth-century reformers who led paradigm shifts that altered the church and history. As an historian, Kurt has underscored the meaning of the Reformation as a rediscovery of the gospel. Luther in fact helped lead the church and the world to a new day, letting God be God and releasing the human spirit from ecclesial captivity. In a similar manner, by getting to know the lesser known people behind the scenes in the Reformation, Kurt Hendel as a teacher has helped people understand not just the complexities of such a momentous time, but also how ordinary life and extraordinary relationships merge to make possible the continuing reformation needed by each generation. This third act, "Fruition," would not have been possible without leaving the "better known" parts of history to seek and learn what happened behind the scenes.

ACT IV—Inter-relationships

Kurt's research has always begun with the need to know the facts—i.e. what was happening at any given time, what were the precipitating issues, who were the key participants, and how the confluence of those realities affected people. However, Kurt's historical scholarship has also been wed to theological interpretation—i.e. what is God up to in history, what do the facts mean, what does the situation tell us about the re-vealed–hidden God? For Kurt, "God talk" means revisiting "human talk." Kurt leads dialogue between what God is initiating and doing and what God's actions mean for people—i.e., "So what?" "What does one make of the world, life's happenings?" and "How does one respond?"

A professor may probe and challenge the intellect, engage in research and writing, lecture, consult, and mentor—and all would be well. And Kurt has certainly been a professor, but he has been so much more. Formed, shaped, and nurtured by the parish, he has valued and been engaged in true parish partnerships, spending a significant portion of each year vis-iting and interacting with pastors and people in congregational settings. As a scholar of history, Kurt takes the time to help people wrestle with the question, "What do we know from the past that can be helpful for the present?" as well as "What can be learned that will keep us from re-peating the past?" Kurt responds, "Dear people, the good news teaches us that God so loved and gave and forgave. The gospel is always about sec-ond chances, about finding the lost, empowering the gifts and energies of people." He loves the church. And while he knows its flaws and shortcom-ings throughout history, he believes the church to be the body of Christ in the world—the body that God has entrusted with the ministry of recon-ciliation. This fourth act, "Inter-relationships," would not have happened without leaving the "library or podium" to be engaged and connected to those in the pew, to friends of theological education, to the many faithfully living out their baptismal calling as children of God.

Esteemed among his colleagues and respected in academia, admired by students, affirmed by the Evangelical Lutheran Church in America and the holy, catholic, and apostolic church, admired by congregations where he provided insightful seminars and workshops on the theology and meaning of the Reformation, and—above all—loved by God, Kurt has been a true friend and partner in ministry with pastors and laity alike. In retrospect, none of the journey, Acts I-IV, would have happened without leaving:

> His homeland for a new beginning
> A beloved institution for conviction
> The familiar for new learning
> The narrow academic role for broader engagement

Leaving and becoming—a journey and work well done—helping others also to live out what it means to be a child of God!

"Kurt, child of God, you are sealed by the Holy Spirit and marked with the cross of Christ forever."

CHAPTER THREE

In Appreciation of Kurt Hendel

Lu Bettisch

I am a former M.Div. student of Kurt K. Hendel at LSTC. I am a parish pastor. I am not what you would call an academic. So if you are looking for a mind-blowing revelation in all things theological, I suggest you turn the page. My hope for this letter is to thank Kurt Hendel for the way he impacted my faith, my education, my call, and my life.

Dear Kurt,

I never realized how Lutheran I truly was until I met you in the fall of 2006 at the Lutheran School of Theology at Chicago. My first day on campus was for orientation in the Master of Arts program. As a church musician of seventeen years, my goal was to get my degree and become a rostered Associate in Ministry in the Evangelical Lutheran Church in America. However, upon my arrival at LSTC, at each and every turn, people assumed I was entering into the Master of Divinity program in order to become an ordained minister.

I grew up in a very conservative wing of Lutheranism which did not ordain women, so the possibility of pursuing ordination was not even on my radar. You were the advisor for the Master of Arts program, so our group met with you the first day for an overview of the program. Later in the week I was assigned an academic advisor—you. When you met with me, I shared with you my frustration over the whole Master of Arts versus Master of Divinity issue. I remember that you gently suggested I listen for God's voice, as God might be suggesting a different path for my life. I said, "But the Bible says women can't be leaders in the church!" At that moment, miraculous things seemed to happen. I liken that moment to the encounter of the Ethiopian eunuch and Philip from the Book of Acts. Like the eunuch, I thought I had a basic understanding of the scriptures, but I really didn't know the whole story. I believe that same Holy Spirit that prompted Philip moved in you to teach me what the good news of Jesus Christ was really about. You taught me that Luther believed in looking at the scriptures through the lens of the gospel. In other words, how did Jesus treat people? For me, this concept was both freeing and terrifying! It meant that instead of the literal words of the scriptures telling me what to do or not do, I was now responsible to read them and interpret them as Jesus would. This obviously changed not only my career path, but my life.

I have been an ordained pastor now for over four years. Not a day goes by that I don't think, "Now there's something I didn't learn in seminary!" I'm sure you are aware that my colleagues and I often joke about how ill-prepared by seminary courses we feel for the real world of the local parish and our jobs as pastors. In just this past year I have had to deal with a tornado blowing most of the roof off of our church building, a homeless guest hacking into our internet and downloading child pornography which resulted in detectives in the building and his arrest, three broken furnaces all on the same day, and having to remove a board member/treasurer. I don't ever remember a class at seminary that covered even one of those items. However, that is the kind of stuff we deal with in the parish every day. In a dream world, I would love to sit at my desk and do an in-depth study of the gospel for the coming Sunday and spend days preparing the perfect sermon. But in reality, it just doesn't happen that way. I often think back to my seminary days and wonder how Greek, Hebrew, systematic theology, and studying the book of Revelation help me in my everyday life and call. It's kind of like learning Algebra in high school. The teachers said, "Yes, you will use this in your everyday life." I cannot remember the last time I needed to find the answer to $x + y = 2$. For me, it was the process of seminary that taught me what I needed to know to be a pastor. As I worked my way through all the classes, papers, and books, I found who I am as a person—as a beloved child of God—and as a called pastor in Christ's church. That wouldn't have happened without you.

My whole goal and life changed once I was reminded of what it means to be Lutheran. Much like Martin Luther himself, I have a very heavy sense of guilt, and I often find myself wondering why God would love me. You reminded us in class that, yes, we all are "rot gut sinners" and certainly don't do anything to earn God's love and salvation. But, because of God's gracious love and mercy we are given the gift of life through grace. Pure unadulterated grace: Nothing we can say or do is enough to win our way into God's grace. As it says in Ephesians 2:8-10, "For by grace you have been saved through faith, and this is not your own doing; it is the gift of God—not the result of works, so that no one may boast. For we are what he has made us, created in Christ Jesus for good works, which God prepared beforehand to be our way of life." Verses 8 and 9 are the promise we as Lutherans hang our hats on. But it is verse 10 that changed my life. For Luther, and for me, this lifted a heavy burden. Instead of going to God and confessing all our shortcomings, then doing penance to pay for our sin, now we are free from sin and can respond to God's amazing love by doing the "good works, which God prepared beforehand to be our way of life." And that is a perfect statement of what I believe. It isn't something I do; it isn't a checklist of dos and don'ts. It is a way of life. And as you so often reminded us, it is so deeply rooted in our identity as children of God through our baptism.

In class you would often remind us that remembering our baptism even on a daily basis was powerful. When we stand in the shower every morning with the water running over us, you suggested making the sign of the cross on our forehead to remind us of just how much God loves us. At first I thought it was a bit strange, but I have shared that in my sermons and children's messages several times. And I have taught the kids how to make the sign of the cross by dipping their hands in the font after worship when we have a baptism. What a wonderful blessing to see the joy on those little faces as they dip their hands in the water and know how much Jesus loves them!

I'm just an ordinary parish pastor who tries on a daily basis to live out that calling. In preparing for this letter, I looked back over all the papers and essays I wrote for candidacy entrance, endorsement, and approval, and found this from my entrance essay before I met you.

> I'm not really sure where God wants me to go from here, but I have a deep sense that God is not drawing me but *pushing* me in a new direction. One of my previous pastors said he sensed God gave me a "hard call" and that there was no doubt in his mind that I should serve the church in my vocation. I pray for God's guidance, strength and courage to take that leap of faith and see what God has in store. I don't have any answers, just questions. I'm not sure I want to do it, but

I sense God does. I don't know where I fit, but God knows. I pray for help and discernment from those around me to help me hear God's heart beat for my life as I discern a call to the position of Associate in Ministry in the ELCA. It scares me to say that because I feel so inadequate, but as a good friend of mine reminds me, "God doesn't call the qualified. He qualifies the called!" From one of my favorite passages from the call of Isaiah:

And I said: "Woe is me! I am lost, for I am a man [woman] of unclean lips, and I live among a people of unclean lips; yet my eyes have seen the King, the LORD of hosts!" Then one of the seraphs flew to me, holding a live coal that had been taken from the altar with a pair of tongs. The seraph touched my mouth with it and said: "Now that this has touched your lips, your guilt has departed and your sin is blotted out." Then I heard the voice of the Lord saying, "Whom shall I send, and who will go for us?" And I said, "Here am I; send me!"

So, when all is said and done I honestly believe I would not have made it through seminary without your encouragement, love, and guidance. And I know that, as the Holy Spirit uses each one of its children, you are most certainly being used powerfully as you touch the lives of your students.

From the bottom of my heart, thank you Kurt!

Just a fellow "rot gut sinner" and saint,
Lu Bettisch

CHAPTER FOUR

A *Festschrift* Tangent

Memories of Professor Hendel in the Classroom

Jonathan Wilson

As a former pupil of Kurt K. Hendel, I took extra pains to demonstrate my knowledge of scholarly convention in writing an academic essay for this *Festschrift* in his honor. It would be poor style to open an essay with a tangent that is off point. And yet to fully honor Kurt in the *Festschrift,* there is something needful about including a tangent *somewhere*. It seems best to make this tangent a separate excursus set as an interruption in the midst of these scholarly contributions.

Those privileged to attend a Kurt Hendel class are able to relate to each other across the decades about the experience. LSTC alumni confirm that in many ways Kurt has remained unchanged from when he began teaching in the 1970s. His exuberance about the material, his awe of the means of grace, his pastoral humility, his convictions on issues of the moment, all lent themselves to entertaining tangents during his lectures. When he stepped away from the lectern, students knew they could rest their hands from taking notes.

Even at 8:00 a.m. if one chose not to pay attention to the lecture one had to work hard to maintain one's diffidence; it was riveting the way Kurt would move around the front of the room, getting worked up on some issue related to creation care or a national election, interjecting an ethical exhortation that we, "dear people," should take to heart. He would then stop suddenly to fix an individual with a hawk-like frown as he enumerated a particularly compelling, dramatic, and serious point.

It made me wonder why on earth Kurt was blaming ME that American car-makers built only gas-guzzlers. This glare would be followed immediately by a sniff and a smirk and a stroll back to the lectern to pick up the morning's theme once more: "Now where were we? Yes. We were speaking of Luther's rhetorical exaggerations in Bondage of the Will. . . ." Kurt's energy was extreme, especially so early in the morning. Still, this only camouflaged but did not diminish the efficiency by which his pupils received all they needed. Students arrived at the end of the semester able to articulate for themselves the progressions of the Christian movement over the millennia and to set the church's myriad theological squabbles and institutional reformations into context.

I was privileged with the Kurt Hendel experience in these most recent years of his long and rich teaching career. Johannes Bugenhagen notwithstanding, I can claim to be his last piece of unfinished business, his final advisee in the Ph.D. track. I could not have asked for a more supportive mentor, especially as he cheered me on to finish my dissertation (hawk-like frown) "sooner rather than later" (sniff, smirk). I was fine with that plan; at forty-six years of age at my graduation in 2015, I am not a spring chicken. That I was not a Lutheran did not trouble him. That I came from a Pietist theological heritage was more problematic, although he held nothing against me academically. His remarkably gracious ways created space for our disagreements to remain, while our shared commitments enabled us to work together closely and productively. I learned from him through our disagreements as much as through our agreements.

What this *Festschrift* is showing you by now is that Kurt Hendel is, above all, a highly effective teacher. He has told the story of the church in a way that has triggered the imagination of each of the scholars in this volume and hundreds beyond. His former pupils have gone in many different directions, but we all somehow remember a statement in a lecture that we could not let go, or a reading Kurt assigned and let us wrestle with, or a conversation in his office or over the phone when came that "Aha!" moment of inspiration. I know when that happened for me: While trying to find a way to adequately study the Lutheran chaplains who served in the American Revolution, we came to the realization that there can be no meaningful conversation about the Lutheran church in colonial America without a thorough knowledge of the life and writings of Heinrich Melchior Muhlenberg. That is the independent study we arranged—and the rest, for me and for many, is history. My thanks to my teacher, Kurt Hendel.

CHAPTER FIVE

Lutherland

Reminiscences from a
Reformation Educational Tour

Ruben Dominguez

It was a remarkable tour Dr. Kurt Hendel led throughout Lutherland in September 2001. I believe it also was an extraordinary tour for the others who filled the bus that traveled throughout the German region which became the center of Luther's Reformation movement. The tour became especially unforgettable because of the appalling terrorist attacks of September 11. In fact, those who took the tour became aware of the attacks on just the first of the ten-day tour. We were visiting what used to be the home of Dietrich Bonhoeffer's parents in one of Berlin's neighborhoods. That same day we were scheduled to stay in one of Wittenberg's hotels. Upon arrival to our hotel, we saw on the lobby TV the first images of the airliners hitting the World Trade Center towers in New York. What we watched on that TV was unbelievable. Several of us thought we were watching a Hollywood movie.

As a continuing expression of his academic skills, Dr. Kurt Hendel throughout his career has led educational tours to Germany. The purpose of them all is to see and learn first-hand about the sixteenth century Reformation.

The brief account of my personal experiences of that educational tour will follow in the next few paragraphs. I am writing these memories from the fond retentions that I have treasured in my thoughts.

Out of the approximately thirty-five people that packed the tour bus, I was the only Hispanic. During our tour of Wittenberg on September

12, the local guide began his presentation with sympathetic words to our American group on the day after the terrorist attack. He also affirmed that the German people felt as though the attacks were done to their own country. Indeed, this sympathetic gesture was repeatedly shown to us during the following days in different locations. We noticed how some German people went to local churches to pray for the families and for those who had suffered one way or another from the terrorist attacks in America.

The local German woman who served as the tour manager knew her job well. She had been contacted by Dr. Hendel during previous educational tours. Upon arrival in every town, among her many other tour duties, she made sure to distribute all sorts of tourist information brochures, particularly those pertaining to our sites of interest. There were also local dignitaries and important persons who were invited to greet our group while in their respective towns. Also, some expert individuals were invited to lecture our group on a variety of Reformation topics. For example, a former Evangelical German Church leader reviewed the whole history of the Lutheran church in Germany. He also included information about important details for many Germans' immigration to America and other countries. These immigrations are part of the global history of Lutheranism, and gave birth to the Lutheran church in the United States and other countries as well.

Not all sites we visited were directly connected to the history of the Reformation. We visited some towns that were the birthplaces of some renowned Lutherans. In Halle, the tour included visits to two important sites. First, the house in which the musician Georg Frederich Handel was born and raised. The second was the building that housed for many years the huge schools and other related institutions which the Pietist pastor, August Hermann Francke (1663-1727), helped to establish. Being on this site, our group members became more aware of how influential the Pietist Movement was in its heyday and how they gained a considerable number of followers. It is also significant to note former students of Halle, Bartholomew Ziegenbalg and Heinrich Pluetschau became the first international Lutheran missionaries to India, and later other missionaries ventured to several countries. One in our group, after carefully touring the Pietist school, commented ironically: "And we thought that mega-churches were born in America. Indeed, this place is the birth of the mega-churches movement, and the Pietists were the first to have a mega-church right here in Halle."

In Leipzig, we visited two historic churches, the first of which was St. Nicholas Church. In this church we also listened to a lecture by one of the pastors who happened to be at the center of the prayer vigils movement that eventually led to the fall of the Berlin Wall and the re-unification of Germany. His stories were outstanding. We had a glimpse of how important religion can be in social movements. Unfortunately, the church pastors and leaders lost their influential role after the re-unification of Germany. It seemed to some in our group that part of the blame fell on the same church leaders and pastors who appeared inca-pable of providing continued leadership and influencing people once the goal of the prayer vigils was accomplished. The second church we visited was the Thomaskirche (St. Thomas Church) where the great Lu-theran musician Johann Sebastian Bach was cantor for many years. His tomb is located within the sanctuary of this church. During the time of our visit to St. Thomas Church, we witnessed a worship service featur-ing one of Bach's cantatas. The sermon was preached in German by one of the church pastors. Once the worship service ended, Dr. Hendel gave us a summary in English of that sermon. Just across a side street of the church, some of us visited a building that holds a museum dedicated to the great musician.

On the second day in Leipzig, just before our departure, our group was called to a place to have the chance to listen to some young locals talk about how they saw their future in a reunified Germany. What I re-member about their speeches is the somber tone of their experiences of as they continued living in the eastern side of Germany. For example, they emphasized that the young people at that particular time did not have a bright economic future if they were to remain in the Leipzig area, or even in what used to be East Germany. They mentioned that a signif-icant number of young people had immigrated and still were moving into the western part of Germany in pursuit of a brighter future. After listening to the young peoples' dull outlook for their lives in Leipzig, I dared to ask them about the opportunities and optimistic perspectives they surely had in their own town.

During our visit to Eisenach, and before going up to nearby Wart-burg Castle, our group visited the so-called Johann S. Bach birth house. The Bach house is a museum today displaying old musical instruments. Bach's music is played daily by staff members and invited artists. We also visited the house where Martin Luther supposedly lived for a few years while attending school and before going to the University of Erfurt. It is said that Luther's mother, Margaret, had some family members in this town. The most important site, however, in the vicinity of Eisenach is Wartburg Castle. This castle, we learned, was the site of some important medieval historical events even before housing Luther as a refugee in 1521. The tour included a visit to the rooms where Luther worked on his translation of the New Testament into German.

In Weimar, we made a significant stop at the nearby Buchenwald concentration camp created by the Nazi government. The intention of this stop was to pay homage to those who died within the camp. Our group had a devotion in the small remaining prison cells section which included a reading from the writings of Lutheran pastor Martin Niemoeller, who was a prisoner in a similar Nazi camp for his active anti-Nazi stand. Most of the camp buildings and barracks had been demolished. Our group visited one of the buildings that still stands; it is now a museum exhibiting personal belongings of those who were prisoners in this hideous camp. We also saw ovens where the bodies of those who died were incinerated. A final stop was made to a symbolic mass tomb where there is a memorial flame. Also we stood at a spot whose surface indicates the normal temperature of the human body. The purpose of these symbols, I gathered, is to invite visitors to remember, never forget—so that another concentration camp will never be built again.

As we left, our bus passed through a gate where not distant from it was another repulsive site. At the time of the war, the prisoners themselves referred to that site as *Carajo*, a Spanish word that could be translated as "the most miserable place." This word gave me another clue that the Nazi regime intended to get rid of all opposition even beyond German lands. Most probably one of the first prisoner groups arriving at Buchenwald was one of Jewish descent living in Spain.

While I don't recall the professor's name who lectured us about Luther and his impact in the European people then and through time, two of his comments still resonate in my mind. When responding to the question of how common German people see Luther today, he said that most tend to consider him as a sectarian leader. He gave some explanations for this observation: One is that Luther basically lived and led the Reformation in a restricted geographical area. Most people admit, however, that his Reformation ideas spread quickly to other countries, but Luther himself remained confined to the protection of his princes during his lifetime. Second, and related to the first observation, most of his followers were German people from specific principalities (Saxony for example). It is true that Lutheranism grew after Luther's death, mostly in the North European countries.

The observation portraying Luther as sectarian leader impressed me deeply since I had never considered myself being a member of a sectarian group. I assume most Lutherans would find it difficult to entertain the thought of being supporters of a sectarian leader. The professor's observation, however, was made from the perspective of today's German people, and I should add that it came from academic circles.

I also expressed interest in getting some information about the Spanish Reformation-inclined leaders who sought support from Luther and Melanchthon in Wittenberg. The professor admitted he did not know much about this topic. I acknowledge this is a special field of interest of which many non-Spanish speakers would not be aware—or interested in—but I also wanted to remind him that I am a member of the Spanish-speaking world.

After his lecture, the professor remained in the hall for a few moments, so I took the opportunity to approach and ask him if he happened to know about Francisco de Encinas (1518-1552). The professor remembered that he had run into this name a number of times in his readings but was not fully aware of who Encinas was. I took the opportunity to briefly review with him Encinas' main scholarly work and contribution to the Reformation in other European countries. Encinas was a classical language scholar who received a humanist formation. He completed the translation of the New Testament into Spanish directly from Greek while living at Melanchthon's Wittenberg home. Melanchthon encouraged him to publish it in 1543 at Antwerp. Furthermore, Encinas translated into Spanish some of Luther's writings, among them *The Freedom of a Christian;* most probably he participated in the translation of *The Commentary to the Epistle to the Galatians.* Both translations circulated mainly in Spanish academic circles, like the one at the University of Alcalá de Henares. Encinas returned to Spain and asked to be received by the Castilian King Charles I, the Emperor Charles V. When he was finally received by Charles, he dared to present him with his own translation of the New Testament, seeking to have support for the reformation of the church in Spain. This action made him suspect of heresy by the Inquisition, and soon he was imprisoned. Since he was a member of a prominent family from Burgos, he was able to escape from prison. He returned to Wittenberg and continued living in Melanchthon's home for some time. Encinas enjoyed Melanchthon's friendship and respect. From Wittenberg he traveled to other countries until his death in Strasbourg in 1552.

Our tour ended at the Frankfurt airport. Dr. Hendel had completed a job well-done. On returning to the United States, and, based on my tour experiences and videos that I took, I wrote a course in Spanish on the Lutheran Reformation for the Hispanic Institute of Theology, then located at Concordia University–River Forest. Yes, that educational tour is unforgettable.

CHAPTER SIX

God's "Dear People" Includes Everyone—Even the Children

Inviting Children and Youth into the Preaching Act without Losing the Adults

Carrie L. Lewis La Plante

Introduction

One of the things that I loved about sitting in courses that Kurt K. Hendel taught was his signature expression with which he would address us during class. Whenever he wanted to be sure that we heard his point, he would address us as "Dear People." And while this was his convention, we also knew that it was not just a convention but really how he viewed his students. We really were, and are, "dear people" in his sight. Because we are people dear to God, we are people dear to Kurt, and in his address to us, he would remind us who we really are.

In the spring quarter of 2002, I was sitting in the Lutheran Confessions course Kurt was teaching. We were studying the sacraments, looking at *The Book of Concord*[1] and *The Use of the Means of Grace*,[2] among other texts. On this particular day, we were having a conversation on Holy Communion. Our discussion centered on the theological basis for the various practices of this sacrament. We talked about how often congregations have Holy Communion and how those various intervals came to be. We talked about the elements that are used in the sacrament including the use of leavened or unleavened bread and wine or grape juice. We talked about the gift of the sacrament in the midst of an emergency and what to do when we do not have the "proper elements" to use. Finally, we talked about who could receive the sacrament, whether one had to be a member of a particular congregation or denomination, whether they had to be baptized or not, and how would a pastor necessarily know.

In the midst of this discussion, we began to talk about the age at which it is appropriate for people to begin to receive the sacrament of Holy Communion. Should it be at the time of confirmation or after a time of intentional instruction in fifth grade or at some other time agreed upon by parent and pastor? In the midst of this lively discussion, as we talked about the pros and cons of each practice, Kurt shared with us a personal story.

He told us that he had felt that there should be some understanding of what was happening when one of God's "dear people" received the sacrament of Holy Communion. Therefore, receiving communion for the first time after a period of instruction had made sense to him. Then, one day, he was worshipping with his grandchildren, and his mind was changed. On that day, as he approached the table with one of his young grandchildren, this child, who had never received communion nor instruction for communion, simply held out his hands ready to receive the sacrament. He had never done this before, and Kurt admitted that his first instinct was to instruct this beloved grandchild to put his hands down; however, Kurt's mind was quickly changed. He realized that this grandchild had never before put out his hands for this sacrament, so there must be something that was prompting him to do it on this morning. Kurt wondered whether the Holy Spirit was working through this grandchild on this particular morning and drawing this child to the meal in a fuller way. If this was the case, who was he to stifle the movement of the Holy Spirit? On that morning, this beloved grandchild received the body and blood of his Lord and Savior, Jesus Christ. Kurt reminded us in that moment that "dear people" includes everyone, that all of God's "dear people" are invited to worship together, and that God often uses children to remind us, as adults, what is really central to faith. Yes, "dear people" includes everyone—even the children.

This lesson made an impression on me and remained with me through the rest of my seminary career and into my ministry as I have sought ways to incorporate children and youth into the weekly worship life of the congregations that I have served. This has been done through children's messages, music leadership, worship leadership for special services, and participating in special homiletic presentations. I realized, however, as I began my work toward my Doctor of Ministry in preaching, the one place where children and youth were not included was in the weekly preaching event. It felt to me as though this was a place where we told the children and youth to simply "hang on" while we talked with the adults for a while, and they simply had to endure until we were ready to sing the next hymn or song together.

As I looked back at lessons I had learned from my coursework and our confessions, I began to wonder whether there was a better method of preparation and performance of preaching that would invite, connect with, and engage all of God's "dear people," and would help us, as adults, to learn about faith and God's love from the children and youth in our midst. In the work that I did through the Association of Chicago Theological Schools (ACTS) Doctor of Ministry of Preaching program, I have found a method of sermon preparation and performance that invites children and youth into the preaching process and preaching act, connects with children and youth through conversational tone and storytelling, and engages children and youth by addressing their concerns and using media in the preaching. Along the way, I have been delighted to find that the adults in the congregation also have a greater sense of being invited into the preaching, are better connected, and feel more engaged in the preaching act, so that all of God's "dear people" are better able to hear the gospel.

While this essay does not allow for a full description of this method, here are some of the ways in which inviting, connecting with and engaging children and youth have helped to include all of God's "dear people" in the peaching act.[3]

Invitation

Inviting the Youngest of God's "Dear People"

When I first began to think about inviting children and youth into the preaching process, I had to find ways to purposefully listen to the children and youth in the congregation in order to understand the concerns that they carry on a daily basis and to hear how they connect scripture to their lives. I began by finding specific opportunities to work with each age group through Bible studies on the assigned scripture for a particular Sunday and focused a given sermon on that particular age group. Since then, I have found it more important to listen carefully to each age group whenever I have an opportunity to spend time with them so that I can hear their concerns and burdens and include those concerns and burdens in sermons in appropriate and less forced ways. Each age group (high school, middle school, elementary, and younger) presents its own joys and challenges, but the insights that they provide into the realities of their lives and the questions of their faith are invaluable resources for the pastor who desires to include all of God's "dear people" in the preaching act.

Once we have invited the children and youth into the preparation for preaching, we preachers are called to find ways to invite the children and youth into the actual preaching act. I have found that the most effective way of doing this is through the children's message. Instead of doing object lessons which are too abstract for many young children, I have begun to closely connect the children's message to the "regular" sermon, usually including something for the children to listen for in the sermon or some way that they can participate in the sermon to help all of God's "dear people" to hear the message of the gospel that day.[4] Asking them to look for something in the worship space, listen for a specific word in the sermon, respond to a cue given in the sermon, or participate in the sermon in some way gives the children and youth a specific way in which to be active in the sermon. I have also found that giving them something tangible to take with them at the end of the children's message helps them to remember the central message of that particular sermon.

I have found that an interesting thing happens when a preacher begins to consciously invite the youngest of God's "dear people" into the preaching act: more of the congregation is reached by the message of the good news of God in Jesus Christ. That may seem like an obvious conclusion, but not only does the preacher reach the children and youth that he or she is consciously considering for the preaching act, but the preacher also can reach adults in a new way. In broadening the demographic and the range of examples that are used to illustrate an idea or concept, some adults who have rarely been reached by preaching may find themselves in the story, either in their current situation or by relating to an experience from their younger years. Preaching with the youngest of God's "dear people" in mind often results in preaching relationships rather than concepts, and even those adults who appreciate sermons *about* God and faith find new ways to *relate to* God, bringing them to deeper faith. Inviting children and youth into the preaching act can help the preacher to bring the good news of God in Jesus Christ to more of God's "dear people" in a more effective way.

What the Youngest of God's "Dear People" Have Taught Us

As I have invited the youngest of God's "dear people" into the preaching act, both in preparation and in the preaching itself, the congregation has gained insight into the relationship that children have with God, and has come to realize that perhaps sharing the good news with others is not as difficult as they sometimes make it out to be.

By considering real examples of how children in our congregation live out their faith, question God, and wonder about how and why the world works the way that it does as illustrations in the sermon, older members of the congregation are brought back to the basics of faith. Permission has been given to the adults of the congregation not to know all of the answers, but to ask questions again. We also have been reminded that our children and youth face real trials that require God's presence in their lives to get through, and we are reminded that all of God's "dear people" need God's presence in the trials that we face.

Connection

Connecting with the Youngest of God's "Dear People"

Once avenues of communication have been opened up between the preacher and the youngest of God's "dear people," then connections need to be made between the preacher and the children and youth, as well as the adults, in order for the sermon to make an impact on the hearers. While there are many ways this can be done, I determined that I needed to move away from sermons that were experienced more like lectures taken from written notes to conversations that were had between the preacher and the congregation. All of God's "dear people" prefer to be talked *with* rather than talked *at*, and for my preaching getting out of a manuscript provides that conversational tone and removes a barrier between the preacher and the congregation that helps to reveal the gospel message that is being preached.

As Joseph Webb writes, preaching without notes "makes possible the fullest and most intense bonding between the preacher and those who share the preaching."[5] My hunch was that if I could remove those pieces of paper that drew my attention away from the people I was trying to reach, I could deepen the relationship between me—the preacher—and the listening congregation, and my preaching would be more authentic. The listeners would know that I really believed what I was saying rather than wonder if I was just doing a good job of repeating what others have said. They would be able to sense in my tone of voice and body language what aspects of my faith are important to me and how I understand it to be important for them. It would become more obvious that I really was listening to their concerns and hearing their joys and fears because, as I would speak of these joys and concerns in the sermon, I also would be looking into their eyes rather than looking at a piece of paper in front of me helping them to believe that I saw them as God's "dear people."

This was a frightening prospect for me because I was unsure whether I could keep a whole sermon in my memory, and I worried that I would lose depth in my preaching without my manuscript because I have important theological insight on the paper in front of me. What I had to realize was that I had to find my own method of writing and rehearsing the sermon and not attempt to mimic other preachers. It took time to gain confidence and find my own rhythm of preparation and performance to make it natural, but the connection that I now have with God's "dear people" gathered in my congregation as I preach far outweighs the fears that had previously held me back.

Beyond preaching without a manuscript, in most cases, I also have come out of the pulpit and into the midst of the congregation during the preaching act. This has helped me to feel that I am one who has been called out from among the priesthood of all believers[6] to preach among and with my fellow believers, rather than one who preaches at them. I can look into their eyes, feel how they are reacting to the preaching, see the nodding and shaking of heads, note the turn of the little heads of the children as they relate to something that I am saying, and even once in a while, hear an "amen" come from a corner of the congregation—none of which I could do as fully when I had the manuscript in front of me standing in the pulpit. I feel that without the manuscript and being in their midst, I am able to "not only speak *to* [my] congregants, [but also] speak *with* them, on their behalf, and as one of them," which makes my preaching stronger and (I hope) more effective.[7]

I have also found greater passion in my preaching again, and much of this is because I sense this connection with God's "dear people" of all ages with whom I am preaching. As Joseph Webb writes, "In order for one's Christian witness to be as moving as it can possibly be, that witness must appear to those who receive it to come 'from the preacher's heart' and 'not from a page of the preacher's sermon.'"[8] Because my passion is engaged, the congregation's passion is becoming engaged as well, and the children and youth are engaged in worship in a new and different way. All of God's "dear people" are connected to God's Word in new and exciting ways. [9]

What the Youngest of God's "Dear People" Have Taught Us

Since I have stopped using a manuscript, have risked being appropriately vulnerable in my preaching and have engaged more conversationally with the congregation, the children and youth have become more involved in the preaching act. The primary lesson that the youngest of God's "dear people" have taught us in this experience is that it is okay to make the preaching act a real conversation with interaction.

The children and youth will answer questions posed in the sermon, whether or not I am expecting a response. They will ask questions at times when they do not understand. They nod and shake their heads. In most cases, there is evidence that at least something in the sermon has connected with them, and they feel the urge to respond.

The children and youth have begun to show the adults that preaching can be a conversation during which it is okay to say what you think and not just think it. This has led to a more interactive and authentic experience of the preaching act and engaged more of God's "dear people" in the preaching act.

Engagement

Engaging the Youngest of God's "Dear People"

Having found ways to invite God's "dear people" of all ages into the conversation—both in preparation and presentation of the sermon—and to connect with the congregation through authentic preaching, I came to realize that I also must find ways to engage the members of the congregation in the preaching act, especially the children and the youth. The one consistent message that I received from the youth with whom I worked was that they wanted to see visual images and media presentations as part of the preaching act. The world in which they live functions in sound bites and media clips, and they desired to have similar engagement in their worship experience. As a result of this, I have begun to incorporate media into my preaching through the use of social and news media in my sermon preparation and through the use of visual images and presentational technology in the preaching act.

As preachers, we want the connection that we make between the texts and the lives of our hearers to be relevant—we want it to make a difference in their lives. As Karyn Wiseman notes:

> In the biblical accounts of Jesus' preaching he passionately told stories that matched the context and the experiences of those to whom he spoke. . . . He spoke from his heart and brought people into a new understanding of who God meant them to be and how they could experience God's grace and abundant love. He went where the people were. He spent time in their houses of worship and in the homes of friends. He walked the roads with his followers and met people where they were. His words changed people; his touch healed people; his acceptance transformed people; and his life, death, and resurrection changed the world. His words were relevant—before relevant was something cool to be.[10]

Like Jesus, we want our preaching to connect to the context and the experience of our people. However, in these days, to be where our people are includes not only visiting their homes and walking the road with them, but it also includes meeting them in the digital world in which many of them spend so much time.

The world around us is changing at a rapid pace, which is made all the more obvious by the speed at which information is shared on the internet, through social media, and over the air waves in news media. Thus, to engage our listeners, it is important for the preacher to pay attention to what is going on in popular media and social media in a very deliberate manner to be more in tune with the issues that concern all of God's "dear people" in our congregation, from the youngest to the oldest, as well as the ways that those same "dear people" are relating to those issues. Once the preacher is in tune with the concerns of the congregation, the preacher then can find ways to "relate the text to the lives of [his or her] parishioners, to help make concrete meaning where there might not be any or where there might be confusion."[11] The preacher can also address these concerns in ways that comfort the hearers with the promises of the gospel or challenge the hearers to consider new perspectives on the issues informed by scripture.

Once we have an understanding of the issues and images that are speaking to the members of our congregations of all ages, we are then freed to consider how those issues and images might be incorporated into a visual presentation that might add meaning to the preaching act. While there definitely are issues with the use of media and technology in preaching, I still believe that it can be a helpful way to engage and enhance the preacher's message. As Quentin J. Schultze notes, "Presentational technologies can appropriately highlight sermon points and focus attention on particular liturgical practices."[12] My goal is to enhance and highlight my messages, when appropriate, through the use of presentational technologies as an additional way to engage the congregation by capturing the attention and imagination of the listeners of all ages.

I do not use video or visual imagery for every sermon. Sometimes this is because I simply do not have the time in a week to put together an effective presentation. At other times, I am unable to find a visual image or series of images that speaks to me on a given topic or text. Because I want the visual images to have meaning and purpose in the sermon, I do "not use visuals for the sake of using visuals," but I want the visuals to "grow naturally out of the text study and other preparation for the sermon."[13]

When it is determined that there are visual images that could enhance the preaching act, then a video clip that speaks the needed message, or more often, a video that I create is used to help make the desired point for the sermon. It is strategically placed in the sermon in order to make the most impact, which differs from sermon to sermon. It is also important to note that not all visual imagery needs to be technological in nature, but can simply be symbols or signs that help to make a point. In some cases, items that the youngest of God's "dear people" can touch and manipulate better aid in making the desired point and leave a more lasting impression.

Regardless of the types of images, hearers of all ages connect with the images in ways that help them to remember the sermon in the following week. Parents comment that the images give them something to talk with their children about throughout the week. For children, it gives them something to focus on, if only for a few minutes, and helps them to connect the message of scripture to their real world. When a preacher is able to reach people in this way, then he or she is able to engage them in the preaching and draw them into the message. The images draw emotional responses, in most cases, which often leads all of God's "dear people" to a more profound experience of the gospel.

What the Youngest of God's "Dear People" Have Taught Us

With their insistence on the use of visual images in preaching so that they can better understand and relate to the sermon, the children and youth have helped to teach, or at least remind, older members of the congregation that no one experiences God in the exact same manner. God comes to us in many and various ways, and God comes to us using means that help us to understand God and God's love for us. For some of us, we experience God most profoundly through the reading of scripture and the proclamation of the gospel in preaching. For others, God is most present to us through the sacraments, through Baptism and the Lord's Supper, where we can tangibly touch, taste, smell and hear God's grace through the water, the bread and the wine. For still others, it is in the singing of hymns and praise songs, through the music of the choirs, the organ, or the band that God comes to us most clearly. And for many, especially our children and youth, God and God's love become real to them in the images that they see. So, while none of us experience God's presence in worship in exactly the same way, as we have incorporated imagery into our worship, particularly during the preaching act, the children and youth have helped the older members of the congregation recognize the ways in which visual images can enhance the message of the sermon so that all of God's "dear people" can experience God's presence with them.

Conclusion

I admit that not every sermon that I preach will adequately invite, connect, and engage all of God's "dear people" in my congregation in a way that everyone will hear a sermon spoken directly to them. However, even on my worst days of preaching, there will be something that will resonate with the hearer, as long as I am faithfully sharing the good news of God in Jesus Christ through my experience of scripture and life as well as the leading of the Holy Spirit,. Even when I have more questions than answers, the grace and promise of Christ will be shared. As Barbara Lundblad says well:

> The Spirit hovers over the lingering text and beckons a conversation with the preacher and with those who will hear the words in the midst of worship. This particular conver-

sation has never happened before; this text speaking to this preacher and these people in this time and place. Through such Spirit-born conversation, God is at work transforming memory into presence.[14]

By inviting, connecting, and engaging with the congregation I serve with the good news of Jesus Christ, I am better able to preach in authentic ways that resonate and help all of God's "dear people" in my congregation, from the youngest to the oldest, find themselves in God's story. I now can see the passion, the hope, the joy, and the relief in the eyes of a child struggling at school or a father who has just lost his job, because they now can trust that they are beloved children of God, that God is there with them, and nothing in all of creation can separate them from the love of God that is in Christ Jesus our Lord. In these ways, my passion for the gospel is renewed, as I seek to invite, connect, and engage all over again so that everyone can know that lesson that I learned so many years ago from Kurt Hendel: God's "dear people" includes everyone—even the children.

Endnotes

1 Robert Kolb and Timothy J. Wengert, eds., *The Book of Concord: The Confessions of the Evangelical Lutheran Church* (Minneapolis: Fortress Press, 2000).

2 *The Use of the Means of Grace* was a statement that was adopted for guidance and practice of Word and Sacrament in the Evangelical Lutheran Church in America at the 1997 Churchwide Assembly.

3 More detail about this method of preparation and performance of the preaching act can be found in my thesis: Carrie L. Lewis La Plante, "Preaching with the Whole Congregation: Inviting Children and Youth without Losing the Adults" (D.Min. thesis, Lutheran School of Theology at Chicago, 2015).

4 Carolyn C. Brown, *You Can Preach to the Kids Too! Designing Sermons for Adults and Children* (Nashville: Abingdon Press, 1997), 28-30.

5 Joseph M. Webb, *Preaching Without Notes* (Nashville: Abingdon Press, 2001), 25.

6 While the term "priesthood of all believers" was never actually used by Martin Luther, this concept has been used by Lutherans to describe Luther's understanding that all Christians, by virtue of their baptism, are called by God to their vocations, whatever those might be. As we serve in those vocations, whether as a teacher, a doctor, an auto mechanic, a pastor, a housewife, a student, or anything else, we serve one another to bring health and wholeness to the body of Christ. In all we do, we are to encourage one another in our vocations and in our life in Christ, for, as Paul writes in Romans, "For as in one body we have many members, and not all the members have the same function, so we, who are many, are one body in Christ, and individually we are members one of another" (Romans 12:4-5). More can be read on this topic in Luther's 1520 treatise, "To the Christian Nobility of the German Nation Concerning

the Reform of the Christian Estate." Martin Luther, "To the Christian Nobility of the German Nation Concerning the Reform of the Christian Estate," trans. Charles M. Jacobs, rev. James Atkinson, in *Selected Writings of Martin Luther: 1517-1520,* ed. Theodore G. Tappert (Minneapolis: Fortress Press, 2007), 264-266.

7 Charles L. Bartow, *God's Human Speech: A Practical Theology of Proclamation* (Grand Rapids: Wm. B. Eerdmans Publishing Co., 1997), 114.

8 Webb, 30.

9 Ibid., 26.

10 Karyn L. Wiseman, *I Refuse to Preach a Boring Sermon! Engaging the 21st Century Listener* (Cleveland: The Pilgrim Press, 2013), 81.

11 Ibid., 84.

12 Quentin J. Schultze, *High-Tech Worship? Using Presentational Technologies Wisely* (Grand Rapids: Baker Books, 2004), 39.

13 Richard A. Jensen, *Envisioning the Word: The Use of Visual Images in Preaching* (Minneapolis: Fortress Press, 2005), 92-3.

14 Barbara Lundblad, *Transforming the Stone: Preaching through Resistance to Change* (Nashville: Abingdon Press, 2001), 147.

Engaging the Christian Tradition

CHAPTER SEVEN

The Ethical Rationality of Luther's Theology of Family

Dean M. Apel

One of the challenges of contemporary theology is how to access and appropriate the gifts of theologians of bygone eras or other cultures for questions of other times and places.[1] If we consider each theological artifact (book, article, sermon, artwork, hymn, counseling session, Sunday school class) as an instance of contextualization, we may learn as much or more from how that theologian addresses his/her context as we do from the specific conclusions that a theologian makes.[2] In ethical questions, we may refer to the theologian's way of negotiating his/her context as that person's ethical rationality. Over the centuries, many have considered Luther's ethics to be paradoxical, if not contradictory. But is there an underlying tectonics to how Luther deals theologically with his complex and foreign (to us) context?[3] In fact, many attempts have been made to understand Luther's ethical rationality. Is there an interpretation of Luther's ethical rationality which best accounts for his theology of marriage and family? In this essay, I will examine several possibilities.

The Two Regiments

Many Luther scholars consider Luther's doctrine of the two regiments to be his primary ethical dialectic. The interpretation of this dialectic is much more problematic than many assume.[4] For the purposes of this section, we will consider the two regiments scheme to be that scheme which distinguishes between how God rules worldly matters and how God rules spiritual matters. An examination of Luther's voluminous writings shows that marriage and family is not restricted to one regiment or the other, but that God "rules" family life through both.

The secular nature of marriage/family. In discussing the impediments of the medieval Roman Catholic canon law, Luther rejects the impediment which forbids a Christian from marrying a non-Christian because of marriage's civil nature.[5] A Christian is permitted to do other bodily things, such as eating, drinking, and business, with non-Christians who are just as much God's good creation as any saint. Therefore, one may also marry a non-Christian (LW 45:25).The fact that marriage and family are basically secular matters is one reason why Luther is reluctant to expound so much on them.[6] As part of the ecclesiastical order, his sphere of responsibility does not technically include marriage and family. Instead, the governing authorities are to enforce the cultural customs relevant for their time and place. This is why the marriage ceremony proper takes place outside of the church (LW 53:111-112).[7]

The Advantages of Being a Christian in Marriage/Family

Despite the essentially secular nature of marriage and family, in Luther's theology there are important Christian dimensions to it as well. Since natural reason[8] and the Bible have opposing evaluations of marriage, family and women, those who have access to the Bible have access to God's positive evaluation (LW 1:70). Another aspect of seeing marriage and family from God's point of view is that one lives one's spirituality in that context. It is the place where one learns to cast off the old self and rely more and more on God. The Christian also has the blessing of being able to appeal to God in prayer in the midst of the difficulties of marriage. So even though the marriage ceremony proper takes places outside of the church, the marriage of Christians is also blessed within the church (LW 53:113). Perhaps because of their knowledge of God's Word, part of the preachers' vocation is to instruct people how to live in their estates. The preacher: "checks the rebellious; teaches obedience, morals, discipline, and temporal estates and offices. Of all the good things a pastor does these are, to be sure, the least. Yet they are so high and noble that the wisest of all the heathen have never known or understood them, much less been able to do them" (*On Keeping Children in School,* 1530, LW 46:226).[8]

Although non-Christians were created good, much is distorted in marriage and family life because of sin. In the context of explaining why it would be disadvantageous for the Germans to be ruled by the non-Christian Turks, one of Luther's main points is that they have perverted the marriage estate through polygyny, dowry, and sodomy.[9] So although marriage and family belong to creation and not to salvation, Christians have many advantages over non-Christians in living within the estate.[10]

The Civil Use of the Law

The civil use of the law is related to Luther's temporal regiment. In Luther's thought, this use of the law is how God constrains even the ungodly to care for other people. As such it is also active in family life. The estate of family life is one of the means by which God cares for others:

> As an example of how work in all such stations is conducive to the good of others, Luther points to a mother who cares for her children, and a father who must arise in the morning and labor to give support to his family. . . . The human being is self-willed, desiring that whatever happens shall be to his own advantage. When husband and wife, in marriage, serve one another and their children, this is not due to the heart's spontaneous and undisturbed expression of love, every day and hour. Rather in marriage as an institution something compels the husband's selfish desires to yield and likewise inhibits the husband's selfish desires to yield and likewise inhibits the egocentricity of the woman's heart. . . . it is the 'station' itself which is the ethical agent, for it is God who is active through the law on earth.[11]

The civil use of the law, then, is another aspect of the secular nature of marriage and family; it is how God "rules" marriage and family in the temporal regiment. And Christians do not hold a special position in regards to the civil righteousness which the civil law compels and inculcates. Indeed it is also operative among Christians who are *simul justi et peccatores* in this lifetime; as sinners they will need the constraint of the civil use.

The Three Estates

Oswald Bayer argues that the three estates doctrine is more central to Luther's ethical rationality than the two regiments doctrine.[12] For example, Luther uses it, in a way similar to the law and gospel, as an important interpretive key to the Bible.

> First, the Bible speaks and teaches about the works of God. About this there is no doubt. These works are divided into three hierarchies: the household [*oeconomiam*], the government [*politiam*], and the church [*ecclesiam*]. If a verse does not fit the church, we should let it stay in the government or the

> household, whichever it is best suited to. (Winter 1542-43,
> LW 54:446, #5533)

Luther believed that the reorientation of spirituality from monastery to the three estates was one of the most significant achievements of the Reformation.[13]

Perhaps because Luther never devoted a treatise to the subject, he uses and writes about the three estates in quite different ways. The following things can be said about the relationship between *oikonomia* and *politia.* (a) Along with *ecclesia, oikonomia* is, strictly speaking, an order of creation. *Politia* is God's way to restrict evil after the Fall and therefore not a part of God's original creation. (b) When parents and clergy fail in their callings, Luther allows and almost enjoins disobedience within *oikonomia* and *ecclesia.* However, disobedience within *politia* is usually strictly forbidden to Christians.[14] (c) Especially in his many statements about education, Luther emphasizes that *oikonomia* is the source of leaders within *politia* and *ecclesia.* (d) The authority structures (i.e. between ruler and subject) of *politia* are ultimately derived from the parent-child relationship within *oikonomia.*[15]

Also, it is not easy to correlate the three estates doctrine with the two regiments doctrine. It might appear that *oikonomia* and *politia* belong to the temporal regiment and *ecclesia* to the spiritual. But we have already seen that the estate of marriage has a very significant spiritual/ Christian dimension. And, of course, insofar as clergy are humans with needs for food, clothing and lodging, they belong also to *oikonomia* and *politia.* This is significant for Bayer:

> By [lumping *ecclesia* with *oikonomia* and *politia*]—essentially opposing the rigid polarities of dialectical theology—he makes it possible, and indeed necessary, to consider Christianity as a religion, as an institution and as a temporal phenomenon. . . . the status ecclesiaticus is not identical with the spiritual governance. For after the fall and before the eschaton, the Christian church is not the pure kingdom of God as the church invisible is; rather, visibility and invisibility permeate each other. In this world and ages, the status ecclesiasticus is also a governmental order [pastors are paid, dismissed according to disciplinary procedure, etc.].[16]

Luther encouraged the heathen to construct the outward forms of their own *ecclesia* (*Psalm 117,* 1530, LW 14:17-24).

Luther can highly evaluate pagan wisdom, to the point of the hyperbolic supposition that pagans are both wiser and more righteous *coram hominibus* in *oikonomia* and *politia* (*Psalm 101*, 1534, LW 13:199-201). This would seem to predispose Luther to appreciate pagan forms of marriage and family. In fact, however, Luther is quite judgmental of the opinions about marriage found in the pagan classical philosophers and ethicists and of the marriage practices of the Turks.

Bayer helpfully refers to a commentary on Psalm 127 from 1532/3 which is not translated in the LW. There Luther uses the Aristotelian scheme of the four *causae* to describe what pagans can and cannot know about *oikonomia* and *politia*:

> Insight into the material and formal cause of social life and the arts, in short, the exercise of reason, is conceded to Aristotle, Demosthenes, and Cicero.[17] This praise, however, is not unqualified. It is their failing—as it is the failing of all the godless—that they desire themselves to be the efficient cause and the final cause to create and perfect economy and politics. "This, however," says Luther, "is not for you"; yours is but to "be an instrument." But anyone who is not content to be God's instrument and mandatary, and one who is not satisfied with the ascribed "judicial and governmental dignity of a political animal," corrupts and perverts, by his arrogance and ingratitude, the exercise of the reason given to him.[18]

The ancient sages' misuse of the efficient and final causes is only part of the story. Sin normally drags a good thing down. And we should not be surprised that both Christians and non-Christians can pervert the estates which God intends for good. "Even though we do not condemn civil and political activities, the human heart nevertheless taints these good works when it uses them for vainglory, gain, and oppression either against its neighbor or against God" (LW 2:119). In fact, Luther's occupation with the problem can probably be traced as his reaction to a Christian (not a non-Christian) perversion of the estates, i.e. monasticism. Again, if Christians have some advantages vis-a-vis *oikonomia* and *politia*, it is not because they are inherently superior to non-Christians. It is instead because they have access to God's revelation and power.

Forell takes exception to an interpretation of Luther which was apparently prevalent in the first half of the twentieth century. "It has been claimed that Luther insisted upon the general and eternal validity of the social system of his time."[19] A careful analysis of Luther's writings reveals that he is far from absolutizing any particular social system. He recognizes and affirms cultural differences in the living out of ecclesia, oikonomia and politia. And he recognizes that the outward expressions of the orders also change over time. In fact, he believes that God raises up cultural heroes from time to time who acting, "under the influence of special divine guidance, . . . are used by God to bring about the necessary changes of the existing political and social conditions. They are the means which God uses to change the concrete expression the natural orders find in any historical situation."[20]

The Reformation itself is obviously aimed at the perversion of the outward forms of ecclesia. And it can be understood as a revolution in a certain sense of the word. Luther engaged politia as well. He condemned those who would misuse public office for their own gain and encouraged Christian rulers to consider their office to be service to their subjects.[21] His insight that love ought to be the spirit of the estates forced Luther to engage his society on all fronts:

> This explains Luther's personal attitude towards the social order. When he tried to reform schools and churches, restrain usury, counsel fair trade practices, and organize the rehabilitation of the poor, he merely put into practice what he had preached and tried to bring his Christian insights to bear upon the social order.[22]

If Luther nevertheless was tempermentally conservative,[23] we might put the best construction on it and understand that he feared the graver potential consequences of political and social revolution and that he was not optimistic that the world would last long enough to make real improvements.[24]

The advantages of Luther's three estates social ethic are clear. By separating ecclesia from oikonomia and politia, the latter estates are not cosmicized and are therefore relativized. The further distinction between the universal estates (natural law/ten commandments) and their cultural manifestations (positive law) allows modification of those cultural manifestations.[25]

The way to test whether the stations are functioning correctly is love or, as Bayer prefers, a discipleship ethic. Love focuses and relativizes the estates and conceives them properly.

The two terms [Discipleship Ethos and Table of Duties Ethos] do not address different substantial ethical fields, but refer to different dimensions of one and the same thing. "Discipleship" here means the intensity and radicalism with which the commandment to love is fulfilled. The "table of duties" directs our attention to forms of existence which fulfill basic needs and the applications of which are in a constant process of renewal; the material content of these concerns Christians and non-Christians alike.[26]

Gustav Wingren's *Luther on Vocation* (1942)

Wingren attempts to describe Luther's understanding of the Christian's primary ethical obligations in terms of vocation or one's station in life. The Christian's situation is between God and the devil and between earth and heaven.[27] The following table summarizes some of Wingren's complex understanding of Luther's ethics and theology.

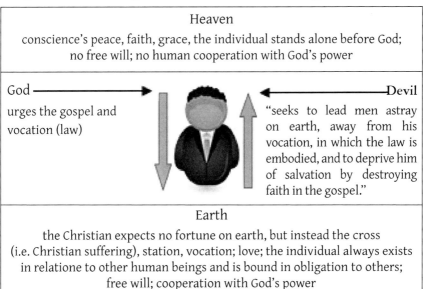

Heaven
conscience's peace, faith, grace, the individual stands alone before God; no free will; no human cooperation with God's power

God ⟶		Devil ⟵
urges the gospel and vocation (law)		"seeks to lead men astray on earth, away from his vocation, in which the law is embodied, and to deprive him of salvation by destroying faith in the gospel."

Earth
the Christian expects no fortune on earth, but instead the cross (i.e. Christian suffering), station, vocation; love; the individual always exists in relatione to other human beings and is bound in obligation to others; free will; cooperation with God's power

Luther's Interpretation of the Human Condition According to Wingren

For our purposes, I want to highlight only three aspects of this complex scheme. First, marriage and family are between heaven and earth. In Wingren's interpretation, marriage and family do not belong to heaven; they are not the vehicles through which one is saved.

Second, marriage and family exist between God and the devil. On the one hand, the devil seeks to disparage these God-pleasing vocations as detrimental to spiritual life and salvation and to draw us away from the exercise of love *in relatione*. On the other hand, marriage and family are some of the ways in which God acts in this world in order (a) to restrain sin and evil, and (b) to give the Christian exercise for prayer and faith. For Luther the most insidious idea is that our works in marriage and family or elsewhere might somehow contribute to our salvation.[29] Such an idea disrupts both how God intends to save us and how God intends that we serve each other.

Third, Wingren emphasizes and illustrates how Luther's ethical rationality is open to change in a number of ways:

> We often come upon Luther's varied efforts to make it clear that man's outward conduct must not be bound and fixed by any scheme determined in advance. Such concepts as "freedom in externals," "freedom to do or to leave undone," "fairness," etc., can all be comprehended within the idea of God's ceaseless recreation of earthly relationships. Through such concepts the system is kept open for ever new beginnings.[30]

Wingren writes that the "pull of God," i.e. service to others through the vocations, "makes unchanging conservatism impossible."[31] Change arises and is inevitable not necessarily because God wants to change the system nor because the system was built for change. Instead, change is inevitable because God counteracts the devil's attacks in new ways as they arise:

> God by himself would be able to let the world continue as it is, steady, unchanging, and without fresh beginnings; but the devil does not permit it. We live in a world that is always being destroyed and always made new. Fresh creation takes place all the time *contra diabolum*, against the devil. God's new measures in the external world are combative actions, and as such they are unexpected and sudden, springing forth from *Gottes Freiheit*, from God's freedom which is not fenced in by any lines laid down in advance.[32]

The devil corrupts previously good orders and vocations and therefore God creates things anew in order to counteract the devil's corruptions.[33] The love which God demands in vocations can never be satisfied with the vocation itself or find the ethical content of the vocation in the vocation itself. Love determines and qualifies how the vocation is exercised.[34] Wingren cites the testamentary passage in the *Confession on Christ's Supper* (1528) to substantiate this interpretation of Luther.

Imitation of another person's godliness (i.e. imitation of saints) is excluded when the goal of such imitation is to manipulate God into saving instead of looking toward the needs of the others.[35] Prayer is the struggle to receive God's wisdom and power in discerning the best course of action *in relatione*.[36]

One must also maintain a certain distance from the positive law.[37] The positive law can be abused, and Luther encourages a practical reason approach in many cases of its application. The ethical virtue of fairness (*epieikeia*) is crucial for Luther in applying the positive law.[38] Since ethical human subjects move through unique moments (*Stündelein*) nothing can be determined in advance. Instead, it is in those unique moments that the human is required to act. In Luther's understanding of history, God sometimes raises up heroes whom God empowers to make fundamental societal changes.[39]

Wingren's interpretation of Luther's ethical rationality is classic not the least because he is able to incorporate so many elements of Luther's theological ethics into it. Although he does not give focused attention to the contexts of Luther's writings on the subject of marriage and family, his approach goes a long way to explain how Luther's ethical rationality is open to context, i.e. how Luther understands God as a kind of strategic general in a battle with the devil and humans and ready to modify the strategy as the battle proceeds.

George Forrell's *Faith Active in Love: An Investigation of the Principles Underlying Luther's Social Ethics* (1954)

Forell attempts to describe Luther's ethical rationality in four principles. The *methodological principle,* that we are justified by grace alone through faith alone, provides the presupposition of Luther's ethics.[40] It is certainly an advantage in describing Luther's ethical rationality to mention explicitly the central doctrine of Luther's system. Almost all that Luther has to say about marriage and family can be traced back to that central idea. Likewise the two regiment and three estates schemes described above both presuppose this doctrine. Wingren's interpretation of Luther's vocational ethics is also built on justification by grace, viz. freedom from self-justification makes space for the true exercise of love in the vocations.

The *ethical principle* simply means that for Luther our works are not about making us happy or holy or saved. Instead, our works are evaluated by how they benefit the neighbor. In terms of marriage and family, we exercise our freedom, rights and responsibilities in our familial relationships in order that the other, not we, might benefit.

The *practical principle* concerns the three estates scheme as described above, but also includes Luther's view of the law. Forrell especially plays up the distinction between natural law and positive law in Luther. Although it cannot be completely equated with the Decalogue (especially the second and third commandments have some characteristics of Jewish ethnic law), the natural law is best found there. The positive laws in which various leaders and cultures attempt to codify the natural law are subject to change. Susceptible as they are to sin, the positive laws must be constantly modified and corrected in order to serve God's purposes in the world. And occasionally God sends a heroic man (*vir heroicus*) in order to overthrow the currently reigning positive law and replace it with a law more in tune with the natural law and less susceptible to abuse by the people of that time and place. Furthermore, Luther advocates that the law always be exercised and applied equitably. The operative words for Luther here are *epieikeia* (Greek), *aequitas* (Latin) and *Billigkeit* (German). Forrell's practical principle is helpful in reminding us of Luther's resistance to reify any particular ethical or legal decision, i.e. any positive law. Because sin and the devil learn how to use even good things, Christians and society have to be constantly vigilant in discerning God's will in the "natural law."

The *limiting principle* refers to Luther's expectation of the imminence of the end of this age. On the one hand, the eschatological horizon led to Luther's reluctance to expect our work to yield any significant and lasting societal or cultural transformation.[41] On the other hand, the realization of the (relatively) imminent death of each Christian explains Luther's advocacy for the toleration of suffering—an advocacy which may have had unintended consequences for suffering and oppressed people in the later history of Lutheranism.

Willliam Lazareth's *Christians in Society: Luther, the Bible, and Social Ethics* (2001)

Lazareth takes the law-gospel dialectic as one of the primary undergirding planks in Luther's ethical rationality. Therefore, the Law has a spiritual function to judge Christians in society and a temporal function to preserve them. The gospel has a spiritual function to justify Christians in society and a temporal function to sanctify them. These four functions are all operations of God's grace on Christians in society, but Satan attempts to impact Christians with sin,[42] chiefly by confusing law and gospel and the ways God rules heaven and earth through the same.[43] Lazareth complicates the law-gospel dialectic by overlaying two forms of the two regiment teaching: the two regiments as God vs. Satan (in Luther's earlier work) and as Christ and Caesar (in Luther's later work). One advantage of Lazareth's book is how he roots these four operations of law and gospel and the four kinds of rule (God, Satan, Christ, Caesar) in Luther's work on specific biblical characters and books. Luther's work with Romans and Genesis are important parts of Lazareth's analysis.

Lazareth also helpfully includes an introductory chapter describing the post-Nazi recovery of Luther's ethical rationality. From Ernst Troeltsch through Max Weber to Karl Barth and beyond, the Nazi Holocaust provided the basis for much critique of Luther's ethical rationality. The main accusation against Luther was that he had made government and culture autonomous unto themselves (*Eigengesetzlichkeit*) and therefore unassailable by the church.[44] The post-Nazi recovery (of which Forrell and Lazareth are representatives) attempts to show that whatever else Luther might have meant in separating types of rule (two regiments, law and gospel), he did not mean that the God of the Bible and the church was not active in the government and culture. On the contrary, preachers had the "auxiliary service" of correcting governments and culture which had gone astray from God's will. But even Lazareth admits that Luther's fear of social disorder may have led him to emphasize the inviolability of government and cultural configurations: "While rightly championing temporal authority, Luther's own culturally conditioned patriarchal spirit admittedly also led him to oppose social disorder far more fervently than either political or economic injustice. His one-sided tilt needs major current correction."[45]

Lazareth's conceptualization of Luther's ethical rationality parallels Wingren's and Forrell's, but in a way which attempts to urge its relevance on the early twenty-first-century Zeitgeist.

Feminist Approaches to Luther's Ethical Rationality

Rosemary Radford Ruether's *Christianity and the Making of the Modern Family* (2000) includes a chapter on "Family, Work, Gender, and Church in the Reformation Era" which extensively cites Luther as an example of the broader Reformation movement. Luther's ideology of family comes under the same scrutiny which she applies to all family ideologies. "I intend to show that shifting ideologies involving the family and 'family values' are generally coded messages about women and how they should behave in relation to men."[46] Her contextual analysis of the Reformation family ideology includes the following: (a) the Aristotle revival which marginalized women by arguing that they were politically inferior by nature;[47] (b) urbanization and the guilds which marginalized women from the means of production;[48] (c) city and territorial based reformations which stood to gain from the acquisition of church-owned properties, including the monasteries and convents which Luther, among others, helped to permanently close down;[49] and (d) the fear of social chaos and subsequent reliance on the strong arm of the ruling authorities.[50]

All of these things plus an overly pessimistic view of human potential led Luther and others to sacralize marriage, family life and traditional gendered divisions of labor, thus constricting opportunities for women and other "non-patriarchs."[51] Ruether emphasizes Luther's comments where he indicated that women were inferior to men even *ante lapsum*, although she admits that Luther understood the pre-Fall inferiority to be of a different degree than the post-Fall inferiority.[52] Invoking Troeltsch's and Schüssler-Fiorenza's *Liebespartriarchalismus*, she argues that Luther imagined pre-Fall paradise "as a sort of autonomous family farm run by a benevolent patriarch and his docile, hardworking, fertile wife. . . ."[53] Luther's understanding that women were excluded from *politia*, a measure taken by God after the Fall, is understood by Ruether as a sacralization of women's exclusion from political rulership. Less appropriate for an analysis of Luther, she blames the Reformers for disparaging nature and body: "The reformers combined nominalism with a neo-Augustinian theology of fallen nature to radically separate humans from any "natural" connection with God, thereby also denying the sacramental potential of nature. Nothing natural could be a bearer of God's grace."[54] Also not as apropos to Luther is her interpretation of the Reformers as excluding folk ritual and customs from wedding ceremonies.[55] Luther strove to allow local cultural customs in the celebrations of weddings even at the expense of the church's control (see, e.g., LW 53:111-112).

Although nuanced, Ruether's analysis of Luther's theology of marriage and family emphasizes the ways in which he argues for and sacralizes a traditional family system which includes assumptions about male dominance and female subordination. But Ruether's analysis is also helpful in lifting forth some of the economic and political contextual factors which formed a background to Luther's theology of marriage and family.

In 2003, Susan C. Karant-Nunn and Merry E. Wiesner-Hanks edited and introduced a compilation of Luther passages on women, *Luther on Women: A Sourcebook*. They suggest that traditional treatments of Luther biography (Bainton, Plass, Oberman and Ozment are cited) place Luther's views of marriage and family as an interlude between the early Reformation years and the last decade of "theological maturation and elaboration."[56] Most Luther biographies consider Luther's impact on marriage and family as significant and positive. Scholarship on the influence of Luther's theology on marriage and family are grouped in two directions. Older confessionalists and newer church historians trained in Germany "frequently describe Luther as rescuing marriage (and by extension women) from the depths of dishonor created by the medieval Catholic championing of virginity . . ." and the consequence of his theology to improve the status of women and to "heighten their social role. Luther took great care, they note, to highlight the important role women played in both the Old and New Testaments, and specifically and vociferously attacked the scholastic denigration of women."[57]

The second direction taken by a group of scholars, "most of them social historians and literary scholars trained outside of Germany," have viewed Luther's impact much more negatively. In a way similar to Ruether, these scholars emphasize the following features of Luther's theology of marriage and family: (a) by elevating the patriarchal marriage and family, Luther denigrated other options for women (such as life in the convent or other forms of the single life); (b) Luther is supposed to have accepted the tradition received through Aristotle that women are by nature inferior to men; (c) Luther understands female inferiority to be *ante lapsarian*; and (d) "biblical examples of women's preaching or teaching were not to be taken as authorizing such actions among contemporary women."[58]

Ultimately Karant-Nunn and Wiesner-Hanks take the position that as a whole Luther endorsed traditional patriarchy and thereby influenced family ideologies up to the present. "We today are justified in regarding the great Reformer as a force for tradition rather than an innovator."[59]

"Martin Luther renewed many venerable generalities and contributed them to a definition of women and subordination that helped to inform ideals of proper domestic relations down to the twentieth century."[60] He did this chiefly by assuming and advocating the notion that women are by nature fit for home life. In other words, his understanding of the female gender role was as a mother and homemaker. "For Luther, women's anatomy bespoke their destiny as mothers...."[61] "In the abstract, Luther envisioned each woman's and girl's confinement to the home, where, in pious mood, she labored efficiently and frugally. He regarded even the domestic sphere as under the direction of the paterfamilias...."[62]

But Karant-Nunn and Wiesner-Hanks significantly nuance this understanding of Luther's assumption of the traditional patriarchy. For them, Luther's experience of being married to Katie had a profound effect on his practice of patriarchy, even if it had less effect on his understanding of it. "Ideology and stereotype were broken up in the mortar and pestel of daily exigency."[63] To his traditional assumptions, Luther "added the powerful leavening of love, and he left us his beneficent example."[64] So Luther was "a man of his day and yet a creative one,"[65] in other words, he contextually moved the marriage and family ideologies which he had inherited along a different vector.

As important as these feminist critiques are for understanding the impact of Luther's theology on subsequent ideologies of marriage and family, they are less helpful for understanding Luther in his own context. They perhaps help us understand more about Luther's impact on subsequent generations than about his ethical rationality. It is not particularly surprising that he would be blind to some of his culture's proclivities and assumptions about women, marriage, reproduction and family. And in many cases, Luther felt somewhat uncomfortably constrained by Scripture (such as 1 Corinthians 14:34; 1 Timothy 2:14, and 1 Peter 3:7) to advocate views which were accepted by his culture—perhaps not because they were part of his culture, but instead precisely because he understood them as scriptural.

In attempting to understand Luther as a contextual theologian, it is important to note what he explicitly accepts and rejects from his inherited culture. In the development of his theology, he takes a "Christ against culture" approach especially on two fronts: the convent/monastery as a form of works-righteousness and the cultured disparagement of women and marriage. Whether or not the restriction of women's role to reproduction and home life was oppressive must be decided on how one assesses the high medieval compulsion toward the convent. In many, perhaps most, cases, the decision to enter the convent was made by the parents. In Luther's understanding, those who made an adult decision to enter the convent and monastery did so under an oppressive and impossible understanding of salvation—that somehow the monastic life was a quicker avenue to right relationship with God. One may question how astute an observer Luther was of his own culture, but again and again in his writings he describes his marriage and family theology as a campaign against their cultural despisers (both in the rational forms of the ancient pagan sages and in the spiritual forms of the contemporary ecclesiastical hierarchies).

Finally, it is important to point out a fundamental disagreement between some forms of feminism and Luther's theology. For some forms of feminism, oppression results in suffering, and suffering is something which by its very nature must be opposed and struggled against. For Luther, suffering was a salutary part of the Christian life and, while not to be sought, was certainly something which God could use for the improvement of the individual Christian. Luther parallels the suffering of the monastery with the suffering which is part and parcel of household relations and even suggests that household suffering is more spiritually challenging than asceticism. In other words, Luther recognizes with modern feminism that the (patriarchal) household will cause women to suffer. But for him, this kind of suffering is not necessarily bad from a spiritual point of view.[66]

Marriage and Family in Luther's Ethical Rationality

I will not here try to argue for the superiority of one conceptualization of Luther's ethical rationality over another vis-à-vis his marriage and family theology. Instead I will suggest a synthesis of the preceding in four principles:

(a) Luther started thinking about marriage and family because of his Reformation breakthrough. *Justification by grace alone through faith alone* is the origin of his family theology and thus becomes the touchstone for his theology of marriage and family. His endorsement of marriage and parenthood have at least as much to do with his perception that monasticism was an illegitimate form of works-righteousness as it does with the goodness of marriage and family themselves.

(b) Although Luther could never quite bring himself to think that sexual relations were completely free of sin, he consistently wants to emphasize that marriage and family are *God's good creation*. Therefore, views to the contrary need to be opposed. And those who are married but continue to be uncomfortable with the notion that marriage and family life are God-pleasing need pastoral care.

(c) *Laws and customs about marriage* (positive law) ought to mirror God's original intentions for marriage. Over time, positive laws are susceptible to exploitation and thus must be revised. An inequitable rote application of the positive law often misses the mark of its original intention and, in many cases, it is better to approach certain ethical dilemmas concerning the family afresh with practical reason. However, God's Word and neighbor-love are the ultimate criteria for deciding marriage and family questions.

(d) *A Christian ought to expect suffering* in this world and interpersonal family relationships constitute an exercise field, a "school of character," for some of the most intense human suffering. Human families are where Christians learn discipleship, character and what it really means to love the neighbor.

As we consider how Luther might help us to understand our own questions about marriage and family from a theological point of view, the following three dispositions may be appropriate. (1) Luther's ethical rationality predisposes us to suspect any cultural phenomenon which pretends to produce salvation or any type of ultimate peace and joy predicated on human effort. For Luther, salvation is God's work alone and not a product of individuals or cultures. At the same time, God conveys God's grace through created means like water, bread and wine, words, liturgies, hymns, brotherly consolation. *Finitum capax infinitum.* (2) Luther's contextual approach also predisposes us to consider each cultural phenomenon as good (as part of creation) and a product of the culture's attempt to reach civil righteousness. There is no one way, i.e. there are any variety of positive laws, to reach this civil righteousness and thus Luther's theology has a high tolerance for cultural diversity. (3) Each cultural phenomenon is also subject to sinful corruptibility. An originally good positive law or piece of culture can be bent to serve private interests as opposed to the common good or neighbor love. Through God's human creators, God must therefore establish a new positive law which is, for the moment, not as susceptible to exploitation. In this way, both God and evil contribute to the formation of new cultural phenomena and moments.

Endnotes

1 This essay is drawn from a chapter of the author's doctoral work: Dean M. Apel, "Contextualizing the Family: The Theologies of Family of the New Testament, Luther, and the Samburu through the Lense of a Contextualization Model" Ph.D. dissertation, Lutheran School of Theology at Chicago, 2009. The author is grateful to Kurt Hendel for supervising the dissertation. His patience and perseverance through a great diversity of research topics and methods, over nearly a decade and with my residence on three continents was and is greatly appreciated.

2 For a thoughtful meditation on the interaction of past and present, see Adrian Thatcher, *Marriage after Modernity* (Sheffield: Sheffield Academic, 1999), 19, 142, and 24.

3 The following were aspects of his context which Luther was attempting to address in his theology of marriage and family, listed here in descending order of importance: (a) Luther's (re)discovery and retrieval of the gospel from behind a medieval theology and spirituality which, in his understanding, concealed it; (b) medieval Roman Catholic spirituality which emphasized what the individual could do to please and earn credit with God; (c) the Roman Catholic canon law concerning family and marriage which, in Luther's understanding, was exploited for the financial gain of the church hierarchy; (d) sexual immorality and concubinage among clerical "celibates;" (e) negative views of marriage in the ancient pagan authors and among his contemporary Christian theologians; (f) consolidating the achievements of the Reformation including how to get formerly celibate monks, nuns and priests married; figuring out ways to support them when the indulgence system was dismantled and writing marriage and family law when the canon law was eliminated; (g) Luther's own family—his mother, father, wife and children. For a full bibliography for this essay, see Apel, "Contextualizing the Family. . . ."

4 See Per Frostin, *Luther's Two Kingdom Doctrine* (Lund: Lund University, 1994), 3-4. Frostin argues that describing the two regiments as a Lutheran "doctrine" did not come into vogue until Christian Ernst Luthardt's *Die Ethik Luthers in ihren Grundzugen* (1867). Ernst Troeltsch and Max Weber (and, through them, Karl Barth) followed Luthardt's lead and influenced two or three generations of scholarship on Luther. From Melanchthon to Luthardt, the three estates scheme predominated as the framework of Luther's ethics. As Frostin notes (168),

5 The impediments were a complex list of what might prevent one person from marrying another.

6 Luther, *Marriage Matters* (1530), LW 46:266, "Now the whole world knows (praise God) what effort and zeal I have already expended and how hard I am still toiling to see that the two authorities or realms, the temporal and the spiritual, are kept distinct and separate from each other and that each is specifically instructed and restricted to its own task. The papacy has so jumbled these two together and confused them with each other that neither one has kept to its power or force or rights and no one can disentangle them again."

7 LW 53:111-112.

8 Luther, *Psalm 111* (1530), LW 13:370, ". . . nowhere among men on earth is there a people like the Christians, who understand so well and can teach so well what worldly stations are. They alone know and teach that these are divine ordinances and institutions. Therefore they alone can truly thank and pray for them in their churches. Outside of that, all human beings despise them as dangerous stations which arose by chance, contrary to the will and command of God."

9 Luther, *On War Against the Turk*, (1529), LW 46:181-182, 239.

10 Luther, *Confession Concerning Christ's Supper* (1528), LW 37:365, "We are saved by Christ alone; but we become holy both through this faith and through these divine foundations and orders. Even the godless may have much about them that is holy without being saved thereby."

11 Gustav Wingren, *Luther on Vocation* (Philadelphia: Muhlenberg Press, 1957), 5-6. Wingren refers to WA 15:625 which has not been translated in the LW. On the issue of the law in family life, see also Marc Kolden, "Luther on Vocation" *Word and World* 3 (1983): 384-385. On how God uses our parents, *inter alia*, to serve us, see the extraordinarily important passage in the Large Catechism, 1529, *The Book of Concord* edited by Kolb/Wengert (Minneapolis, Fortress, 2000), 389.26-27.

12 See Oswald Bayer, "Nature and Institution: Luther's Doctrine of the Three Orders," *Lutheran Quarterly* 12, no. 2 (1998): 129.) See also Frostin (*Two Kingdom Doctrine*) who believes that the two regiment framework is actually a nineteenth century attempt to understand Luther's ethical rationality.

13 See *Confession Concerning Christ's Supper*, 1528, LW 37:363-364.

14 The exception is when *politia* restricts the free course of the gospel in its territorial realm. This is the theme of October 1530's (published April 1531) *Dr. Martin Luther's Warning to His Dear German People* (LW 47).

15 The following table attempts to summarize some of the relationships between the three estates in Luther's theology:

	OKONOMIA	POLITIA	ECCLESIA
Is it an order of creation?	yes	no, created after the Fall	yes
Is disobdience to superiors allowed?	yes	not usually	yes
Leaders	the source of leaders for politia and ecclesia	originate in oikonomia	originate in oikonomia
authority structures	existed in the pre-Fall creation	derived from Oikonomia	existed in the pre-Fall condition

16 Bayer, "Three Orders," 130.

17 Luther sometimes speaks of the estates in terms of natural reason and natural law. On the limits of natural reason and law according to Luther, see Öberg "The Problem of Natural Religion in Luther" and "The Witness of Natural Religion in Luther Source Material" in Ingemar Öberg, *Luther and World Mission* (St Louis: Concordia, 2007), 37ff.

18 Bayer, "Three Orders," 146. Bayer refers to WA 40/III: 202-69.

19 George W. Forrell, *Faith Active in Love* (Minneapolis: Augsburg, 1954), 135.

20 Ibid., 136.

21 Ibid., 152.

22 Ibid., 154 "The task of the church includes a continuing renewal of the worldly orders, a never-ending alertness in all vocations, from the princely to the meanest labor." Wingren, *Luther on Vocation*, 48.

23 If one wants to try to make Luther consistent, the conservative aspect of his ethic would apply to other cultures as well as his own. In other words, an African ethnicity, for example, would be encouraged to preserve its traditional *politia* and *oikonomia* instead of casting it aside for a Western or another configuration. Of course, the Christian "prophet" would need to critique the local political and domestic configurations in the same way, i.e. by the Word of God.

24 Forell, *Faith Active in Love*, 135-36.

25 Of course, determining the universal and local in culture and law is a motor which drives much inquiry and, at times, bitter debate.

26 Bayer, "Three Orders," 149.

27 Cf. the titles of two recent biographies of Luther: Heiko Oberman, *Luther: Man between God and the Devil* (New Haven: Yale, 1989) and Richard Marius, *Martin Luther: the Christian between God and Death* (Cambridge: Harvard University, 1999).

28 Wingren, *Luther on Vocation*, 162.

29 Wingren, *Luther on Vocation*, 14, "God receives that which is his, faith. The neighbor receives that which is his, works."

30 Wingren, *Luther on Vocation*, 20.

31 Ibid., 37.

32 Ibid., 160.

33 Wingren, *Luther on Vocation*, 37, "In earthly orders God and the devil are both actively at work. Therefore these orders never stand still. They are always corrupted because men depart from God's will. But they are improved and reformed anew by God, among other things, in true Christian faith and love." In much of Wingren's later theology, the Gospels' portrayal of the Pharisees is an example of how originally good laws can be misused and exploited for personal gain.

34 Ibid., 99.

35 Ibid., 171-184.

36 Ibid., 184-198.

37 WA 30/3, 239 (*Von Ehesachen*, 1530) "Freedom from the authority receives, on the whole, unusually frequent expression in this little brochure on marriage; see, for example, 245f." quoted in Wingren, *Luther on Vocation*, 209n85.

38 Wingren, *Luther on Vocation*, 199-210.

39 Ibid., 213-233.

40 See Forell, *Faith Active in Love*, 64, "...never believe that you have a correct understanding of a thought of Luther before you have succeeded in reducing it to a simple corollary of the thought of the forgiveness of sins." Althaus calls justification for Luther "the presupposition of all Christian activity" including ethics. (Paul Althaus, *The Ethics of Martin Luther*. Philadelphia: Fortress, 1972, 3)

41 Forell, *Faith Active in Love*, 157.

42 See diagram in Lazareth, *Christians in Society*, xi.

43 Ibid., 85.

44 Ibid., 5.

45 Ibid., 171. It is interesting that Lazareth writes this while at the same time castigating Reinhold Niebuhr for the following remarks, "'Luther's inordinate fear of anarchy, prompted by his pessimism, and his corresponding indifference to the injustice of tyranny, has had a fateful consequence in the history of German civilization.'" (Lazareth, *Christians in Society*, 27, the quotation is from Niebuhr's Gifford Lectures, 1939).

46 Rosemary Radford Ruether, *Making of the Modern Family* (Boston: Beacon, 2000), 5.

47 Ibid., 262.

48 Ibid., 63-66.

49 Ibid., 67.

50 Ibid., 69,"The challenge of Anabaptism and the Peasants' War of 1525 turned Luther and other reformers to a reliance on princes and town magistrates as their arm of enforcement, and prompted them to shelve the more radical visions of dissent and social equality suggested by their motto 'a priesthood of all believers.'"

51 The reification of male headship family systems is one of the roots of anti-women evil for Ruether. See Ruether, *Making of the Modern Family*, 12, "The anti-family traditions of the gospels and early Christianity can in fact be understood as a critique of oppressive forms of family. In this light, theologies that sacralize family systems of 'male headship' at the expense of women, children, and servants are not legitimate; they are forms of human sin, not divine mandate."

52 Ibid., 73-74.

53 Ibid., 74.

54 Ruether realizes that Luther's sacramental theology is unique among the other reformers. See Ruether, *Making of the Modern Family*, 76, "Luther's spirituality was sufficiently steeped in medieval sacramentalism to resist these further moves [of Zwingli and Calvin]. But even this does not say enough. Luther's teachings on the estates and the two regiments, i.e. his creation theology, also emphasize nature's capacity to mediate God's grace and judgment. *Finitum capax infinitum.*

55 Ruether, *Making of the Modern Family*, 78.

56 Susan C. Karant-Nunn & Merry E. Wiesner-Hanks, *Luther on Women: A Sourcebook* (Cambridge: Cambridge University Press, 2003), 5. If there is an era in which Luther writes less about marriage and family issues, it is probably the early years of his marriage.

57 Karant-Nunn & Wiesner-Hanks, *Luther on Women*, 7.

58 ibid., 7-8.

59 Ibid., 12.

60 Ibid., 13.

61 Ibid., 10.

62 Ibid., 9.

63 Ibid., 13.

64 Ibid., 14.

65 Ibid., 11.

66 Luther, 1 Peter, LW 30:84,"He who is a Christian must also bear a cross. And the more you are wronged, the better it is for you. Therefore you must accept such a cross willingly from God and thank Him." Cf. John A. Maxfield who exegetes Luther's interpretation of the Joseph cycle in Genesis along the same lines: "In his lecture on the rest of the Genesis narrative, Luther treated these themes of Jacob's and Joseph's sufferings in their earthly life as the means by which God worked their transformation and salvation." (*Luther's Lectures on Genesis and the Formation Evangelical Identity, Sixteenth Century Essays and Studies 80.* Kirksville, MO: Truman State University Press, *p.* 131) For Luther, suffering in the vocations of life is not restricted to women. Husbands/fathers will also suffer in family life, albeit in different ways than wives/mothers.

CHAPTER EIGHT

Rehabilitating the Vocation of Cantor with the Help of the Early Church and Johannes Bugenhagen

Mark P. Bangert

Kurt K. Hendel's life-long investment in Reformation history and theology has provided him with concurrent passions, not the least of which are his untiring crusade for attending to a Lutheran view of baptismal vocation and his love for the musical heritage spawned in the sixteenth century, indeed by Martin Luther himself and his circle of compatriots. Falling in line here, a handful of intersecting personal interests, especially the changing role of the church musician, seem to be summoning a re-evaluation of current conceptions of the church musician's identity and vocation. More about those interests below, but helping this process to productive ends necessitates a look at visions accumulated along the way by that host of singers, players, and thinkers who mused their way into matters liturgical. Kurt has taught us to think carefully about vocation and to not take lightly the legacy left by our Reformation forebears. What follows is merely the beginning of what needs to be a larger conversation. For now it is sufficient to venture some foundation pieces prompted by a long and beneficent association with Kurt.

Searching for the Archetype

Sunday service folders give us a variety of titles: musician, church musician, song leader, minister of music, organist, keyboardist, and cantor. Sometimes these titles derive from an attempt to elevate the individual's sense of worth; sometimes they are meant to keep boundaries around the power inherent in musical acts—sad to say for all concerned. All of the titles, and more still, give evidence of some understanding of what or who this person is that leads/makes music in Christian assembly, and what is expected of her/him.

The multiplication of possible titles signifies that there is no one single archetype that is claimed across congregations. What is noteworthy is that only two of the titles above involve keyboards, and yet one could probably venture safely that most people associate musical happenings in church with keyboards. In light-hearted moments I sometimes refer to my respected church musical friends as "lever pushers," intending without malice to nudge us all to ponder what cantors exactly do or should do apart from pressing keys. If not "lever pusher," then what? Responding, one could offer up "song leader," with the implication that the job description needs more attention to vocal dimensions. But then most of these church musical friends would bristle with the claim that such is what they do. This in spite of the following descriptor of a cantor posted on the website of the Association of Lutheran Church Musicians:

> The cantor, the historical term among Lutherans, is the leader of the people's song . . . the assembly, choral groups, solo singers and instrumentalists, among whom *organists have been especially important for Lutherans*"[1] (emphasis mine).

To the extent that musical name-calling demeans faithful people who often do not receive the recognition they deserve—monetary or otherwise, the "lever pusher" moniker serves no good purpose, and if anything diminishes an already faltering self-esteem. But hurtful things are said or thought nonetheless, and when that's coupled to low expectations from congregants, clouds gather above a worshiping assembly. Ensuing gloom stifles potential and eventually everyone sort of gives up. The silence amounts to a cry for help.

Lacking an inspiring sense of vocation, moreover, leaders of the church's song are easily and disproportionately drawn to secondary concerns, such as facilities, quality of the band, pensions, health-care, keyboard skills, preludes, postludes, bell choirs, and drums of many sizes and shapes. These things can be all-consuming for one who has responded positively and hopefully to a well-meaning but ill-crafted advertisement for someone "to play the hymns and liturgy," and now looks to the assembly for direction and a sense of common purpose.

Organizations like the Association of Lutheran Church Musicians do much to nurture their members, keep healthy goals in sight, and challenge congregational expectations. Unfortunately, the process is not much helped by the rites offered for public recognition of these modern day cantors. In the 1982 *Occasional Services* the chance to enhance the church musical vocation resides in an omnibus rite labeled "Installation of a Lay Professional Leader," and then only by a six-line tailored prayer.[2] There is little opportunity here for encouragement, recognition of gifts, or for expanding the vision of the congregation.

Matters improved with the appearance of *Occasional Services for the Assembly,* a companion volume to the 2008 *Evangelical Lutheran Worship.* In this volume the ministry of music in a congregation, to be sure along with other specialized ministries such as administration and education, begins to receive special notice through the laying on of hands in a service titled "Commissioning of Associates in Ministry," especially if the particular ministry entails "a major occupational commitment."[3] The ritual expansion to the laying on of hands signals an intended mark of importance but that now begs more detailed content. Recognizing that church musicians enter the vocation with differing skills and commitments, the editorial team of the newer collection decided in favor of installing a church musician alternately as a Lay Professional Leader, following the pattern of the 1982 book.[4]

When the 1982 book was assembled, the editors faced the difficult challenge of making sense out of the variety of ecclesiastical rosters (and their accompanying rites) from three different church bodies. While the resulting services accommodated the needs of the churches to some degree, the confusing collection of materials in that book also retarded the church's understanding of and appreciation for the role of the cantor. The newer book has done much better, but the really good news is that the national church body, the Evangelical Lutheran Church in America, through its Word and Service Task Force, is proposing to combine three separate existing lay rosters into one, members of which would be called "deacons."[5]

Simplifying bureaucracy has its own rewards but what's even more important here is the opportunity to rehabilitate the vocation of cantor, for the sake of cantors themselves, for the sake of congregational and pastoral expectations, and for the sake of the whole church. One place to begin the process of rehabilitation is the proposed title of deacon.

Diaconal Ministry as Matrix for a Leader of the Church's Song

Whatever hesitation may emerge from considering a single roster under the title of deacon, equivocations doubtlessly derive from the title's spotty history. Those old enough remember that the use of "deacon" and "subdeacon" for identifying various participants in "high church" liturgical events implied for some a subversive attempt to reinstate a multi-step clerical hierarchy. Lutheran aversion to such ranking carried over to the title itself, so there is a lurking hesitancy about using "deacon." Susan Wood reminds us that a fixed pattern of sequential elevations is something from the high Middle Ages and not necessarily inherent to the notion of deacon.[6] Historically speaking, "a deacon is not someone who is almost a priest but not quite; he [sic] is, rather, someone who is authorized to exercise a distinctive public Ministry in the church."[7]

To see the benefits of rethinking the church musical vocation as diaconal ministry it is necessary to clear a path back to the emergence of that ministry in the church. There one can discover at least three distinct personal qualities that attracted the church's attention as it sought to fulfill its local ministries through the gifts of individual members: enthusiasm for Christian formation, charitable demeanor, and a passion for apostolicity.

Enthusiasm for Christian Formation

Early Christians soon recognized the variety of gifts they communally possessed and realized that many of their individual talents and aptitudes were essential to continued existence together. In Romans 12:4-8 the apostle likens people with particular talents to the human body, explaining how the members are all different from one another but together comprise the local body of Christ. He calls out administrators, preachers, almsgivers, among others, and includes the grace or gift of teaching.

In subsequent generations that gift of teaching manifested itself in a variety of ways. Teachers thought to have the gift commonly sought to proclaim the gospel, whether that be through the enlightenment of catechumens, the instruction of young presbyters, or engaging in evangelistic acts.[8] Because of this core goal, the practice of Christian formation (as we might call it today) took on liturgical dimensions as the assembly welcomed these teachers to read the gospel during its gathering around Word and Sacrament.

The teaching gift, like the other two qualities here considered, was understood to be an apparent "grace," a charism, publicly and ritually acknowledged or prayed for by the entire assembly so that it might be held in high regard by all the members of the body.[9]

Schillebeeckx suggests that the notion of team ministry is one way to comprehend how the church of the first three centuries addressed its perceived needs.[10] Receiving this charism as a gift of the Spirit, one among many, believers anticipated an invigorating passion as its driver, together summoning the teacher's innate abilities for the building up of individuals in the body of Christ. This charism served therefore as a compass for its bearer and as witness to the Spirit's presence.

Charitable Demeanor

Susan Wood reminds her readers that "originally . . . *diakonia* broadly refers to 'service,' and is descriptive of the ministry of the whole church prior to its later more technical use."[11] At the heart of diaconal ministry, then, reside charitable works--feeding the hungry, serving the widows, and taking care of the poor. A deacon without a heart for such charity is unthinkable in the early church as shown in Acts 6:16. The setting aside of seven Hellenists to serve at the tables of the widows soon took on the role of a kind of "proof text" for those on the "diaconal roster" of the church. Just how definitive charity turned out to be for this ministry of service comes clear in the annals of the Synod of Rome (595) where the participants officially ordered the deacons to "no longer chant [psalms] in order to consecrate themselves again to preaching and charitable work."[12]

This blunt call from diaconal pleasantries back to the diaconal core echoes across the centuries. Augustine, in an effort to link God's activity and human response, observed that the Psalmist used both the psalterium and the cithara as accompanying instruments, the former to reveal the ordinances of God, the latter to urge from the faithful works of justice and love.[13] Finding a lesson there for contemporary church musicians, Christoph Wetzel writes, "The charisma of singing is therefore not a means for pleasure-seeking enrichment or pious self-expression of a congregation, but one among many manifestations of ministry that builds up the congregation."[14] Legitimacy for the vocation of church music, he further argues, can only emerge from "the unity of liturgy and diaconia."[15]

Whether musical or not, the activities and gifts usually associated with diaconal ministry embrace if not end in charitable activities. Serving the poor is the essence of deacon-hood, as it were, the fabric of the diaconal demeanor.

Passion for Apostolicity

To be known as an apostle among the first Christians meant that one was reckoned to have authority. For Paul, witnessing the resurrection prompted and sealed that authority (1 Corinthians 15:5-9). He counted his apostleship as essential for his ministry, even though some of his contemporaries were not sure he qualified.[16] Before other distinct offices were in place, apostleship constituted a sufficient focused ministry because apostles served the immediate needs of the church. The pastoral letters of the New Testament, Schillebeeckx noted, reflect concerns about structuring alternative ministries but still simply say "the ministry is needed to preserve in a living way the apostolicity of the community's tradition."[17] That growing sense of staying true to what is shared and passed on intensifies in the next generations, especially as the apostles and other leaders one by one die and are no longer on the scene. The prime concern then becomes a passion for preserving the content of faith, the success of which often eluded the communities seeking it. In the face of heresies and divergent alternatives, however, there remained among many the trust that the Spirit would prevail in the quest for apostolicity. Passion for that eventually generated creeds, examinations before ordination, and a host of other safeguards to do everything possible to stay true to what was handed down from the beginning.

The passion for apostolicity became essential especially for bishops and presbyters (pastors or priests) but had as much to do with diaconal ministry also, simply because deacons also taught and administered the Word, albeit in other ways. To entrust oneself to a deacon means that one has confidence in the deacon's commitment to apostolic faith. Such was the hope and expectation of the early church.

And Now a Word from Johannes Bugenhagen

In addition to his prolific output as a theologian, Johannes Bugenhagen prepared church orders for over fifteen towns or areas of northern Europe. While some of these orders overlapped in content, he carefully strove to be sensitive to local needs, all the while providing practical ways of disseminating Luther's liturgical principles. His own pastoral bent and prior vocation as teacher in Treptow led him to see the importance of Morning Prayer (Matins) and Evening Prayer (Vespers) as a means to widen use of the languages in the city schools.[18] The high profile he gave these services in his church orders came also from the musical benefits he saw in their regular use by students.

Bugenhagen's musical interests can be traced to the education he himself received in the German university system. Immersion in the quadrivium (arithmetic, geometry, astronomy, and music) meant that he would have read and digested some of the influential medieval music treatises whose authors nearly unanimously traced the origins of music to God's beneficence. In this way he was no different from his Wittenberg compatriots, Martin Luther, and the composer/cantor Johann Walter (1496-1570—who, while based chiefly in Torgau, might just as well be counted as a Wittenbergian) and the publisher Georg Rhaw (1488-1548).

Rhaw, for a time cantor at the famous *Thomaskirche* of Leipzig, moved to Wittenberg in 1523 to set up a printing business to service the emerging needs of the Reformation. Like Bugenhagen he supported musical education in the schools especially through the continued use of Vespers and its traditional musical components. On his own Rhaw commissioned a composer by the name of Balthasar Resinarius (c.1486-c.1567), also known as Balthasar Harzer, to compose a set of Responsories for the entire church year, including feast days of important saints. The composer designed these polyphonic pieces to be sung after the lesson(s) in Vespers, like their medieval chant predecessors.

Resinarius wrote in the style of his teacher, Heinrich Isaac (c. 1450-1517), both steeped in the musical practices of the Maximilian court where Resinarius had also sung in the choir. He later became bishop of Leipa in Bohemia, converting from Roman Catholicism to the Lutheran faith. Texts for these compositions, not surprisingly, came to Lutheran use from traditional sources, unpurged.

Rhaw published the collection in 1544.[19] Johannes Bugenhagen wrote the preface ("Doctor John Bugenhagen to the adolescent students").[20] He simultaneously introduced the collection and intimated a theology of music that, while making no direct claims on the history of the cantorate or diaconate, clearly resonates with notions of leadership among the early generations of Christians, especially as those notions intersect with the church musical vocation.

Throughout the preface Bugenhagen shows respect for the young students and has their best interests in mind. He recognizes that they require constant motivation to stay on the educational track and assures them that music will provide excitement, cheer, joy, and delight as they honor their vocation as students.[21] One suspects that he is writing from experience and that he enthusiastically endorses this publication as a means for forming the faith and character of its users. They are the audience and it's for their welfare that Rhaw, Resinarius and Bugenhagen are making this effort, "For whoever truly is not cheered by singing music cannot be believed to be a human being."[22]

If, like a deacon of old, Bugenhagen enthusiastically looks after the formation of the young in faith, he likewise manifests beliefs in the positive outcomes the act of music making provides (also is sure of the positive ends of music). A major part of his essay deals with behavioral problems observed among the students, their scope not sufficient for disciplinary action, but probably common enough in a boarding school to merit a blanket concern. "There are a few students, and I mean a few," he writes, who "at all hours" conduct their lives via all sorts of Sybaritism: "fighting, feasting, drinking, seeking pleasure, dressing up, posturing, dancing, nocturnal clamoring, giving in to base desires, and the life that goes with that."[23] Not wanting to turn them all into monks, he writes, he nonetheless offers these songs so that with rejoicing they might delight in all honesty and every good work. "Therefore, to this end we offer you these holy songs, composed with the art of music, which will, as we hope, be holy delights for you."[24]

Support for this gesture emerges from the belief that by engaging with this music the young students would be able to resist all the temptations their educational endeavors offer. In so far that these songs might induce better behavior one can congratulate Bugenhagen for his charitable demeanor, observing also his conviction, widely held at the time, that music is a means by which God addresses the needs of individuals, citing David's musical cure for Saul's ailments.[25]

It is clear that Bugenhagen was not altogether happy about the publication of this volume. As a theologian he suspected liturgical texts that could lure worshipers back into old patterns. Consequently he disfavored liturgical components such as Responsories because they had little importance for parishes outside of city churches with schools, and, more significantly, because he considered the texts of some Responsories to be unscriptural. No doubt he thought of himself as being a champion of apostolicity in this regard; indeed, the drama between the lines indicates how serious he was about all of this.

For one thing, he was not able to excuse himself from the invitation (presumably) to write an introduction to this collection, because the composer had dedicated his work to Bugenhagen. Nevertheless, he marched on. He complained in the preface that the texts for Saints days are unsuitable (*incommoda*), and therefore have been changed, some by Resinarius himself, and others by an un-named typographer—who is, of course, Georg Rhaw. Just what kind of negotiations occurred between Rhaw and Bugenhagen is not made clear, but Rhaw's opinions on all of this were certainly not as severe as those of Bugenhagen, since he was the one who commissioned the collection. No matter the complications Bugenhagen, desired to have the texts "pure and good from the sacred writings and the Word of God."[26]

From a current perspective, filled with the desire to find hints for re-envisioning the vocation of the cantor, we might conclude that Bugenhagen's zeal is distasteful. Any critique of his radical reconstructions, however, should also include a measure of sympathy once we think of him as dedicated to preserving the apostolicity of the faith. His critical penchant is a reasonable self-check for any pastor, theologian, deacon, or cantor, especially when it proceeds from a passion for passing on the faith to novices. Texts do make a difference, after all, and the responsible leader in the church's worship will strive to get congregants to repeat week by week what will be true and helpful for a lifetime.

While the vocation of cantor is not a concern for Bugenhagen in this preface, he wrote and behaved in accord with the standards he described. He wrote as one who is enthusiastic about formation, has a charitable demeanor, and is passionate about apostolicity—all prompted by musical matters. He moved the tradition along under new circumstances and thereby offered the beginnings of a blueprint for rehabilitating the vocation of the cantor. The resources are there, the need is clear, and the energy resides in the prospect of looking to the cantor as deacon of music.

Endnotes

1 www. ALCM.org/home/marketplace/poster.

2 "Installation of a Lay Professional Leader," *Occasional Services* (Minneapolis: Augsburg Publishing House and Philadelphia: Board of Publication, Lutheran Church in America, 1982), 136-42.

3 "Commissioning of Associates in Ministry," *Occasional Services for the Assembly* (Minneapolis: Augsburg Fortress, 2009), 213-223.

4 Ibid., 101-05.

5 According to "Report and Recommendation of the Word and Service Task Force to the ELCA Church Council," November 2013, action on this matter will take place at the 2016 Churchwide Assembly.

6 Susan K. Wood, *Sacramental Orders* (Collegeville, Minnesota: The Liturgical Press, 2000), 167.

7 Ibid., 170.

8 Ibid., 144.

9 Edward Schillebeeckx, *Ministry. Leadership in the Community of Jesus Christ,* trans. from the Dutch by John Bowden (New York: Crossroad, 1981), 69 and 139.

10 Ibid., 34.

11 Wood, 144.

12 Ibid., 175.

13 Christoph Wetzel, "Musik und Diakonie der Kirche nach Augustin," *Musik und Kirche* 25/1 (January-February 1955): 34.

14 *Das Charisma des Singens ist also nicht ein Mittel zur genußsüchtigen Bereicherung oder frommen Selbsdarstellung der Gemeinde, sondern eine unter den vielen Ausrüstungen zu Gemeinde bauendem Dienst.* In Christoph Wetzel, "*Die Träger des liturgischen Amtes im evangelischen Gottesdienst,*" *Die Musik des Evangelischen Gottesdienst,* vol. 4 of *Leiturgia,* ed. Karl Ferdinand Müller and Walter Blankenburg (Kassel: Johannes Stauda, 1961), 277.

15 Ibid., 300.

16 See Wayne Meeks, *The First Urban Christians* (New Haven, Connecticut: Yale University Press, 1983), 131.

17 Schillebeeckx, 19.

18 Victor H. Mattfeld, *Georg Rhaw's Publications for Vespers* (Brooklyn, New York: Institute of Mediaeval Music, 1966), 85.

19 Balthasar Resinarius, *Responsoriorum Numero Octoginta,* ed. Inge-Maria Schröeder, vol. 1 of Georg Rhau, *Musikdrucke aus den Jahren 1538 bis 1545,* ed. Hans Albrecht (Kassel: Bärenreiter, 1954).

20 "*Studiosis Adolescentibus Doctor Johannes Bugenhagius Pomeranus S. P. D.,*" *Responsoriorum,* XVII-XVIII.

21 *Haec omnia, studiosi adolescents, vobis in vestrum usum offeruntur, ut excitati et delectati hisce Musicis cantibus, gaudentes et alacres, aliis artibus et disciplinis operam detis, ad quod officium Deus vos vocavit,* ibid., XVII.

22 *Qui vero Musicis cantibus non delectantur, ne hominess quidem esse crederim,* ibid.

23 *Sunt pauci adolescents, et adeo pauci, . . . horum omnia sunt plane Sibaritica, gestus, victus, ebrietas, voluptas, vestitus, incessus, saltationes, nocturni clamores, turpitudines et ipsa vita,* ibid.

24 *Ideoque ad hanc rem offerimus vobis haec pia cantica, arte Musica composita, quae vobis (ut speramus) sanctae erunt voluptati,* ibid.

25 *Nam Musica sacris verbis ornate, fugat spiritum malum, ut vides Davide 1. Reg. 16,* Ibid, XVIII.

26 *Puriora . . . boni ex sacris literis et verbo Dei,* ibid., XVII.

CHAPTER NINE

Not a *Festschrift*, but a *Streitschrift* for John Calvin

Jerome Bolsec's *Histoire*

Ken Sawyer

Lutherans will not be surprised to read that the earliest biographical portraits of John Calvin reflected the polemical agendas of that highly contentious era, since sixteenth-century biographers of all confessions were all drawing from rhetorical traditions concerned with praise, blame, and persuasion.[1] The "Lives" of Calvin produced by Calvin's fictive sons Theodore Beza (1519-1605) and Nicolas Colladon (1530-1586) in three redactions (1564, 1565, and 1575) defended their *"Pater"* against a wide array of critics. Their efforts provoked several responses, notably from Jerome Bolsec (1520?-1584), whose *Histoire de la Vie, Moeurs, Actes, Doctrine, Constance et Mort de Iean Caluin* (1577) was a not a *Festschrift*, but more a *streitschrift* of the Genevan reformer and his colleague Theodore Beza, published with other anti-Protestant biographies.[2] As Beza and Colladon's stolid hagiographic portrait of Calvin informed the Protestant traditions, so Bolsec's defamatory portrait set the tone and terms for much subsequent anti-Calvin polemic.[3] Bolsec's life and work still stands in the shadow cast by his dispute with the Genevans. The intensity of the rhetoric has obscured the substantial areas of *agreement*, since Bolsec's theological commitments long remained Reformed in spite of his break with Calvin, and he participated in Reformed theological communities until his final (re)turn to Roman Catholic sponsors.[4]

The Life and Works of Jerome Bolsec

Bolsec was a Parisian, born in the 1520s, but perhaps earlier. He came of age when the French reform was undergoing dramatic changes with the passing of a generation of leaders: the younger Guillaume Briçonnet (1472-1534), Jacques Lefèvre d'Étaples (1455-1536), and the great exemplar, Desidarius Erasmus (1466-1536). In these same years the alliance of the Paris Parlement, authorities of the Sorbonne, and a broad spectrum of nationalists, traditionalists, royalists, papalists, and reformist monastics collaborated to control the books, ideas, and bodies linked to the French humanists, "Lutherans," and a growing circle of lawyers and humanists devoted to Reformed theology. Many individuals and families were driven into exile: Gérard Roussel (1500-1550), Lefevre, and Pierre Viret (1511-1571) in the 1520s, Cop and Calvin in the 1530s, and waves of promising lawyers, clerics, and teachers in the 1540s.

In 1545 or 1546 Bolsec joined these exiles in leaving France for safety in Ferrara at the court of Renee of France.[5] Between 1546 and 1550 he was connected with the court of Renee, perhaps among the almoners—a broad category that might have combined duties as chaplain, advisor, and courtier. The turmoil of that royal family encouraged subterfuge and indirection, leaving many questions concerning Bolsec and others hosted/protected by Renee. Bolsec is not mentioned by name in contemporary records.It may be during this time that Bolsec trained to be a physician, since when he established himself near Geneva in 1550/51, Bolsec served as private physician to the family of Jacques de Bourgogne, Seigneur de Falais et de Breda (d.1556). It is unknown how or where Bolsec met de Falais, but the later efforts of de Falais on Bolsec's behalf indicate a strong and abiding affinity.[6]

There is no reason to consider Bolsec's theology remarkable, except that his emphases differed from Calvin. Indeed, the Bolsec conflict was *not* unusual in its origins or its substance—since Paris, Bourges, Lyons, Geneva, Basle, Bern, Strasbourg, were all centers of theological debate and conflict—each town filled with past and potential converts, with alliances shifting year by year. Bolsec, like many of his generation in an age of reform, blended scholastic training, a particular readiness to debate, and a profound unwillingness to defer on doctrinal points.

The Conflict in Geneva 1551

Bolsec's public conflict with Calvin began when he offered his opinions on predestination at one of the "Congregations" in March of 1551 in

Geneva. "Congregations" were clergy-led discussion groups, providing some opportunities for interaction among clergy and laity on theological topics. Philip Holtrop notes Bolsec's statement that he had spoken at two of these meetings. [7]The pastors in attendance admonished Bolsec in private conversation, perhaps at Calvin's house. Whether Bolsec continued to attend the "Congregations" during the spring and summer is unknown. He attended the "Congregation" of October 16, 1551, and spoke again on the issue of predestination. This time he offered a pointed critique of Huldrych Zwingli, and, by implication, of Calvin. Since the resolution of theological disagreements usually became a referendum on Calvin's leadership in the city, the result was rapid and certain. Bolsec was arrested and made the center of a criminal trial.

Throughout the trial, issues of authority, freedom of expression, and doctrinal specificity combined with the complex situation of the political relationship of Geneva to other cities, especially Bern. Trial documents show Bolsec's various strategies to find support and obtain release. He was required to respond to questions posed to him by the Genevan authorities, but Bolsec responded in questions, answering by accusing his accusers. Bolsec also sought to gather help from friends in order to sow discord among his opponents. By appealing beyond Geneva, Bolsec drew attention to the points of tension on some doctrinal perspectives within the Reformed alliance, thereby exposing the Genevans to criticism by their own allies. Advice was solicited from some, with silence expected from others. For example, Heinrich Bullinger's response strained his relationship with Calvin. By December 23, 1551 the case had been settled, the sentence pronounced: Bolsec was banned from Genevan territories.

Especially damaging to Bolsec was the release (through Philibert Bonna and/or de Falais) during the trial, of a ten-stanza meditative poem he had composed during his imprisonment. This *Lamentation* was not the reason for his trial, but it became a factor in his conviction and expulsion from Geneva. Bolsec's complaint that Calvin and his allies were agents of injustice spoke as loudly, if not louder, as his own theological arguments:

Stanza 1   *Mon Dieu, mon roy, ma force et ma fiance*
            Mon seul appuy et ma seule esperance
            Vers moy ton serf qui reclame ta grace
            Tourne tes yeulz: et monstre moy ta face.
            Charité dort et crualté m'assiege
            Pour me tirer en ses filletz et piege.

Stanza 5 *Chrestiens sont ilz devenuz tyranniques?*
Chrestins ont-ilz zeles pharisaiques?
Chrestiens ont-ilz perdu leurs meurs si belles?
Brebiz de christ sont elles si cruelles?
O durs assaulx, o mortelles allarmes
Qui font mon cueur tout consumer en larmes.[8]

Bolsec's strategies escalated the conflict by exposing the Genevans to critique by Reformed allies in other cities. Bolsec also personalized the conflict through his *Lamentation*, presenting the Genevans as tyrants. Predictably, the Genevan authorities closed ranks, rejecting both Bolsec and the implied argument that the Genevans should accept dissent or diversity on points of doctrine.[9]

After his expulsion from Geneva, Bolsec moved to Thonon, within Bernese territories, in January of 1552. Though banned from Geneva, Bolsec was free to continue his critique of Calvin, reaching out to potential Bernese allies while maintaining contact with some Genevans. Holtrop reports Bolsec offered to write a treatise against Calvin in 1552, and that he petitioned (unsuccessfully) the Genevan authorities to be allowed to return to Geneva in 1552 and 1553. In 1554 Bolsec joined with two allies, Andre Zebedee (d.1555), and Jean Lange , to publicly denounce Calvin and the Genevan teachings on predestination. In response to repeated Genevan prompting, this broadside was met by a general Bernese reprimand of Bolsec, followed by an ineffective prohibition of discussion of the topic of predestination in Bernese territories. Throughout the first months of 1555 the Genevans repeatedly complained to the Bernese, seeking to prompt the Bernese to deal with Bolsec's continuing campaign against Calvin. Though Bernese pastors and magistrates found little merit in Bolsec, they did not all agree with Calvin, and, because of political considerations, Bern would not quickly accede to Genevan requests. Finally the Bernese did agree to banish Bolsec on March 31, but allowed him a generous three months to leave Bernese territories.

Bolsec's exact whereabouts in the next six years are not known. In the fall of 1561 Bolsec was in Bern, requesting permission to pursue some form of ministry. While it is known Bolsec lived in Bern throughout 1562, and into 1563, it is uncertain whether he attended the national Synod of the Reformed churches in Orleans in April of 1562, though he apparently submitted a request for a ministerial appointment. In that year Bolsec published his *Mirouer envoyé de vérité au roy Charles neufieme* (Paris,

1562), dedicated to Charles IX, appealing for reform in France, just after the Colloquy of Poissy and the Edict of 17 January.[10] This treatise was presented as a message from the goddess Veritie, presented as having appeared to Bolsec in the similitude of a dream at Christmastide, 1561. In spite of its unusual form, and in spite of Bolsec's break with Calvin, his message to the young king presented a recognizably Reformed line of argument, requesting freedom from idolatry and reporting on the recent troubles in Paris.

From Bern, Bolsec moved to Lausanne in April of 1563, but his Genevan opponents had not forgotten him. In August he was among a group deposed at the national Synod of the Reformed churches, meeting in Lyons. Bolsec was denounced as an infamous liar and apostate, though it remains unclear whether and from what status or office he was deposed. Bayle suggested his deposition indicates Bolsec had earlier obtained an appointment in some ministry, while others are less sure, suggesting that the persistent opposition of the Genevans was enough to secure his deposition. In Lausanne Beza prompted another trial to test Bolsec's conformity to the city confession, leading to another banishment in December 1563. His whereabouts in the next years are difficult to trace, though Beza's later writings indicate that the Genevans watched him in these years, perhaps because of other publications.[11] With the death of Calvin in May 1564, the conflict between Bolsec and the Genevans entered a new phase, a phase now completely directed by Beza.

The "Lives" of Calvin

Three months after Calvin's death in May 1564, Theodore Beza published a brief *Vie De Calvin* as a preface to the Calvin's *Commentary on Joshua*. Written as part lamentation, part defense, and part consolation for all who had lost a father in Calvin, Beza's *Vie* opened with a brief prologue in which Beza blended the personal with the polemical. Beza then placed the outlines of Calvin's life and death as a summary and continuation of the broader work of Reformation. Beza sounded the themes of Calvin's honorable fidelity to the work of God, and claimed that Calvin's fidelity to the gospel had somehow protected him from personal animosity and anger, even when confronted with many opponents. Furthermore, Beza's recounting of the many intense controversies and the problems stirred up by vociferous opponents were cited as indications that Calvin played a particular role as God's champion.

Glossing his own devoted friendship with Calvin, Beza appealed for a broadly public reading of Calvin's life, and claimed that all who knew Calvin would testify to Calvin's ability to focus only on the central issues concerning the enemies of God, rather than upon personal sleights or affronts. Shedding this line of argument in the last portion of the work, Beza changed tactics and defended Calvin's anger as righteous, rather than as something base and personal. Beza also defended Calvin against charges of cruelty, avarice, and excessive control. Bolsec was brought into this narrative after Beza mentioned Anabaptists, Pierre Caroli (1480-ca.1545), and Miguel Servetus (1511?-1553). Briefly listing the main outlines of Bolsec's career before moving on to the next opponents, Beza then listed a group of anti-Trinitarians, political opponents, and others, before invoking the formulaic opening words, "He was born in . . ." A second edition of the *Vie de Calvin* appeared in 1565. Debate continues as to the relative roles of Beza and Nicholas Colladon in the composition of this work. This second redaction expanded the 1564 work, adding details, names and dates to the text, continuing the character defense of Calvin by stressing the equanimity with which Calvin dealt with those with whom he disagreed. Where the 1564 account had dealt briefly with accusations of a controlling nature in Calvin, the 1565 redaction took a longer line of defense by offering damaging details about several of Calvin's opponents. This tactic acknowledged that Calvin was sometimes a man of anger and occasional intemperance, but implied that his (righteous) anger was directed against their (unrighteous) attacks. In this expanding defense of Calvin, this redaction provided examples from Calvin's life to counter the charges listed briefly in the earlier redaction. This 1565 redaction described Calvin's youth, education, and early ministry, his years in Strasbourg, and then considered his publications down to the year 1551. Bolsec is the first mentioned (CO 21:72-75) in the long section (CO 21:72-93) on Calvin's opponents. Beza/Colladon expanded the treatment of Bolsec, drawing upon the 1551 trial record, and referring to Bolsec as "Mr. Monk" (Monseur le moine), or as exhibiting "monkish" foolishness (impudence Monachle).

Beza published a third redaction of the life of Calvin with his edited selection of Calvin's letters in 1575. This Latin text, the *Vita Calvini*, revised the 1564 and 1565 editions with a new preface and incorporated materials from the earlier redactions to provide a picture of the early life of Calvin, including his acquaintances in Noyon, Paris, Strasbourg, and Geneva. This *Vita* presented episodes of Calvin's life as illustrations of virtue, his calm responses to opponents, his nobility in suffering, and his good death. This redaction became the standard biography of Calvin, building on the previous redactions, trimming some sections, expanding others, rearranging the narrative and emphasis. Beza's preface acknowledged, then dismissed, accusations that Luther, Zwingli, and Calvin were regarded as gods among the reformers, and worshipped as if gods. Beza artfully described his own work as an artless and simple narrative. Beza's 1575 treatment of Bolsec (CO 21:143-145) is both briefer and more cutting than the earlier redactions. Beza drew upon events from 1551 through the date of composition to complete his effort to present Bolsec as a man without standing or scruple. Beza listed two banishments from Bernese territories, Bolsec's presence at the Synod of Orleans, and added a gratuitous swipe that Bolsec had allowed his own wife to be a prostitute.

For polemical and rhetorical purposes, the personality of Calvin receded in the narrative of his work and words in these three successive redactions by Beza and Colladon. The rhetorical strategy which heightened the central issues/ideas of Calvin's life, likewise flattened the presentation of Calvin's personality. The resulting portrait was of a reformer in little need of change or emendation of his theological position or language.Beza's *Vita Calvina* presented an active life without much of an actor. As William Bouwsma has observed:

> The canonization of Calvin began as early as Beza's *Life*, a work that, from an author who had known Calvin so long and so closely, is curiously lifeless and lacking in human insight. Beza was sensitive to the charge that, after accusing Catholics of idolatry, he had made Calvin into a "god." But his response seems rather to support than to refute this charge. [12]

Bolsec's Response

Bolsec is not known to have published any works between 1562 and 1577. The occasion for his re-entry into the public arena was Beza's 1575 provocations in published correspondence and the *Vita Calvini*. Bolsec's issues with the Genevans were longstanding: mistreatment he suffered during the original trial; the subsequent hounding by Beza and a network of Genevan allies, including involvement at Lusanne and possible involvement in the national Synods of Orleans at Lyons; the insult to his wife; the publication of Calvin's letters in 1575; and finally, the defamatory portrait in the *Vita*.

Bolsec published his *Histoire de la Vie, Moeurs, Actes, Doctrine, Constance et Mort de Iean Caluin* in 1577, a response to twenty-five years of contention and provocation. Holtrop notes Bolsec followed the basic order of the 1564 *Vie de Calvin*, rather than the *Vita Calvini* of 1575, and this may indicate Bolsec may have had his manuscript in preparation for some time.[13] The 1577 *Histoire* brought Bolsec back into print with a very public confirmation of Genevan fears. Drawing upon his direct experiences with Calvin, sources from Beza and others, and his own imaginings, Bolsec offered a portrait of Calvin as the ambitious, cruel, arrogant, and vindictive chief of sinners. Bolsec pursued at least four goals in his work: to portray Calvin as a heretic; to destroy Beza's reputation and his (Beza's) authority as Calvin's interpreter; to present a counter narrative "*streitschrift*"; and to defend Bolsec's own reputation and theological views.

To portray Calvin as heretic, Bolsec followed a long literary/theological tradition that painted only in negative tones. Pfeilschifter notes the medieval genre of the "Ketzerschema," the scheme of the heretic, by which *all* the errors of the past and present are projected onto the targeted person. Bolsec agreed with Beza's claim that Calvin's character was steady and stable, but Bolsec claimed that character was fixed in the form of a heretic, as dangerous to the current church as were the heretics of the early centuries of Christianity. In keeping with the genre, Bolsec labled Calvin's illnesses as the outward manifestation in inward error. Next, Bolsec turned Beza's own words against him, indicting him as a willing liar in service to his unworthy master, Calvin. Playing upon Beza's reverence of Calvin as his "master, teacher, and friend," Bolsec posed a series of difficult questions related to Calvin's politics, personal ethics, and doctrine, in order to undermine Beza's authority as interpreter and biographer. Thirdly, Bolsec neatly inverted the Genevan narrative of the events of Calvin's life. Where Beza/Colladon had presented Calvin as a stalwart, stable in his pursuit of God's purposes, Bolsec claimed that Calvin been a deceiver since his youth. For example, according to Bolsec Calvin had resigned his posts at Noyon in the 1530s not because of scruples, but because he had been "outed" by his enemies, exposed as a philandering sodomite and a fraud (Chapter 5). In Bolsec's telling, Calvin was nearly executed because of his crimes, but was allowed to flee Noyon after receiving a brand on his shoulder.[14] Leaving France for Ferrara, Bolsec's Calvin changed his name to cover his past. Bolsec claimed that because Calvin had been willing to deceive the gullible through elaborate lies and fabricated miracles, and because Beza was all too willing to trumpet falsehood as truth, the church was now troubled by a Calvinian sect. Finally, Bolsec presented a running defense of his own theological perspectives throughout the *Histoire*, beginning first by aligning himself with the broader church against the Genevans (Chapters 1-2), then presenting a defamatory portrait of Calvin as person and theologian, and finally by invoking God as the Judge of history (Chapter 26). For Bolsec, the St. Bartholomew's Day Massacre (1572) was a lamentable but just consequence of the provocative heresies of Geneva. Bolsec's *Histoire* presented Calvin's heresy, Beza's perfidy, and Reformed credulity. Bolsec's slander was a direct answer to the slanders of the Genevans, like some defamatory call and response.

History and Biography

Biographies, histories, and martyrologies reinforced the confessional lines that separated increasingly self-contained Reformation communities, whose members freed themselves from the burden of reading opposing viewpoints, except for purposes of denunciation. The polemical *Vita Calvini* traditions served these purposes after Calvin's death. Beza's 1575 *Vita Calvini* became the [15]standard within the Protestant camp, and Bolsec's *Histoire* served as the standard source for many subsequent writers among non-Protestants. Writers professed their preferences, and readers confirmed their prejudices, through selective but reinforcing presentations of the "other." As Mario Turchetti has shown, description often yielded to polemical need in these texts, as "personality" supplanted the actual persons involved. These competing interpretive traditions continued in Beza's and Bolsec's successors. Several defenses of Calvin appeared in the late-sixteenth and early seventeenth-century that prompted and responded to attacks on Calvin. Bolsec's *Histoire* proved useful to the anti-Protestant traditions, joining Francois Baudouin's disciple Papire Masson (1544-1611), Florimond de Raemond (1540-1601) and other champions of resurgent Roman Catholicism. Raemond could easily disown Bolsec's details while retaining the basic portrait of Calvin as heretic. Charles Drelincourt's *La Defense de Calvin* (1667) relied on Beza, but knew enough of Bolsec to dispute his sources and interpretations. Pierre Bayle's summary judgments of the Reformers and the conflicts of the sixteenth century challenged dogmatic excess, but his critical essays gave no comfort to anti-Protestant groups or individuals.[16]

Conclusion

Jerome Bolsec was one of many whose conflict(s) with Calvin and his allies drove him into exile and opposition. The intense rhetoric and the substantive disagreements between Bolsec and the Genevans have tempted most to accept the Beza/Colladon picture of Bolsec as a troubled and troubling outsider, rather than as a legitimate dissenting voice within the Reformed tradition. The conflict between Bolsec and the Genevans began in disagreement, moved through denunciation, and culminated in defamatory biography.

The Beza/Colladon portraits presented a reformer with few flaws, while the Bolsec portrait presented a Calvin with no virtues. Because these interpretations were interactive, taking place within a lively and intense polemical context, contemporary students do well to gain a familiarity with both traditions, and to subject both traditions to scrutiny. The Beza/Colladon and Bolsec portraits are neither equal, nor interchangeable. Nevertheless, consideration of either requires recognition of both. Beza/Colladon's three lives of Calvin and Bolsec's streitschrift present the false choice between *either* a sanitized *or* a demonized portrait in biography. Instead we must recognize the inevitable place of polemic within religious biography, even in the best biographies of our most cherished reformers.

Endnotes

1 For a recent summary of classical models of biography, see Richard A. Burridge, "Biography," in *Handbook of Classical Rhetoric in the Hellenistic Period 330 B.C.—A.D. 400* edited by Stanley E. Porter (New York: Brill Academic, 1997), 371-191. See also Irena Backus, *Life Writing in Reformation Europe* (Aldershot, UK: Ashgate, 2008). See also Olivier Millet, *Calvin et la dynamique de la parole* (Geneva 1992). See also, *Histoire de la rhétorique dans l'Europe moderne 1450-1950*, edited by Marc Fumaroli (Paris 1999), including an overview by Olivier Millet, "La Réforme protestante et la rhétorique (circa 1520-1550)," Ibid., 259-312. Of course, the category "confessionalism" is problematic, with the definition changing from decade to decade.

2 See Irena Backus, "Roman Catholic Lives of Calvin from Bolsec to Richelieu: Why the Interest?" in *John Calvin and Roman Catholicism: Critique and Engagement, Then and Now*, edited by Randall Zachman (Grand Rapids: Baker Academic, 2008), 25-58. See also *Calvin and His Influence, 1509-2009*, edited by Irena Backus and Philip Benedict (New York: Oxford University Press, 2011).

3 See Jean-Robert Armogathe, "*Les Vies de Calvin au XVIe and XVIIe siecles*," in *Historiographie de la Reforme*, edited by Philippe Joutard (Paris 1977), 45-59. See also Daniel Ménanger, "*Théodore de Bèze, Biographe de Calvin*," *Bibliotheque d'Humanisme et de Renaissance* 45, no. 2 (1983), 231-255. See also Backus, "Roman Catholic Lives of Calvin ...," 25-58. For details of the three redactions of the *Life* of Calvin, see Frédéric Gardy, *Bibliographie des Œuvres Théodore de Bèze* (Geneva: Droz, 1960), items 172-221.

4 See Frank Pfeilschifter, *Das Calvinbild bei Bolsec und sein Fortwirken im französischen Katholizismus bis ins 20.Jahrhundert* (Augsburg: FDL-Verlag, 1983), which includes a critical bibliography of the editions of Bolsec's main text, 375-397. See also Philip Holtrop, *The Bolsec Controversy on Predestination, from 1551 to 1555: the Statements of Jerome Bolsec, and the Responses of John Calvin, Theodore Beza, and Other Reformed Theologians* 2 vols. (Lewiston, New York: E. Mellen Press, 1993). See also responses to Holtrop, including Brian Armstrong's review in *Sixteenth Century Journal* 25, no. 3 (1994), pp. 747-750, and Richard Muller's review in *Calvin Theological Journal* 29 (1994), 581-589.

5 How far up the academic ladder Bolsec climbed remains an open question. The *Bibliotheca Carmelitana* refers to Bolsec as "Sacrae Theologiae Doctor," but his name is not found among the theology faculty of the University of Paris.

6 See Mirjam van Veen, "'*In excelso honoris gradu*': Johannes Calvin und Jacques de Falais," *Zwingliana* 32 (2005), pp. 5-22.

7 Holtrop, vol. 1, pt. 1, p. 54, quoting CO 8, 154ff.

8 The text of the *Lamentation* is found in CO 8:226-227. See Holtrop's English translation and discussion of the text and its variations, *The Bolsec Controversy* vol. 1, pt. 2, 544-561.

9 See Henri Fazy, editor, *Proces de Jerome Bolsec* (Geneva, 1865). The case texts are printed in the *Corpus Reformatorum* 36 (Calvin, vol. 8), col. 145-248, and have been minutely reviewed by Holtrop, Pfeilschifter, and Fazy. I follow their exposition of the trial and the movements of Bolsec in the 1550s and early 1560s.

10 See Chiara Lastraioli, "Bruits d'armes contre bruits de papier: un rare opuscule de Bolsec adressé à Charles IX," in *Le bruits des armes: mise en forme et désinformations pendant les guerres de religion (1560-1610)* (Tours: Champion, 2012), 39-57.

11 See Lastraioli's assertion that Bolsec authored *Le double des lettres envoyees à Passevent Parisien, par le Noble et excellent Pasquin Romain, contenant en vérité la vie de Jehan Calvin* (Paris: Pierre Gaultier, 1556). See Chiara Lastraioli, "D' un texte inconnu de Jerome Bolsec contre Calvin," *Reformation & Renaissance Review* 10, no. 2 (2008), 157-174.

12 William Bouwsma, *John Calvin: a Sixteenth-Century Portrait* (New York: Oxford University Press, 1988), p. 236, note 8.

13 Holtrop, *The Bolsec Controversy*, vol. 1, pt. 2, 785-800.

14 See Pfeilschifter, *Das Calvinbild* . . . See also Christopher Elwood, "A Singular Example of the Wrath of God: The Use of Sodom in Sixteenth-Century Exegesis," *Harvard Theological Review* 98, no. 1 (2005), 67-93.

15 See Mario Turchetti, *Concordia o Tolleranza?: François Bauduin (1520-1573) E I "Moyenneurs"* (Geneva: Droz, 1984).

16 See Barbara Sher Tinsley, *Pierre Bayle's Reformation: Conscience and Criticism on the Eve of the Enlightenment* (Selinsgrove: Susquehanna University Press, 2001).

CHAPTER TEN

Will African Christians Become a Subject in Reformation Studies?

David D. Daniels

Will African Christians living in Europe during the sixteenth century become a subject within Reformation studies? Africans are key topics within Renaissance and sixteenth century art studies, including African Christians. Titles of major texts in these academic fields capture the theme: *Black Africans in Renaissance Europe*, *Revealing the African Presence in Renaissance Europe*, and *Othello's Countrymen: The African in English Renaissance Drama*. The oldest of these texts reaches back to the 1960s, illustrating that prior to the advent of Black studies as an academic discipline Renaissance studies broached the topic of Africans in sixteenth-century Europe. Yet Reformation studies has been hesitant about following suit. Afro-European and African Christians living in Europe during the Reformation era is a topic awaiting scrutiny.[1]

The life of Father Vicente Lusitano (c.1522- d. post-1561), an Afro-Portuguese Roman Catholic priest, offers a window into the world of sub-Saharan African and Afro-European Christians who lived in Europe during the era of the Reformations, Protestant and Roman Catholic. Vicente Lusitano ranks among the first Afro-European Roman Catholic clergy to convert to Protestantism during the sixteenth-century Reformations, representing the understudied world of sub-Saharan African and Afro-Europeans in the circles that constituted Christianity in Europe on the brink of the modern West.[2]

Reformation Europe within World Christianity

Excavating Lusitano's life provides a means to explore the presence of Afro-European and sub-Saharan African Christians within the Reformations of the sixteenth-century and a way to pursue the study of the Reformations as a topic within the discipline of World Christianity. In this paper, I will argue that the life of Vicente Lusitano and the lives of other Afro-European and African Christians in Reformation Europe were shaped by the European Catholic reception of Ethiopian Christianity as an ancient Christian church and by Europeans and Africans relating to each other through a cultural logic based on religion as the defining marker of African and European Christian interaction in Reformation Europe, instead "race," which would only be constructed as a concept in a later century.

As a topic within the study of World Christianity, the study of the Reformations would seek to become attuned to the multiplicity of voices, including African Christian voices. While the reception of the Reformations within Africa, Asia, and the Americas would be of interest, the presence of African Christians in the Reformations within Europe will be the focus of this current inquiry. In such an inquiry, Reformation studies would be expanded and become more multicultural in orientation.

Lodging the sixteenth-century Reformations as a topic within the study of World Christianity can offer fresh perspective to the study of Reformations, Protestant and Roman Catholic, recognizing the interdependencies or interconnections within the history of the World Christian movement. Including Afro-Europeans and African Christians in Europe on an enlarged and redrawn map of World Christianity prompts the replotting of European Christianity. This new map of the religions of Europe in 1500 is drawn with the Roman Catholic topography of northern, western, southwestern, and central Europe and with the Muslim topography of southeastern Europe. This religious map of the Christian world in 1500 shows Christians living in the Muslim-ruled regions of southeastern Europe, northern Africa, and west Asia; in the isolated Christian enclaves of the Americas; in the independent Christian kingdoms of non-Muslim ruled Europe; and in the Christian-ruled Ethiopian Empire and the Christian Kingdom of Kongo. Among the polycenters of World Christianity in the sixteenth century, then, would be the Christian kingdoms of Ethiopia and the Kongo with Kongelese Christianity, but also the Kongolese diaspora in Europe and the Americas. On this map, Ref-

SUBJECT TO NONE, SERVANT OF ALL

ormation Europe intersects with these different Christian societies and enclaves.

Inserting Afro-Europeans and African Christians into Reformation Europe as a topic within the study of World Christianity can draw insights from human or religious geography. Borrowing from the French philosophers Gilles Deleuze and Felix Guattari to grasp the multiplicity of voices and the plurality of origins that construct the Christian tradition, Dale Irvin suggests the rhizome as a new image. Rhizomes are "plants with subterranean, horizontal root systems, growing below and above ground in multiple directions at once." Irvin contrasts rhizomes with trees to describe the interlocking character of Christian tradition.

> A tradition . . . is not like a tree, organized with a major trunk and smaller (or minor) branches, and drawing primarily from a single, dominant taproot that likewise grows in one direction. A tradition is more like a rhizome, agglomerating and stabilizing at times around common experiences or locations, but then branching off and spreading rapidly at other times, in several directions at once. It is a decentered, or multicentered, system flowing across multiple material and subjective fields.[3]

This image provides a new way to visualize the Reformations within Europe and on various continents, capturing the multiple ways in which European and African Christians in sixteenth-century Europe were intertwined historically. To excavate the African Christian presence within the Reformations requires uncovering the inventiveness of the African and European Christian exchanges that constitute the linkages that fashioned the Reformations.

Studying Afro-Europeans and African Christians in Reformation Europe as a topic within the academic discipline of World Christianity challenges the dominant historiography of the Reformations in which the Reformations are basically interpreted as a European phenomenon, focusing solely on the activities of "white" European Christians while being silent on the presence and activities of the African Christians in Reformation Europe. World Christianity Studies pursues other historiographic directions.[4]

In studying Afro-Europeans and African Christians in Reformation Europe as a topic, the polycentricity of World Christianity and the exchanges within Europe between the Christian movements from continents can garner attention. Rather than only differentiating Christianity by continent and arguing for European Christianity alongside African Christianity, Asian Christianity, or Christianity in the Americas, this perspective warrants accenting the interdependencies and interconnections, for instance, between European and African Christians on one continent such as Europe.

By showing European Catholic reception of Ethiopian Christianity as an ancient Christian church and a cultural logic based on religion as the defining marker of African and European Christian interaction in Reformation Europe instead of "race," this chapter will make various intellectual moves. The chapter offers a biographical sketch of Father Vicente Lusitano. Lusitano's life story will be situated within the European world of elite African and Afro-European Christians, noting the institutions they established, the seminaries and universities they attended, and the "countries" from where they either emigrated or transported through the forced immigration of the slave trade.

As opposed to engaging in a genealogical exercise isolating the building blocks during Lusitano's lifetime that contribute to the rise of modern racism, the chapter will pursue an archeological project by excavating the era in he lives as a Christian clergyperson of African descent serving the church in sixteenth-century Europe. Modern racism as a social system will be introduced briefly in order to supply a backdrop to how the Christian world prior to the advent of modern racism as European Christianity's alliance with it as well as the invention of Western Christianity or Modern Christianity as a project of modern racism.

Central to the argument regarding the reception of African and Afro-European Christians in sixteenth-century Europe is the vaulted status of the African kingdom of Ethiopia and Ethiopian Christians in the religious and political imagination of European Christians during the fifteenth and early sixteenth centuries; this status would especially be extended to the African elite or nobility on the African Atlantic coast. Coupled with this vaulted status in the European imagination of the era was the elite treatment Ethiopian Christians received during this era.

While the argument of this essay is framed as describing a social reality of African and Afro-European Christians in Europe prior to the construction of modern racism, this society reality is, though, already marked by prejudice and by the existence of slavery in the Iberian Peninsula. Africans were sold into slavery in Europe along with "white"

Muslims and Eastern Europeans during this time; these conditions, however, functioned in the sixteenth century differently than they will function within the system of modern racism of the mid-seventeenth century and subsequent centuries. Consequently, how prejudice against Africans was disconnected from a system of racism will be discussed in the chapter.

Sketching the Life of Vicente Lusitano

Born in 1522, Vicente Lusitano was the son of a "white" Portuguese father and African mother. A native of Olivenca, Alentejo, Portugal, his early name reflected his affiliation with his hometown: Vicente de Olivenca. He was one of the 150,000 to 200,000 Africans who lived on the Iberian Peninsula during the sixteenth century. Later he was renamed Vicente Lusitano, probably after he relocated to Rome.

Lusitano and his African and Afro-European Christian contemporaries challenge the popular imagination, and sometimes even scholarly imagination, of the Reformation Europe being absent of sub-Saharan African Christians. They counter the narrative of West and Central Africans who only commence embracing Christianity during the modern missionary enterprise of the nineteenth century and the modern European mass colonialization of Africa during the late nineteenth century. Lusitano symbolizes the community of African and Afro-Europeans who lived in sixteenth-century Reformation Europe. Instead of occupying the lands marked by European exploration, conquest, and colonization during the so-called European age of discovery, Lusitano and his African and Afro-European Christian contemporaries were born and raised in Europe; they were discovering Europe.[5]

Baptized within the diocese of Ceuta, Lusitano was raised a Roman Catholic. In Lusitano's sixteenth-century Portugal, sub-Saharan Africans attended Roman Catholic mass as well as had their baptisms, confirmations, weddings, and funerals held in the church and officiated by Roman Catholic priests. Marriages occurred between "white" Portuguese nobility and Kongolese nobility. The legal system granted sub-Saharan Africans the right to sue "white" Portuguese and, within sixteenth-century legal history, there were a set of legal decisions with sub-Saharans as the victors. Lusitano lived in the diocese of Ceuta whose geographical boundaries crossed the Strait of Gibraltor, creating a diocese that connected parishes in southwestern Europe to parishes in northwestern Africa.[6]

WILL AFRICAN CHRISTIANS BECOME A SUBJECT IN REFORMATION STUDIES?

Lusitano's parents likely were not nobles. Since African noblewomen were not permitted to travel to Europe by most African customs; it is unlikely that his mother was a noblewoman. Since nobles often only married nobles, it is unlikely that his father was a noble either. Born of commoners, Lusitano would still, though, travel as a Roman Catholic priest in elite circles because of his social connections.

Lusitano's family most likely introduced him to the religious and social life of confraternities. The religious life of "white" Iberians, Afro-Europeans, and African Catholics centered around Christian lay groups called brotherhoods or confraternities. Some confraternities were "interracial," even consisting of "white" Portuguese slaveholders and enslaved Africans as members. There were even African-instituted and governed confraternities with the first and most influential confraternity for sub-Saharan Africans being Our Lady of the Rosary; sub-Saharan Africans founded their first branch of this brotherhood before 1494. During the 1500s, they established at least eight other branches in Portugal alone.[7]

A part of the second generation of Africans and Afro-European Christians to be educated for the priesthood in Europe, Lusitano took his vows as a priest in the diocese of Ceuta and was ordained as a Roman Catholic priest of the habit of St. Peter. Throughout the sixteenth century African and Afro-Europeans would continue to join the Roman Catholic priesthood, including other Afro-Europeans such as Andre Friere. The ordination of Africans to the Roman Catholic priesthood was made possible by the papal brief, *Exponi Nobis*, issued by Pope Leo X in 1518. This papal brief suspended as a prerequisite that candidates for the priesthood had to be born to Christian parents. Although it is possible that both of Lusitano's parents had been baptized as infants, *Exponi Nobis* made it possible for Africans who were recent converts to join the priesthood as long as they lived out their vows as priest in the global south and not in Europe. Afro-European clergy were free to serve as priests in Europe.[8]

Among the first generation of African and Afro-European priests to be educated on the cusp of sixteenth-century Europe was a group of young African Christian men who were educated in Lisbon by 1494, the year when sub-Saharan African priests went to the islands of São Tomé to serve as priests. The first Kongolese Roman Catholic priest to be consecrated to the bishopric was Ndoadidiki Ne-Kinu a Mumemba (c. 1495-c.1531) whose baptismal name was Henrique. Pope Leo X was instrumental in fulfilling the request of Henrique's father, King Afonso (c. 1456-1542 or 3), which was to create a Kongolese Roman Catholic cohort of priests and a bishop. Ordained in 1520, Henrique was consecrated a bishop in 1521. The priesthood was also opened to African slaves; one priest of Lusitano's generation, Joao, was born to parents who were both enslaved. Lusitano was following in the path of other African Roman Catholic priests.[9]

The majority of African priests who were educated in Europe would be trained in Portugal. Catering especially to Kongolese Roman Catholics, these theological institutions included the Saint Eloi seminary at the monastery of Saints George and John the Evangelist in Lisbon along with the seminary of Saint Joao in Xabregas. They were also educated at the University of Coimbra as well as the episcopal residence at Evora. By the early 1600s, sub-Saharan Africans studied at St. Jerome College in Coimbra, St. Augustine College in Lisbon, and St. Anthony College in Lisbon. During the sixteenth century, St. Eloi ranked as the most prominent center for the education of sub-Saharan African Christians. At times the student body was even "multi-racial," composed of sub-Saharan African, south Asian, and "white" Portuguese Christians. Education was open to all classes of African and Afro-European Christians; though it is unclear if all schools were open; no extant laws excluded Africans and Afro-Europeans. Literate Africans and Afro-European Christians in Europe pushed the literacy rate within Europe up to the range of 10 to 20 percent of the European population; educated African and Afro-European Catholic priest increased the literacy rate among Roman Catholic clergy since many "white" European priests were functionally illiterate at the beginning of the sixteenth century. In a sense, the educated African and Afro-European Catholic priests were in the vanguard.[10]

Ascribing to the European distinction between the nobility and the peasantry, the Portuguese plotted Africans on both sides of the class divide. The African nobility in Portugal were often from the Atlantic coast African kingdoms of Benin and Kongo. African nobles such as Henrique, a son of the Kongolese King Afonso, constituted the African elite in European society. It appears that Portuguese society as other European societies being stratified by class accepted African nobles as "peers" to Portuguese nobility. Intermarriage between the two nobilities, African and Portuguese, appears to have occurred. So, the admission of African nobles into Portuguese elite institutions squares with this logic of churches, schools and universities.[11]

Besides interacting with African nobles, Lusitano would interface with African freed-persons who lived in Portugal and Spain. African freed-persons traversed the social space above the lowest stratum. As formerly enslaved Africans, African freed-persons constituted a significant community; they were joined to Afro-Europeans, children born often of European fathers and African mothers as well as children born of mulatto parents.

While Lusitano lived on an Iberian Peninsula with a significant sub-Saharan African minority of 150,000 to 200,000 people with the majority of these sub-Saharan Africans being enslaved, there existed a recognizable community of free-born or manumitted African population of approximately 2,580 people in Portugal. By the mid-1500s, Lisbon's municipal population was ten percent sub-Saharan African or 10,000 people, including a segment of the sub-Saharan Africans who were the descendents of the enslaved Africans who arrived after 1444. According to Zurara who lived in Lisbon during the 1400s, sub-Saharan Africans "as soon as they understood our language they turned Christian with very little ado." He furthered noted that he "saw . . . boys and girls (the children and grandchildren of those first captives, born in this land) as good and true Christians as if they had directly descended, from the beginnings of the dispensation of Christ, from those who were first baptized." [12]

After being consecrated a priest, Lusitano interacted with the "white" Portuguese nobility, serving as the tutor to Dinis (Dennis), the son of a nobleman within the Lencastre family. Besides the occupation of tutor, other African and Afro-European Christians were also involved in education. A Kongolese young adult operated a school at the castle in Lisbon where he taught the humanities as a subject between 1522 and 1557 during the reign of King Joao III. The highest ranking educator among African and Afro-European Christians within Lusitano's generation was most likely Dom Juan Latino (1518-1596), a native sub-Saharan African who grew up in Spain. A recognized poet, Latino was a professor of Latin and Greek at the Cathedral of Grenada from 1546-1566 and occupied an academic chair. [13]

Lusitano migrated to Rome around 1550 at the age of 28, accompanying Dinis's father, Afonso de Lencastre, then Portugal's ambassador to Rome. While in Rome, Lusitano circulated in sacred music circles and became a papal singer. In 1551, he became the contestant in a famous debate with Nicola Vicentino (1511-1575 or 1576), a well-known music theorist, about the genre of sacred music. Held in the Sistine Chapel, the debate was judged by Ghiselin Danckerts (1510-1567) and Bartolome Escobedo (1510 1563); the judges designated Lusitano the winner of the debate. Becoming a composer and scholar of sacred Christian music, Lusitano's work played a defining role in Renaissance music. On the Italian peninsula, he taught music in Rome, Padua, and Viterbo.[14]

Vicente Lusitano traveled in the circles of the Italian Catholic reformers. In dialogue with the Italian humanists, these reformers included advocates of moral reform as well as others open to ecclesial and theological reform. Lusitano navigated the transition from Roman Catholic to Protestant through contact with Venetian Catholic progressives and Venetian Protestants. The Venetian region was recognized as a site of the "Lutheran plague" as early as the 1540s. By 1549, Bishop Peter Paul Vergerio (c.1498—1565), was disposed, accused of harboring Lutheran ideas. In the Venetian region lived Roman Catholic reformers who fought for the reform of Roman Catholic practices and the theology of salvation.[15]

Vicente Lusitano converted to Protestantism around 1561. Letters of introduction were written on his behalf, attesting to his embrace of the Protestant cause. Count Julius of Thiene penned a letter to Peter Paul Vergerio, the former Roman Catholic bishop who had converted to Protestantism. A leader within this Venetian vanguard, Count Julius came from the northern part of the Italian Peninsula that includes the Venetian territory. Count Julius left his native Vicenza within the Venetian territory by 1556, finding refuge as a Protestant within Wurttemberg during Duke Christopher's reign. In Wurttemberg, he became better acquainted with the Lutheran cause and served as an intermediary between the Venetian vanguard and Lutherans. In his letter to Vergerio, Count Julius requested that Vergerio introduce Lusitano to Duke Christopher in order for Christopher to welcome Lusitano to Wurttemberg.[16]

Prior to converting to Protestantism, Vergerio was a prominent Roman Catholic official and reformer. As a Roman Catholic reformer, he interfaced with other progressive cardinals such as Reginald Pole (1500-1558) and Gasparo Contarini (1483-1542). As a papal diplomat, he represented the Roman Catholic Church at pivotal meetings with leading Protestants: the Diets of Augsburg in 1530 and Worms in 1541 along with the Colloquy of Regensburg in 1541. At Regensburg, the conference was convened as an attempt to reconcile Catholics and Protestants. Vergerio even met with Luther at Wittenberg in 1535 and John

Calvin and Martin Bucer at Regensburg in 1541. Vergerio also attended sessions of the Council of Trent in 1546.[17]

First appointed a bishop to a diocese in Croatia by 1536, Vergerio received an appointment to the bishopric of the diocese of Capodistria, his birthplace, in the Venetian territory. In 1549, he fled into exile, escaping to the Italian-speaking Protestant region of Switzerland. Visiting Geneva in 1550, he interacted with John Calvin. In 1553, he associated with Duke Christopher of Wurttemberg as an advisor to the Duke. In a letter to Duke Christopher, Vergerio vouched for Lusitano's Protestant convictions and musical expertise.[18]

Navigating the world of the Venetian Catholic and Protestant reformers, Lusitano migrated to Protestantism by traveling the paths blazed by Vergerio and Count Julius. As a Roman Catholic priest embracing the Protestant cause, Lusitano became one of the first Afro-European Catholic clergy to become Protestant. While it is uncertain whether he became a Protestant minister as Vergerio did, his conversion to Protestantism distinguished him among the Afro-European and African Catholic priests of the Reformation era.

The World of Afro-European and African Christians in Europe

How did this world of Vicente Lusitano and his Afro-European and African Christian contemporaries emerge in the first place? The sixteenth-century world of educated sub-Saharan African Christians in Africa and Europe had its origins in the fifteenth century. It was conceived around the 1400, an era when Europe was seized by a deep fascination with the African Christian Kingdom of Ethiopia. By 1400, Christianity had already existed for over 1000 years in Ethiopia whereas Christianity in northern Europe was approximately 400 years old and European tribes such as the Saami still practiced animism or traditional religion. To excavate the place of Ethiopia within Europe and the European imagination an archaeological approach could offer insight.

Lodging Ethiopia at the center of the reconstructed world of Vicente Lusitano and his Afro-European and African Christian contemporaries supplies an angle of vision to the Ethiopian discovery of Europe and the European encounter with Ethiopians in Europe. The Ethiopian Christian encounter of Catholic Europe opens with the Ethiopian "embassies to the Vatican" in 1402 as well as presence of Ethiopian delegations at the Council of Constance (1414-1418) and the Council of

Florence (1441/43). An archaeological way to study the encounter differs from a genealogical approach that might focus on the disembarkation of enslaved Africans in Lisbon of 1444. The archaeological approach would chronicle the reception of Ethiopian Christians in Europe. The manner in which Ethiopian Christians were "well-received" in Europe partially explains the "positive" reception that Kongolese Christians received during sixteenth-century Europe.[19]

The reception of the Ethiopian Christians, who affiliated with the Coptic Church in Egypt, went beyond their full membership at two councils sponsored by Roman Catholic popes. The Vatican authorized the use of a church in Vatican City or Rome for Ethiopian priests to celebrate the Ethiopian Orthodox liturgy in Ge'ez around 1481 and of the adjacent hostel for lodging the Ethiopian priests and pilgrims. The authorization of the church to celebrate of Ethiopian liturgy followed the Vatican sending an embassy to Ethiopia in 1451. Among the names of the church was St. Stephens of the Ethiopians. The Vatican's recognition of the Ethiopian church as Christian and not aberrant was informed by an agreement that grew out of the Council of Florence in which the Vatican mistakenly thought the Ethiopian church acknowledged the primacy of the Rome Catholic pope; by virtue of this "understanding" the Roman church and the Ethiopian were in communion.[20]

Ethiopia being at the center of the excavated world of Vicente Lusitano and his Afro-European and African Christian contemporaries was reflected in the maps of the Christian world that informed European Catholics in 1500. These maps were drawn from earlier mappings based on a Christian imaginary populated by Christian exemplars such as Prester John of Ethiopia and medieval speculation of the geographic location of biblical Paradise, the Garden of Eden, being in Africa.[21]

During the 1400s and earlier, the Christian world was divided by Muslim lands that isolated Christian Africa from Christian Europe. Ethiopia possessed a magnificent reputation in Europe as a great, pious, wealthy, and militarily-equipped Christian kingdom led by a phenomenal king called Prester John. According to Donald N. Levine, "the prestige and renown" of Prester John "was then surpassed by no other Christian prince."[22] Christian Europe anticipated that Ethiopia with its wealth in gold and large military could provide with Europe financial resources as well as be ally in battling Islam.[23] Ethiopia was a savior of sorts for Europe with Prester John resembling a social messiah. European Catholic pilgrims to Jerusalem regularly saw Ethiopian pilgrims while both visited the holy Christian sites; Ethiopians monks had been resident in Jerusalem since the early thirteenth century. Other Ethiopian monks belonged to a monastery in Ehden, Lebanon and others were associated with the Church of the Savior in Nicosia, Cyprus.[24]

In Ethiopia, monastic schools possessed a long and rich history of literacy by the sixteenth-century. Students learned to read and write in the major Ethiopian language of Ge'ez. A robust theological and literary tradition undergirded the written texts that students mastered. Ethiopian theologians and scholars were versed in the ancient Christian texts from early centuries of Christianity. A literate class constituted the Ethiopian clergy and political elite. An estimated 1000 or more students would annually enroll through these monastic schools.

Ethiopia as a literate Christian kingdom became the framework in which Portugal and the Vatican would engage sub-Saharan African kingdoms such as the Kongo, Benin, and Warri. The Kongolese would be classified as "Ethiopians from the Congo." Christian Ethiopia as a concept provided the theological space for sub-Saharan Christian Africans to operate as equals within Portugal, the Vatican, and other European arenas.[25]

Reformation Europe: An Age before Modern Racism

How best to characterize the presence of Vicente Lusitano and other African as well as Afro- European Christians during the Reformation Europe as an era that precedes the invention of modern racism. Without the modern construction of Africans as inferior ontologically, scientifically, theologically, and legally, how are African Christians envisioned by the ecclesial, legal, and social systems? How do African and Afro-European Christians possess rights, exercise freedoms, and occupy a social space inside the same class system erected for "whites" rather than outside the class system being segregated as the excluded? Do the rights they possess, the freedoms they exercise, and the social space they occupy provide a window to a world that warrants interrogation? Will these explanations reveal something about church practices, the legal systems, and social customs that differ from the later developments expressive of modern racism? By excavating the social terrain that the African and Afro-European Christian elite navigated and the environments that they built on these terrains, another dimension of sixteenth-century Reformation Europe is uncovered.

The hegemonic polarities that dominated Lusitano's era and the six-teenth-century Reformation Europe placed Christian over against Jew, Muslim, and infidel. Grounded in religious distinctions and codified in law, these polarities organized and ruled European society or, more exactly, European society as a sixteenth century Catholic invention. Exclusionary practices were based on religious distinctions. These religious distinctions could also have biological referents as in Jews being both a religious and racial or proto-racial category. However, African was not a proto-racial nor racial category in this era. For European Catholics, Africa consisted of three sectors defined religiously: Christian, Muslim, and pagan. During part, if not all, of sixteenth-century Reformation Europe, Ethiopian be-came a term to refer to Ethiopian Christians as well as Kongolese.[26]

While an aesthetic polarity between white and black existed during Lusitano's era, it failed to be codified in the European legal or ecclesial system nor did the white-black polarity oppose Africa to Europe. For Ro-man Catholic Europe in the sixteenth century, there were white Africans such as the Arab North Africans, brown (tawny/swarthy) Africans such as the North African Berbers, and black Africans such as sub-Saharan Africans. Religiously, black Africans included Ethiopian Christians, other Christians, Muslims (blackamoors), and pagans. While civilization as a concept would be developed after the sixteenth century, "civilization" as a contrast between highly organized society and a primal society would be a polarity that would contrast sub-Saharan Africa to Europe either because Portugal and the Vatican recognize that "civilization" marked the Ethiopian Empire and the such kingdoms as those of Kon-go and of Benin. During the era of Lusitano and his Afro-European and African Christian contemporaries, terms that later marked modern rac-ism were fluid. The term slave, for instance, lacked association with any particular color, being applied to the people of southeastern Europeans, Arabs, North Africans, Asian Indians, Chinese, American Indians as well as sub-Saharan Africans. The term Negro, likewise lacking an associa-tion with a specific "race" or color, referred to American Indians, Asian Indians as well as sub-Saharan Africans. Consequently, Negro applied to a variety of people of color. A polarity between white and black as well as Africa and Europe failed to develop in a hegemonic way that would be inscribed in legal or ecclesial system possibly because of the fertile concept of Ethiopia and the term black and Africa were rendered fluid, complex and multivalent within Portuguese, Vatican, and, possibly, European discourse by the place of Ethiopia in the European imagination and mapping of the Christian world.

Conclusion

The study of World Christianity recasts the history of the church in profound and provocative ways, introducing to our times generative historical moments that had been long forgotten and are in dire need of being remembered. The world of Lusitano and his Afro-European and African Christian contemporaries was a world that was conceived before the modern European construction of race, the invention of modern racism as an ontologically based, "scientifically" grounded, theologically legitimated legal codified caste (and beyond-caste) system, and the engineering of modern chattel slavery with Africans as the exclusive property. This world privileges a "multi-racial" Catholic Portugal, Portugal where Kongolese and other African Christians were members of every strata of the society, joining "white" Portuguese Christians in erecting ecclesial and socio-cultural communities within Reformation Europe. This world generated a new historical moment in sixteenth-century Reformation Europe where Afro-European and African Christians like Vicente Lusitano served as priests, a historical moment that later would be overwhelmed and eclipsed by the modern construction of race and attendant system of racism.

Endnotes

1 T. F. Earle and K. J. P. Lowe, eds., *Black Africans in Renaissance Europe* (New York: Cambridge University Press, 2010 [2005]); Joaneath Spicer, ed., *Revealing the African Presence in Renaissance Europe* (Baltimore: Walter Arts Museum, 2012); Eldred D. Jones, *Othello's Countrymen: The African in English Renaissance Drama* (Oxford: Oxford University Press, 1965).

2 Maria Augusta Alves Barbosa, *Vincentius Lusitanus: Ein portugiesischer Komponist und Musiktheoretiker des 16. Jahrhunderts* (Lisbon: Estado da Cultura, 1977). Robert Stevenson, "Vicente Lusitano New Light on His Career," *Journal of the American Musicological Society* 15, No. 1 (Spring 1962): 72-77; Robert Stevenson, "The First Black Published Composer," *Inter-American Music Review* 5 (1982): 79-103; Philippe Canguilhem, "Singing upon the Book According to Vicente Lusitano," *Early Music History* 30 (October 2011): 55-103.

3 Dale T. Irvin, *Christian Histories, Christian Traditioning: Rendering Accounts* (Maryknoll: Orbis Books, 1998), 47.

4 Since the concept of "race" and "whiteness" will only emerge after the sixteenth century, "white" and "race" will be placed in quotation marks. "White" as an adjective is the author's attempt to distinguish between indigenous Portuguese and African immigrants.

5 See David Northrup, *Africa's Discovery of Europe: 1450 to 1850* (New York: Oxford University Press, 2002).

6 A. C. de C. M. Saunders, *A Social History of Black Slaves and Freedmen in Portugal, 1441-1555* (Cambridge: Cambridge University Press, 2010 [1982]), 149-150.

7 Saunders, 150-156.

8 Leo X, "Exponi Nobis", 12 June 1518, *Corpo Diplomático Portugues, Contendo os Actos e Relações Políticas e diplomáticas de Portugal com as Diversas Potências do Mundo desde o Século 16 até os Nossos Dias*, . 9-10.

9 John K. Thornton, "Rural People, the Church in the Kongo and the Afroamerican Diaspora (1491-1750)" in *Transcontinental Links in the History of Non-Western Christianity*, edited by By Klaus Koschorke (Weisbaden: Harrassowitz Verlag, 2002), 38; John K.Thornton, "The Development of an African Catholic Church in the Kingdom of Kongo, 1491-1750," *Journal of African History* 25 (1984): 147-167; Saunders, 157.

10 Saunders, 157.

11 C. R. Boxer, *Church Militant and Iberian Expansion, 1440-1770* (Baltimore: Johns Hopkins University Press, 2001 [1978]), 3-7.

12 Saunders, 60; Willie J. Jennings, *The Christian Imagination: Theology and the Origins of Race* (New Haven: Yale University Press, 2010), 19.

13 Gerald Moser, "The Portuguese in Africa," in *European-language Writing in Sub-Saharan Africa*, vol. 1, edited by Albert S. Gerard (Budapest: Akademiai Kiado, 1986), 45, 51-52.

14 Stevenson, "The First Black Published Composer," 92.

15 Antonio Santosuosso, "Religion More Veneto and the Trial of Pier Paolo Vergerio" in *Peter Martyr Vermiglio and Italian Reform*, edited by Joseph C. McLelland (Waterloo, Ontario, Canada: Wilfred Laurier University Press, 1980).

16 Stevenson, "The First Black Published Composer," 98.

17 Santosuosso, 43-47.

18 Frederic Corss Church, *The Italian Reformers* (New York: Columbia University Press), 154; Jules Bonnet, translator and editor, *Letters of John Calvin* (Burt Franklin: Research & Source Series, 2007), 245, 276.

19 C. F. Beckingham, "Ethiopia and Europe, 1200-1650" in *European Outthrust and Encounter: The First Phase c.1400-c.1700*, edited by C. H. Clough and P. E. H. Hair (Liverpool: Liverpool University Press, 1994), 81-86; Lamin O. Sanneh, *Disciples of All Nations: Pillars of World Christianity* (Oxford: Oxford University Press, 2008), 98.

20 Beckingham, 81.

21 Jean Delumeau, Matthew O'Connell, trans., *History of Paradise: The Garden of Eden in Myth and Tradition* (Urbana: University of Illinois Press, 2000 [1992]), 90-91.

22 Donald N. Levine, *Greater Ethiopia: The Evolution of a Multiethnic Society* (Chicago: The University of Chicago Press, 1974, 2000), 9.

23 Jan Nederveen Pieterse, *White on Black: Images of Africa and Blacks in Western Popular Culture* (New Haven: Yale University Press, 1992), 25.

24 Stefan Goodwin, *Africa in Europe:Antiquity into the Age of Global Expansion*, vol. 1 (Lanham, Maryland: Lexington Books, 2009), 150.

25 Boxer, 83.

26 Bernard Lewis, *Cultures in Conflict: Christians, Muslims, and Jews in the Age of Discovery* (New York: Oxford University Press, 1995).

CHAPTER ELEVEN

Driving Away the Devil

God's Word as Provision for the Future of the Church

Elizabeth L. Hiller

A hidden treasure found in my grandma's belongings when she passed away was a set of church council minutes from 1874-1885.[1] These minutes, translated for an anniversary celebration of the congregation from the original Norwegian to English, chronicle the earliest years of Norwegian Lutheran immigrants in rural, southwest Minnesota. They detail the formation of Wang's Evangelical Norwegian Lutheran Congregation of Renville County, Minnesota. This congregation, like so many others, was an outpost for Christian formation. They took this task seriously. They provided for the education of their youth in the English language and provided significant social services for their community.

The minutes of Wang are not different from the minutes that you would read in a Lutheran church today. As with many churches, a significant part of the council's work included attending to the financial business of the church, working through fiscal challenges and maintaining and updating church property. The congregational council of Wang also formulated plans to address community issues. They shared care, compassion and funds for those suffering after a grasshopper plague, for a Swede who worried about his family in his home country, and they also addressed the alcoholism that was preventing parents from attending to their duties with their children.

Nostalgia for a mythic Christian world might tempt us into imagining that every person in Renville County, Minnesota, was a member

SUBJECT TO NONE, SERVANT OF ALL

of one of the dozens of small Lutheran churches that dot the country-side there, but the council's minutes tell a different story. The minutes chronicle that many souls in the community were unaffiliated or uninterested in its Christian fellowship. Yet the church of 1880 also makes very different assumptions than the councils that many of us lead and serve on today. For example, the assumption then was that those addicted to alcoholism would return to Christian fellowship if and when they were able to leave drinking behind. The expectation was that Swedes, who generally kept their distance from the Norwegian churches, would found their own church when they had sustainable numbers to do so. The assumption was that no matter one's current reality, all people belonged in the Christian fold. These church leaders trusted that all people belonged to God.

Today, few people assume Christian faith in others. According to the latest Pew Study,[2] belief in God is dropping at an unprecedented rate.[3] Affiliation with the church, certainly for people under thirty years old, is not expected. Biblical and theological literacy is not and cannot be assumed in our wider culture, in our churches, even among incoming seminarians. This is a markedly different cultural and church reality than the reality found some one-hundred-odd years ago. In Wang, nearly all of the members had had strong catechetical training in Norway as youth. Whether they were pious or not, their world views were shaped by the church. They had a vocabulary for speaking about significant issues in their faith.

Ashburn Evangelical Lutheran Church, the church I pastored for over five years, and the church Kurt and Jobey Hendel call home, exemplifies the changing face of American Protestant Christianity. Ashburn's congregation includes Anglo-Americans of German, Swedish, and Lithuanian descent, African-Americans whose grandparents moved to Chicago during the Second Great Migration, and a smattering of refugees from Liberia and immigrants from Ghana. Theological diversity and literacy is broader still than the ethnic and racial diversity in the congregation. Like Ashburn Lutheran Church, congregations everywhere are increasingly comprised of people from widely different backgrounds, with widely different theological and biblical understandings of God, life, the universe, and everything else. Bemoan or celebrate the changing face of American culture and American Lutheranism, it is the reality of every church and every Christian today.

Speaking the Truth in Love

Today, church councils represent the diversity of backgrounds, theologies and theological literacies that are present in our churches. A significant difference from the Wang church council of 1880 and the majority of councils today is the amount of time and attention given to theological debate. One of the major concerns of the Wang church council regarded predestination.

May 28, 1883

The first matter to come before the meeting was the "*Naadevalget*,"[4] as follows: Man's free will to gain salvation. Congregation asserted itself that man cannot by his own reason or strength do anything towards soul's salvation, it must come from God. That man must accept God's call, for man's will is to do that which is evil. The good must come from God. Man's fall is his own fault for he will not accept the call from God who grants everlasting life to those who believe in him.[5]

We might dismiss the theological focus of this old school church council as something that is possible when churches are homogenous and when their members were all raised as Lutheran Christians. We might scoff at the time devoted to theological issues like predestination, the issue which instigated the formation of Wang as an independent congregation. As pastors, we might sigh with relief when parishioners do not want to argue about the theological implications of sex and definitions of marriage! Yet, there is something admirable in the Wang church council capacity and willingness for conversation and debate concerning the foundations of faith. Every man, and they were all men, on the Wang church council was a farmer or laborer. There were no trained academics, they were baptized theologians and philosophers. The church council minutes reveal frequent and spirited conversation on the 28th Article of the Augsburg Confession on the power of bishops, and frequent and considerable consideration of predestination and human's role in salvation. Further, this church, a small group of fifty families, had little pastoral support. Their pastor served four other congregations, leading worship and "reading" with their confirmands on a monthly basis. Yet this group of Christians followed their theological instincts and was able to articulate their beliefs. They were able to speak through and about the most complex aspects of faith.

As a pastor, I have served three significantly different calls: a 3,000-member big steeple congregation in the Quad Cities of Illinois and Iowa, a small and diverse congregation in urban Chicago, and my current call in a bedroom community of Fargo, North Dakota–Moorhead, Minnesota, in the heart of the Lutheran belt. Each of these churches has had faithful, energetic church councils who take seriously their calls from God to serve their congregations. I am grateful and humbled each day by the gifts that God provides the leadership of these churches. While acknowledging these gifts, theological conversation and making decisions through the lens of our faith was and is difficult in each of these different contexts. Speaking about God and using biblical story as the source and norm for our lives as churches was and is out of the comfort zone for many church council members. As a young(ish) pastor, I've struggled to articulate my own theological instincts and convictions in difficult decision-making processes. Discerning God's direction for us and talking about God while avoiding arrogant pronouncement of the full knowledge of God's will for our church is simply a difficult thing.

God Will Provide: What You Are to Say Will Be Given To You

If you doubt the difficulty of speaking about God and the difference God makes in your life, try an experiment.[6] At dinner with friends, in your next adult education class, or with colleagues, ask, "What difference does God make in your life?" Share the difference that Christ makes in your life. Most Lutheran Christians speak well and fluently about the great things their churches are doing. They speak with passion about caring for those in need and providing nets to prevent malaria in Tanzania. They are proud of the work of their churches, but it is very difficult for most Lutheran Christians to articulate how God gives them life or joy or peace or purpose each day. It is often difficult to share the most compelling parts of our faith stories.

Nearly every job I have held since I was eighteen years old has been at a college, church, camp or organization affiliated with the Evangelical Lutheran Church in America. It sometimes seems the number of times that St. Francis' apocryphal words, "Preach the gospel at all times and when necessary use words," has been shared with me and other young people in these ministry contexts is greater than the number of stars in the sky and the grains of sand on a seashore. This mentality discouraged many of my peers and me from speaking about our faith, casting suspicion on those who spoke openly about their faith as people who were somehow less thoughtfully Christian or too evangelical. Further, this mentality creates a false division or rivalry between speaking about faith and living out our faith through acts and lifestyles of justice and mercy.

Our world needs to hear the good news of Jesus Christ. Jesus' last words, a command echoed in our baptismal liturgy, enjoin us to baptize and teach about Jesus to the ends of the earth. The suspicion of the spoken good news of Jesus Christ must stop in our churches. Our difficulty, reluctance, or refusal to share the way that God makes a difference in our lives must change. Too many people in our communities do not know God, or like God, or believe in God. Too many people in our communities need to know the grace and love of God. Speaking about faith and growing the confidence of laity to have a deep, relational sense of faith in God is necessary now. We cannot wait. Years of limiting the sharing of faith to good deeds, justice work, and service have limited our proclamation of the gospel.

God's Word is Our Great Heritage

Our culture and our own challenges with sharing the gospel are formidable foes. Luckily, we have a God who is more powerful than the sin, death, and the devil in and around us. Martin Luther writes in the *Preface to the* Large Catechism,

> Nothing is so powerfully effective against the devil, the world, the flesh, and all evil thoughts as to occupy one's self with God's Word, to speak about it and meditate upon it, in the way that Psalm 1 calls those blessed who 'meditate on God's law day and night.'[7]

As leaders of churches, both lay and ordained, it is incumbent upon us to foster communities and environments where people have the opportunity, knowledge, and support to grow deep, relational faith in God. It is incumbent upon us as individuals to practice disciplines where we grow in deep, relational faith in God. Being able to share the gospel depends upon trusting the power of the gospel in our lives, in our churches, and in our communities. Being able to share the gospel depends upon trusting God to give us the words to share God with others.

There is no magic formula for occupying one's self with God's Word. We trust that the Holy Spirit will work through our efforts to encourage disciplines of prayer, study of Scripture, and congregational opportunities for faith formation. Few pastors have the time or resources to build faith formation programs for the home and the congregation. Luckily, dozens of useful resources exist for disciplined, focused efforts at growing peoples' faith, love for God, and love for their neighbors.[8]

It matters that pastors and church leaders commit to cultivating faith in ourselves and our churches as we continue engaging our communities. It matters that pastors develop and focus on forming people in faith in Christ. People who are growing in their faith will have the energy, enthusiasm and spiritual maturity to engage our congregations and communities for the sake of Christ and for the sake of the world. It is not enough to be a socially-active or socially-conscious congregation. We need to be faith-inspired, active, and conscious congregations.

In order to further ground my current congregation in faith, this year our congregation will use Luther's Large Catechism as a specific resource and devotional guide for our life together. The church council will focus its monthly devotions on the familiar scripture of the Lord's Prayer and its exposition as found in the Large Catechism. Our secretary's minutes will reflect our biblical and theological contemplation! Our confirmation mentors and parents each will receive excerpts of the Large Catechism and a short exposition and guide to them in order to give these leaders direction and insight as they lead middle school youth in growing in their faith. We live in an area where confirmation is culturally "mandatory" for youth, and I receive this as a gift from God and as an opportunity for serious biblical and theological reflection. While many congregations have moved away from catechetical training to relationship-based models for confirmation ministry, the necessity of strong content for confirmation ministry cannot be overemphasized. Youth need to build relationships at church, yet these relationships are a part of a larger web of relationships that they are building in school and basketball practice. They will not receive God's Word or be shaped by a unique Lutheran worldview in these other activities.

Our world needs the gospel, and Jesus commissioned all Christians to share it. Pastors and congregational leaders need to take focused, disciplined care to provide and model methods and ministries where congregation members can grow in a deep sense of faith in God and feel confident in speaking of their faith. The world needs the gospel. God provides us with God's very self, God's Word, to grow the kingdom of God among us and through us. It is my prayer that churches are bold enough to proclaim it.

Endnotes

1 "First Secretary's Record of The Wang Lutheran Congregation in Renville County: 1874-1885," translated by Mr. and Mrs. Tom I. Loe. Unpublished.

2 Pew Research Center: http://www.pewresearch.org/fact-tank/2015/05/12/millennials-increasingly-are-driving-growth-of-nones/ (accessed on July 7, 2015

3 A useful introduction to changes in the conditions for belief is in James K. A. Smith's *How (Not) to Be Secular: Reading Charles Taylor* (Grand Rapids: Wm. B. Eerdmans Publishing Co., 2014). This summary and reflections on Taylor's assertion of the changes in conditions for belief in God is formative in this reflection.

4 *Naadevalget*, a compound Norwegian word combines *God's grace* and *election*. This term refers to the predestination or "pro-Missouri" controversy of the 1870s and 1880s in North American Lutheranism. See E. Clifford Nelson and Eugene L. Fevold, *The Lutheran Church Among Norwegian-Americans* (Minneapolis: Augsburg Publishing House, 1960), 241ff.

5 This minutes is found in Wang Lutheran Church, Renville County, Minnesota.

6 I am indebted to Martha Grace Reese's excellent *Unbinding* series for its encouragement to take seriously the baptismal promise to "proclaim Christ in word and deed." Reese's books include significant portions of the fruits of the Lilly Endowment's Mainline Evangelism Project. This project concluded that mainline churches can and do grow by developing three key practices: 1) Laity have a deep, relational sense of faith in God. 2) Laity can articulate their faith comfortably. 3) Pastors and lay leaders hold a laser-like focus on people beyond church. For the full report on the Mainline Evangelism Project, see http://www.gracenet.info/documents/120501%204th%20 Endowment%20Report%20public%20FINAL.pdf and gracenet.info. (accessed on July 7, 2015).

7 Martin Luther, "The Large Catechism," in *The Book of Concord: The Confessions of the Evangelical Lutheran Church,* eds. Robert Kolb and Timothy Wengert (Minneapolis: Fortress Press, 2000), 381.

8 Series, books, and programs that have been used widely and adapted for specific contexts in mainline denominations for sharing the foundations of faith and for encouraging significant trust in God are noted below, including brief descriptions of their content provided by the author or publisher:

Unbinding the Gospel: Real Life Evangelism and the *Unbinding Series* (www.gracenet.info) arise out of the only major study of evangelism in mainline churches, funded by the Lilly Endowment. It is a book for pastors who want to know the truth about the state of evangelism. It is a book for Christians who want a hopeful, powerful, prayerful, joy-filled way to learn to share their faith. It's also a book for people who cringe when they hear the E-word! Based on thorough research, sparkling with life and practicality, and steeped in spirituality, this workbook for congregational use has been enthusiastically endorsed by seven heads of denominations, professors of evangelism, leading experts, and pastors.

ALPHA series (alphausa.org/) *Alpha* is a series of interactive sessions that freely explore the basics of the Christian faith in a friendly and honest environment. No pressure. No follow up. No charge. *Alpha* runs in churches, homes, coffee shops, and bars all around the globe. Typically *Alpha* has ten sessions, which include food, a short talk, and a time of small group discussion where those attending can share their thoughts.

It covers topics such as, "Who is Jesus?" "Why and how do I pray?" and "How can I resist evil?"

Faith Practices Series (http://www.practicingourfaith.org) The *Faith Practices Series* includes books for people of all ages to engage in historic Christian practices. Christian practices are not activities we do to make something spiritual happen in our lives. Nor are they duties we undertake to be obedient to God. Rather, they are patterns of communal action that create openings in our lives where the grace, mercy, and presence of God may be known to us.

Augsburg Fortress's *Animate* series, David Lose's *Making Sense* series, Philip Yancey's *What's So Amazing About Grace*, the *NOOMA* films, and Kelly Fryer's *Reclaiming the "L" Word: Renewing the Church from Its Lutheran Core* are further resources for pastors and church leaders who need easily adaptable and compelling resources for growing faith and discipleship in their lives and in their congregations.

CHAPTER TWELVE

Whose Supper Is It?

Keith Killinger

For Martin Luther and his successors, the "Lord's Supper" was not just a name but a confession of faith. In all their discussions of it, they were conscious that they were talking about the *Coena Dei,* the "Supper of the Lord." Its institution was his, its definition was his, and its rules, shape and use were his and his alone.

The church makes bold to claim that this meal of bread and wine truly communicates Christ's Body and Blood to the recipient *and* that the believing recipient receives from God not just a promise but the actual gift of forgiveness for his or her sins. Such claims strain the limits of believability, as Luther himself was aware, asking in his Small Catechism, "How can bodily eating and drinking do such a great thing?"

On what grounds can the church make these bold claims? According to Luther and his successors, it is not on the strength of its own authority or the weight of precedent, nor under the aegis of popes or councils, but solely on the say-so of the Lord Jesus himself—specifically in the words by which he instituted the Supper. Paul Althaus called the Words of Institution, the Verba, Luther's "final fortress" in his battles over the sacrament.[1] These words of Christ trumped all other claims, even those boasting centuries of acceptance in the church. According to Luther,

> If we desire to observe mass properly and to understand it, then we must surrender everything that the eyes behold and that the senses suggest—be it vestments, bells, songs, ornaments, prayers, processions, elevation, prostrations, or whatever happens in the mass—until we first grasp and thoroughly ponder the words of Christ, by which he performed and instituted the mass and commanded us to perform it.

For therein lies the whole mass, its nature, work, profit and benefit.[2]

The definition of what the sacrament is lies solely in the words of Christ; if other definitions contradict or add new ideas to those words, they are to be abhorred. In his *Babylonian Captivity of the Church* Luther warns, "Whoever sets aside these words and meditates or teaches concerning the mass will teach monstrous and wicked doctrines, as they have done who have made of the sacrament an *opus operatum* and a sacrifice."[3]

Jesus' Words of Institution were not a bulwark only against perversions and distortions of the sacrament that Luther and his successors saw the Church of Rome having made, but also against the "left wing" of the Reformation, particularly the Sacramentarians who denied that Christ's Body and Blood could actually be present in the physical elements of the Supper. In his treatise, *Against the Fanatics,* Luther wrote that his opponents had all found a stumbling-block in three of the central words of the Verba: *hoc est corpus (meum)*—"this is (my) body."[4] Andreas Rudolph Bodenstein von Karlstadt (1486 –1541) stumbled on the *hoc*, offering a tortured explanation that with "this" Jesus had actually indicated, not the bread, but his own body at the table with his disciples. While "take and eat" referred to the bread, "This is my body, which is given for you" began a *separate* discourse on his approaching passion.

Huldrych Zwingli (1484-1531) and Johannes Oecolampadius (1482-1531) argued in more sophisticated fashion on the basis of metaphor. Fastening on the *est,* Zwingli insisted that Jesus had intended this in a metaphorical sense, as "symbolizes." For Oecolampadius, the metaphor lay in the word *corpus:* "my body—so to speak." Luther acknowledged that Scripture does sometimes use "is" poetically or metaphorically; but one must show—beyond a doubt—that Jesus intended his words *on this occasion* to be so understood, because their clarity and specificity—reported by three evangelists and St. Paul—require clear and unequivocal proof from Scripture itself that *these words* should not be taken as they stand. Later, Martin Chemnitz (1522-1586) pointed to the solemnity of the words of Christ and how they were his "last will and testament."[5] No one setting down a last will and testament, he wrote, "would speak in such imprecise, obscure, and ambiguous language as to cause the minds of the heirs, after the death of the testator, to be led astray by various arguments over the meaning of the words of the will." [6] Dismissing the radical reformers' arguments, Luther advised, "Let them go . . . and let us adhere to the words as they read: that the body of Christ is present in the bread and that his blood is truly present in the wine."[7]

Whether his opponents were the "fanatics," with their philosophically-based denials that a truly *human* nature of Christ could be in more than one place at one time, or that the finite and physical can communicate the divine, or whether they were the supposed authorities and precedents of the Church of Rome, Luther saw all of them as seeking to take the sacrament under their control—first of all, to define its nature and purpose, and then to expand (or limit) its power and effect—so that they might use it in whatever manner *they* saw fit.

The Supper, however, does not belong to the church, to its theologians, to the weight of tradition, or to the logic of philosophers like Aristotle. It remains the *Lord's* Supper, and if it is used or presented as anything other than that for which the Lord instituted it, and to which he attached his promises, then it is an empty exercise, and the claims made about it are equally empty. Such efforts are not merely futile, they are acts of rebellion against Jesus' own express command.

But if *hoc est* laid the foundation for understanding the *nature* and the *effect* of the Lord's Supper, equally significant were the words *hoc facite*—"do this." It is these words that establish the Supper as the *Lord's* Supper. On the night in which he was betrayed, Jesus not only defined the Supper, but also gave clear instructions for how it was to be used: he said, "Take, give thanks, distribute, and consume it" and thus—and only thus—receive its benefits.

Hoc facite demolished the Roman Church's claim that the Mass was a sacrifice. In his *Babylonian Captivity of the Church,* Luther lays the clear words of the Verba against Rome's claims that the Mass is a good work or a sacrifice. He encouraged believers to distinguish carefully the *core* of the Mass, the sacrament that Jesus instituted, from the many additions, embellishments, and accretions added by others. "For," he writes, "as you will see, we are going to overthrow all the godless opinions of men which have been imported into this most precious sacrament.[8]

The Words of Institution show clearly that in the night when he was betrayed, Jesus did not "offer" up a sacrifice to God, nor do a good work for others, but rather gave his disciples a "testament" and a "sign."[9] Another Lutheran reformer, Johann Brenz (1499-1570), asserts the same thought in lively language in his catechism of 1556:

But it should be stated very specifically in this description of the supper that in the Supper Christ offers and gives his Body and Blood to US—to us, I say! For the Lord's Supper was not instituted so that in it the priest should offer up Christ's body and blood to God the Father for the sins of the living and the dead. But far more properly: that the Body and Blood of Christ should be given to Us—to us, I say—to be eaten.[10]

Jesus' *hoc facite* also demolished the practice of the "private mass." Luther describes a "nightmare" he said he experienced in which the devil accused him of having "effected conversion [i.e., transubstantiation] *contrary to the ordinance and intention* of Christ":[11]

Christ's intention is that we should celebrate the sacraments or the mass in such a way that it might be distributed among his Christians and administered to others. . . . Now you, contrary to the intention of Christ, have received the sacrament alone in every instance and administered to no one for fifteen years.[12]

Instead of offering the sacrament to the faithful as Jesus' own "testament" to nourish faith and hope, the church and its priests had rather sought to offer it to *God* as a meritorious work and had encouraged people to place their trust in this act. The devil's trump card in this instance was to deny that the bread in such a "sacrament" is really the Body of Christ.[13]

Similarly, the Lord's *hoc facite* prohibited withholding the cup from the laity. If the notion of sacrifice sought to add something to what Jesus had commanded, withholding the cup was a bald attempt to *take away* from what he had explicitly commanded. In fact, it was specifically in regard to the cup that he had added, "*all of you.*" For the church to reinterpret those words to mean "only some of you" was to claim an authority equal to Christ's own. In his *Treatise on the New Testament* of 1520, Luther wrote, "The pope does not have a hair's breadth of power to change what Christ has made; and whatever of these things he changes, that he does as a tyrant and Antichrist."[14]

Another teaching that went beyond the express command or promise of the Lord was the claim that the mass permanently transformed bread and wine into Christ's Body and Blood. This opened the door to additional "uses" of the Blessed Host such as expositions, devotions, processions, and benedictions. Luther did not deny that the elements are *transformed* from "mere" bread and wine into Christ's Body and Blood, as he instructs Philipp Melanchthon (1497-1560) to tell Martin Bucer (1491-1551) in 1534. "Our understanding is this: . . . that everything that the bread does or experiences also pertains to the body of Christ. Therefore, one may truly say that the body of Christ is carried, distributed, received, or eaten. That is what the words say: 'This is my body.'"[15] Because of his conviction that Christ's Body and Blood are present in the liturgical celebration, Luther retained practices such as adoration of the sacrament[16] and its elevation.[17] But these reflected the nature of the elements *within the use* mandated by Christ: taking, giving thanks, sharing, and consuming. The Lord gave neither instruction nor promise regarding the elements apart from or after the celebration of the sacrament. If it was taken to the sick within a reasonably short time after the conclusion of the worship service, it was, in effect, a continuation of that service, that mandated "use." But the church had no grounds for locking it in a cabinet or keeping it on an altar to be given out should a need arise; nor was it to be displayed, worshipped, or carried in procession as if it were indeed Christ's Body. Responding to the Council of Trent's decisions, Chemnitz rejected the claim that an eventual eating of such a host, even weeks or months after its "transformation," properly completed the action mandated by Christ; guaranteeing that his body had indeed been present all along.[18]

For the reformers, the only way to be able to trust the church's mind-boggling claims regarding the sacrament was to listen to what the Lord had commanded and promised on that night in which he was betrayed, and then obey that command *and* make no claims or promises beyond those which he had expressly stated.

So Whose Supper Is It?

Jesus did not institute the Supper and then hand it to the church for it to define, alter, or use as it saw fit or found expedient. For Lutherans it is held in trust and used for those purposes which Christ established for it. The mainstream of Lutheran Reformation thought running from Luther through Chemnitz and others and encapsulated in the Formula of Concord is in agreement on this.

Yet if saying this merely sums up certain arguments from several centuries ago, then this is really little more than dead "data," and one may legitimately ask, "So what?" What relevance does it have for now?

In truth, the church has always been susceptible to the siren-call to take the things of God and claim them as its own, to use for its own purposes. The temptation to do so with this sacrament: to take hold of it, modify or use as it wishes, is always with us.

Some such attempts are egregious. This writer recalls from his college years a suggestion that one might see in bread and wine relatively common and basic elements of daily life in Jesus' time, so that his choice of them for the sacrament of his Body and Blood was profoundly "incarnational," and "coming to people where they were." Thus it was suggested that to be relevant to modern life, the church might consider using doughnuts and coffee—or pretzels and beer—for at least an occasional celebration of the sacrament to emphasize a similar presence of Christ in very "ordinary" life.

Most attempts to take control of the sacrament are less obvious, but no less an effort by humans to alter—or even "improve"—it, especially under the rationale of "just as good as." Substituting grape juice for the sacramental wine, which was popular in certain corners of American Lutheranism, is one example. Without access to stable grape juice, Jesus had to inaugurate his meal using an alcoholic drink. But today's juice—possibly even from the same kind of grapes as wine—is not only "just as good" as wine, but perhaps even superior to it, as using it does not give an impression of sanctifying alcohol.[19]

Another "improvement" over what Jesus commanded is making intinction the sole form of distribution of the sacrament, on the grounds that intinction is "just as good as"—and more practical or efficient—as separate eating and drinking.[20] But to what extent may we modify the Lord's command because we consider an alternate "just as good"? To a seminary class the sainted Arthur Carl Piepkorn (1907-1973) stated that a minimal definition of "drink" in the sacrament requires "a quantity of wine sufficient to run down the back of the tongue and into the throat."[21]

Especially seductive for clergy are temptations offered in the "consecration" of the sacrament. A study of the sixteenth-century regional Lutheran "church orders" reveals something remarkable: virtually no gesture of any sort is commanded for the celebrant at the recital of the Verba apart from facing the congregation, holding paten and cup "about breast high," and speaking the words in a loud, clear voice. There is no dramatic "speaking into the bread," or signing with the cross. This is how important the reformers held the Verba to be: at supper that first night,

Jesus' words had *forever* instituted the Supper, and the reformers repeatedly cite John Chrysostom (349-407) that Jesus' words are comparable to "the command, 'Be fruitful and multiply,' which, once spoken, has efficacy in the article of creation for all time."[22]

Reciting the Verba "did" nothing to the elements of bread and wine; rather, it confessed what *Jesus* did—forever—to bread and wine that are taken with thanks, shared, and consumed in a community of faith. To add gestures implying that the celebrant is somehow "blessing" or "consecrating" the elements is to suggest that the authority and creating power of Jesus' words—by themselves—are insufficient without human "help." Signing the cross over the elements would not enter Lutheran church orders until well into the 1600s when the sacramental elements were now ceremonially "set aside" to *become* Christ's Body and Blood in the moment of eating and drinking—per Melanchthon's "receptionist" view of the sacrament that supplanted Luther's sense of Christ's real presence in the whole liturgy.

Another temptation is to break the bread in concert with the words in the Verba. This suggests that Jesus' own words defining the sacrament, which were so important to the reformers, need improvement or augmentation by the celebrant dramatically reenacting just that one part of what Jesus did. The reformers, by contrast, wanted nothing to distract hearers from the *words* of Christ that that are the warrant and assurance of what this sacrament is said to be.

Other examples abound, but these at least remind us how the sacrament can easily become so familiar to us that we start to feel we can modify, alter, or even "improve" this mystery entrusted to our fallible stewardship. As they did for the reformers, the Words of Institution remind us just *whose* Supper this really is.

Endnotes

1 Paul Althaus, *Theology of Martin Luther,* trans. Robert C. Schultz (Philadelphia: Fortress Press, 1966), 384.

2 Martin Luther, *Treatise on the New Testament, That Is, the Holy Mass,* LW 35:82.

3 Martin Luther, *Babylonian Captivity of the Church,* LW 36:37.

4 Martin Luther, *Against the Fanatics,* LW 36:346.

5 Martin Chemnitz, *Lord's Supper: De Coena Domini,* Translated by J. A. O. Preus, Index by Delph Holleque Preus (St. Louis: Concordia Publishing House, 1979), 81ff.

6 Ibid., 82.

7 Martin Luther, *Against the Fanatics*, LW 36:346.

8 Ibid.

9 Ibid., 37, 51f.

10 Johann Brenz, *Heylsame vnnd nützliche erklerung des Ehrwirdigen Herren Joannis Brencij / vber den Catechismum*. Durch Hartman Beyer / allen Christlichen Hauszuettern zu gefallen verdeutscht. Nürnberg / M. D. LVI, [page:] Dd iiij.

11 Martin Luther, *Private Mass and the Consecration of Priests*. LW 38:151. (Emphasis added)

12 Ibid.

13 Ibid., 153. Cf. 193f.

14 Martin Luther, *Treatise on the New Testament, That Is, the Holy Mass*. LW 35:106.

15 *D. Mart. Luthers Bedenken Über die von den Zwinglianern gesuchte Vereinigung in der Lehre vom heiligen Abendmahl, zu der handlung in Cassel dem Melanchthon mitgegeben. Den 17. December 1534.* (St. Louis Edition, XVII: 2053n.)

16 Martin Luther, Martin Luther, *Adoration of the Sacrament*, LW 36:293f.

17 Martin Luther, *German Mass*. LW 58:82. Cf. WATr 5:308; #5665.

18 Martin Chemnitz, *Examination of the Council of Trent*. In four parts. Translated by Fred Kramer. St. Louis: Concordia Publishing House, 1978. II.IV.VII.1. (Kramer, 293).

19 In a congregation he served, this writer discovered that berry-flavored drink (like Snapple®) was in the cups reserved for grape juice. The "thought-trail" can be imagined: grape juice is "just as good as" wine; grape-flavored drink is "just as good as" grape juice; any purplish, fruit-flavored drink is "just as good" as grape-flavored drink.

20 Just as offering grape juice to those who abuse alcohol or who take medicine that interacts with alcohol is arguably a separate pastoral issue, so also is that of the *individual* who chooses to intinct, perhaps to keep from spreading his or her cold germs to others. See Luther's pastoral advice regarding lay-persons who, from fear, resist receiving the cup, *Babylonian Captivity of the Church*, LW 36:27; *Receiving Both Kinds in the Sacrament*, LW 36:248ff.

21 An approximation of his words.

22 Martin Chemnitz, *Examination of the Council of Trent*. In four parts. Trans. Fred Kramer. St. Louis: Concordia Publishing House, 1978. II.IV.I.7. (Kramer, 227). See Formula of Concord, Solid Declaration VII: 76.

CHAPTER THIRTEEN

The "Torch of Thuringia"

Introducing a Seventeenth Century Theological Light[1]

Andrew F. Weisner

John Gerhard (1582-1637) was, according to Kurt Hendel's teacher Arthur Carl Piepkorn, "the 'archtheologian' of the Lutheran church."[2] He was 'a most fair disputant of all the Protestants, shedding the greatest light upon the arguments on which he touched,' . . . Robert Bellarmine [Roman Catholic theologian and bishop, 1542—1621] had no adversary more to be dreaded than Gerhard," wrote Heinrich Schmid, quoting the Roman Catholic theologian Louis Du Pin (1657-1719). Schmid adds, "Bossuet [Roman Catholic bishop, 1627-1704] is said to be the author of the often-quoted remark that Gerhard is the third (Luther, Chemnitz, Gerhard) of the series of theologians in which there is no fourth."[3] Gerhard holds a prominent place in, if not actually culminating, a dialectical pattern of Lutheran–Roman Catholic polemics during the first hundred years after the Reformation, which can be described as follows:

1.a. Martin Luther begins the Reformation, aided by Philipp Melanchthon

1.b. The Council of Trent responds to Luther (and other reformers)

2.a. Martin Chemnitz responds to the Council of Trent[4]

2.b. Roman Catholic Jesuit theologian and bishop Robert Bellarmine responds to Chemnitz

3. John Gerhard responds to Bellarmine

John Gerhard was born on October 17, 1582, in Quedlinburg, northern Saxony.[5] His father was Bartholomew Gerhard, an aristocrat and "prefect of the senatorial treasury,"[6] whose death in 1598 Gerhard mourned bitterly. His mother, Margaret Bernd, was the daughter of John Bernd, a municipal assessor of Halberstadt, of whom Gerhard was rather fond, personally paying his funeral expenses upon his death in 1624. His paternal grandfather was Andreas Gerhard, a councilor of the Abbacy of Quedlinburg, known for his erudition and piety. Named after this grandfather was John's older brother of two years, Andreas, who later became a renowned lawyer; and John Gerhard's son, John Andreas Gerhard, saw to the publication of some of this uncle's legal treatises in 1659. In addition, Andreas and John had five sisters.[7]

Gerhard's parents gave serious attention to his education, and as a youth he attended the school in Quedlinburg, where he was taught by the rector, Henry Faber. Years later, in the dedicatory epistle of *Loci Theologici*, Gerhard cites the names of sixteen well-known teachers who credited Faber as being a significant influence on their education. Gerhard remained in school there until 1598, studying humanities (including, of course, languages), and continued his studies at the Halberstadt Lyceum under the direction of the rector, Paulus Dolsch. During this time, when not yet eighteen years old, he composed a Latin poem, *Historica Evangelica*, and a Greek one, a *Passionis Historia* of Christ. This was the beginning of such scholarship, claims Cotta, that would later complete a "harmony of the Gospels," begun much earlier by Martin Chemnitz (1522-86) and Polycarp Leyser (1552-1610), under the final title, *Harmonia evangelistarum Chemnitio-Lyseriana a Johanne Gerhardo continuata et justo commentario illustrata* (in 1626-27).[8]

At about the same time he began his studies in Halberstadt, Gerhard was afflicted by plague. Cotta relates that it was a "fortuitous" double-dose of an antidote that saved his life.[9] Yet, even earlier, at age fifteen, Gerhard was "tormented . . . by a very grave illness," that seemed not only "to exhaust his strength inwardly, but also afflicted his mind that, full of worry [he was] devoid of almost every sense of consolation."[10] During this time he was influenced considerably by the Lutheran theologian and mystic Johann Arndt (1555-1621), his parish pastor in Quedlinburg at that time.[11] Emerging out of this "most serious illness," Gerhard, who had been earlier inclined toward a career in medicine, decided "he should enter, rather, studies of holier doctrine," and therefore "pronounced a vow" to do so.[12]

In 1599, he entered the University of Wittenberg to study philosophy. He also studied history under Wolfgang Franz, logic and ethics from Antonius Euonymus, rhetoric from Martin Helwig, mathematics from Erasmus Schmid, natural philosophy from Johannes Mehlfurer, and anthropology from Jacob Cocus. On his own he studied Aristotle and commentators on Aristotle, which helped prepare him for later disputations. The following year, remembering his earlier vow, he turned his attention to theology, hearing lectures by the distinguished theologian Leonard Hütter and lectures on the Old Testament book of Daniel by Salomon Gesner.[13]

Following the advice of a relative, Andreas Rauchbar, pro-chancellor to the elector of Saxony, Gerhard commenced his original intent in 1601, the study of medicine, and in the brief space of two years he wrote medical propositions for public debate, a whole volume concerning procedures for curing various diseases, and even took up the practice of medicine. Yet, after the death of Rauchbar, he could not forget his earlier vow, and in 1603 he returned to his study of theology, remembering earlier advice from Arndt, who had recommended above all else the study of languages (i.e., sacred philology) and scripture. For such study of "holier doctrine" he developed a great love, and began to include such works in his own library.[14] He then proceeded to the University of Jena, where he gained the attention of Professor Salomon Glass. With Glass' encouragement he studied theology, the church fathers, and the scholastics, and heard lectures by Jena's outstanding theologians George Mylius, Ambrose Reuden, and Peter Fisher. Yet his studies would not continue, for in November, he again became very ill, despairing whether he would recuperate, to the point that he even wrote a last will and testament.[15]

But, beyond hope and expectation he recovered, and, in 1604 with one of his students, Michael Rauchbar, he accepted an invitation to study at Marburg with Johann Winckelmann (c. 1551-1626); with Hebrew Professor Johann Scholli; and the renowned theologian, Balthasar Mentzer (1565-1627), under whom he studied interpretation of scripture. In 1605 he and Mentzer journeyed together, visiting the cities of Giessen, Frankfurt, Darmstadt, Heidelberg, Stuttgart, and Tübingen (among others), meeting some of those cities' most erudite scholars.[16] Probably during this time Gerhard collected material that would later occupy his large and famous library.[17]

When Gerhard and Mentzer returned from their journey to Marburg there was some disturbance in the city, due to a recent proposal of

Maurice, Landgrave of Hesse-Kassel (1572-1632), to introduce Reformed theology into the local churches and university. Therefore Gerhard and his student Rauchbar departed for a brief stay at Hemsendorf, an estate of Rauchbar, at which time Gerhard began to consider seriously an academic career. After brief excursions to Magdeburg, Braunschweig, and elsewhere, Gerhard returned to Jena to continue his studies. During the year 1606 he was elected to the adjunct faculty of Jena and then wrote and publicly defended a dissertation in philosophy, *De Vero* ("On Truth"). In 1607, he wrote and defended at Jena another dissertation, *De Necessitate et Contingentia* ("On Necessity and Contingency").[18]

Also in 1606, at the recommendation of Wolfgang Herder, professor of logic and ethics at the University of Jena, Gerhard was offered the ecclesiastical office of superintendent of Heldburg by the local prince, Johann Casimir, who lived in Coburg, the patron and founder in 1603 of what would become the famous *Gymnasium Casimirianum* (which thrives today). Gerhard was not inclined to accept the position, in part because his mother wanted him to return to Quedlinburg. To overcome this potential obstacle, Prince Casimir himself wrote letters to Gerhard's mother to try to gain her approval of her son's appointment. Finally Gerhard accepted, but not before returning again to Jena to defend yet another dissertation, *Praecipuas de Sacra Coena Controversias* ("Particular Debates About the Holy Supper"), a quite contentious topic at that time; he was granted the degree doctor of theology by the Jena faculty.[19] He then proceeded to his new duties in Heldburg, but added to them was the task of organizing regular theological disputations at the gymnasium in nearby Coburg. This Gerhard continued for the next nine years, while also accompanying Prince Casimir on various journeys as an ecclesiastical counselor, frequently preaching and participating in colloquia, all of it nearly wearing out his health. In 1613 the prince commissioned Gerhard to conduct a visitation to all the parishes in Thuringia and Franconia, the result of which endeared Gerhard even more to Casimir. Gerhard paid close attention to the doctrine and discipline of the churches, which he determined "had slackened too much and was dislocated, . . . through listlessness."[20]

While superintendent at Heldburg Gerhard received, but did not accept, many offers to move. In 1608 he was called to be a counselor to the Archbishop of Magdeburg and to a pastorate in Hamburg; in 1609, to be bishop of Weimar and to a university position at Prague. In 1610 he could have been a theology professor at Giessen, Superintendent General of

Hannover, or Bishop of Eisleben. In 1611 he was offered the position of Superintendent General of Linz in upper Austria; Dean of Mansfeld; and Bishop of Rites at Quedlinburg. In 1612[21] he was asked to become chief ecclesiastical official of Moravia; and in 1613 and 1614 he was offered professorships at the universities of Altdor-Wittenberg and Helmstadt, respectively. The chief reasons Gerhard declined these invitations were his close association to Prince Casimir—who, likely, simply would not let him leave—and his hope of returning someday to Jena, "most dear to him."[22]

The year 1615, however, did include a move for Gerhard, from Superintendent of Heldburg to Superintendent General of Coburg, which was still in Prince Casimir's territory. The move, in fact, was instigated by the prince in order to get Gerhard closer to him (since Casimir resided in Coburg). Yet the prince was not able to keep Gerhard close at hand for long. Even in 1611, the faculty of the university at Jena had expressed a desire to have Gerhard return as a professor of theology, but Casimir would not allow Gerhard leave. In 1615, however, after the death of a senior theology professor at Jena, Ambrose Reuden, the elector of Saxony, Johann Georg I, personally intervened on behalf of the university and obtained from Casimir Gerhard's dismissal to the university. But Casimir made sure, also, to have his way, negotiating that Gerhard would continue to serve as his ecclesiastical counselor; participate in visitations, synods, and other deliberations; and assist in yearly exams at the *Gymnasium Casimirianum*. For these services Casimir promised an annual stipend plus expenses.[23]

Once at Jena, Gerhard applied himself to his theological lectures with great fervor and to the task of shaping students in holy doctrine. He lectured on "theological commonplaces," i.e., *Loci Theologici*, his book on which he had been working since 1609; books of sacred scripture (notably Hebrews and Revelation); and organized theological disputations, arguing especially against Roman Catholic and Calvinist doctrines. Often he served as dean of the theological faculty and prepared for their doctorates such outstanding theologians as Salomon Glass, Frederick and Wilhelm Lyser, Andreas Kesler, and Christian Weber.[24] He also served the university well by enhancing its endowments, especially securing from princes Johann Philipp and Wilhelm, and abbess Dorothea Sophia of Quedlinburg the bequest of their estates. Notable, too, are the many occasions during which he served as an advisor to nobles regarding political issues or as an official representative at state functions (e.g., the funeral of Gustavus Adolphus, king of Sweden, in 1633). His Jena years also included his participation in notable convocations to settle theological disputes, namely, in 1621 at Jena, dealing with Georg Calixtus (1586-1656) and Cornelius Martin, professors at Helmstadt, suspected of heterodoxy; in 1624 at Leipzig, regarding the "self-emptying" of Christ, a controversy ignited by theologians from Tübingen and Giessen; and the "Rathmann controversy" concerning salvation, addressed in 1629, and at the same conference issues stirred up by the Jesuits. Also at this conference, in response to the Jesuits, the Elector commissioned an apologia, the final form of which was published as *Defensionis Pupillae Evangelicae* ("Defense of the Evangelical Pupil") in 1630 under the name of Matthias Hoe von Hohenegg, but Gerhard was the primary organizer of the treatise, to which Polycarp Lyser, Henry Hoepfner, Wilhelm Lyser, and Johann Hulsemann also contributed.[25]

While teaching at the University of Jena, just as when he was superintendent at Heldburg, he received many offers to move: in 1616 to become Superintendent of Schaumburg; in 1617 Bishop of Pamiers in Prussia; in 1621 the University of Strassburg; in 1622 Rostock; in 1624 Uppsala; in 1626 Marburg (at this point, Lutheran again); in 1627 Wittenberg; and on various occasions people of Lübeck, Halberstadt, and even King Frederick of Denmark tried to acquire his talents for their academies.[26]

Indeed, throughout northern Europe during the early seventeenth century, Gerhard's influence—politically, intellectually, and certainly theologically—was powerful and pervasive. His strength of character, especially during the Thirty Years' War, is attested to by Johann Michael Dilherr, once professor at the University of Jena and later theologian in Bavaria: "If any annihilation threatened, the avenger was Gerhard. If any blow was feared, the shield was Gerhard. If any storm was impending, the refuge was Gerhard. If there was any on-rushing shower, the sun was Gerhard."[27]

In May of 1637, Gerhard began to feel a fever coming upon him; by August his condition had become worse. On August 17, writes biographer J. F. Cotta, "he was so sick that he breathed out his pious soul, thoroughly cleansed by the blood of Christ. . . . How full of faith did he commend to divine providence his loves; with what great contrition of heart did he declare his confession of sins; with what great tenderness did he bid farewell to his colleagues. . . ."[28] At Gerhard's funeral, Dilherr declared:

"There is almost no academy in the European world of Protestants, there is no church of any more renowned city, but that it has desired to be illumined by this 'Torch of Thuringia,' and called to it this extraordinary name of Europe," John Gerhard.[29]

By his life and teaching in Thuringia, John Gerhard served as a torch to cast light for the sake of truth. By sharing his appreciation of the church's ministry, history, and theology, may we cast light upon the issues and challenges of our day.

Endnotes

1 An earlier version of this paper was published in *Lutheran Forum*, 43, No. 4 (Winter 2009): 32-35.

2 Arthur Carl Piepkorn, "John Gerhard," in *The Encyclopedia of the Lutheran Church*, vol. II, ed. J. Bodensieck (Minneapolis: Augsburg Publishing House, 1965), 905.

3 Heinrich Schmid, *Doctrinal Theology of the Evangelical Lutheran Church*, translated by Chas. A. Hay and H. E. Jacobs (Minneapolis: Augsburg Publishing House, 1899, reprint, 1961), 668.

4 M. Chemnitz, *Examination of the Council of Trent*, trans. Fred Kramer (St. Louis: Concordia Publishing House, 1971-86), 4 volumes.

5 This presentation is based on the following sources: the brief article on Gerhard by A. C. Piepkorn in *The Encyclopedia of the Lutheran Church*, op. cit.; a section entitled "*J. Gerhards Leben*" in Helmut Claus' *Bibliotheca Gerhardina: Eigenart und Schicksal einer thuringischen Gelehrtenbibliothek des 17. Jahrhunderts* (Landesbibliothek Gotha: 1968), 10-11; Robert P. Scharlemann's *Thomas Aquinas and John Gerhard* (New Haven, Connecticut: Yale University Press, 1964), 37-43; and Johann Friderick Cotta's "*De Vita et Fatis et Scriptis Joannis Gerhardi*," that appears as a preface in an 1868 edition of Gerhard's *Loci Theologici*, Ed. Preuss, ed. (Berlin: Gust. Schlawitz, 1868), vol. I, iii-xxiv.

6 Cotta, iii.

7 Ibid., iii f.

8 Ibid., iv.

9 Scharlemann, 38; Cotta, iv.

10 Cotta, iv; Piepkorn, 905.

11 Scharlemann, 38; Claus, 12. Scharlemann (and Piepkorn, 905) spells the name of this pastor "Arnd," while Claus and certain other scholars, such as Cross-Livingstone, spell it "Arndt." Cp. F. L. Cross and E. Livingstone, eds., *The Oxford Dictionary of the Christian Church*, 2nd ed. (Oxford: Oxford University Press, 1974), 92.

12 Cotta, iv.

13 Scharlemann, 39; Cotta, iv.

14 Scharlemann, 39.

15 Cotta, v-vi; Scharlemann, 39.

16 Cotta, vi.

17 Scharlemann, 40.

18 Cotta, vii.

19 Ibid.

20 Ibid., viii.

21 Cotta's biography, viii, here states 1606, but this date is likely a misprint, since 1606 does not fit in the chronological sequence of the text.

22 Cotta, viii.

23 Ibid., ix.

24 Ibid.

25 Ibid., x-xi.

26 Ibid., xii.

27 Ibid., x.

28 Ibid., xiv-xv.

29 Ibid., viii.

CHAPTER FOURTEEN

"Am I a Deserter?"

A Lutheran Pastor's "Catch-22" from the Revolutionary War

Jonathan M. Wilson

Introduction

Catch-22 by Joseph Heller was first published in 1961.[1] Long considered a classic, the novel satirized the American military's ineptitude, ethical slothfulness, and bureaucratic inertia in the midst of the Second World War. In the novel, the "catch-22" was the code-number for the military rule governing applications for discharge due to mental unfitness: If a person applied for discharge, this was proof of mental fitness and the application was denied. The term "catch-22" now refers generally to any unsolvable bureaucratic, legal, or systemic paradox.

Two centuries before Heller coined the phrase, the military chaplain Friedrich V. Melsheimer (1749-1814) experienced a catch-22 of his own. He was assigned to a German auxiliary regiment aiding the royalists in the American Revolutionary War. In his experience of army life he discovered an unresolvable conundrum: The commands of Jesus were incompatible with the duty of a soldier; for Melsheimer, a ministry of the church that commended a soldier to duty was a *non sequitur*.[2] Melsheimer continued in his call until the defeat, surrender, and scattering of his regiment in captivity made his ministry moot. He opted to resign his call, but his superiors, all of them likewise prisoners of war, refused to accept his resignation.[3] For years he was *persona non grata* to all sides of the American Revolution. When he applied for admission to the Pennsylvania Ministerium, the synod required that he prove he had been formally released from his chaplaincy,[4] but with his regiment judging him a deserter no such commendation would ever be forthcoming. This catch-22 kept his status in suspense until after the war's end.[5]

Burgoyne's Campaign

Melsheimer was born in Negenborn and educated at Helmstedt. His ministry path was typical of many young clergy in Germany in the eighteenth century: Holding a degree but with years to wait for a pulpit, he accepted a call to a military chaplaincy. At the time the army of his native Braunschweig-Wolfenbüttel was mustering several of its units to join British royalists in their struggle against the patriots in North America. As a civilian contractor, Melsheimer received his ordination from the Wolfenbüttel consistory and was appointed to the Dragoons regiment by its commanding officer, Lt. Col. Friedrich Baum (1727-1777).[6]

Melsheimer and the Braunschweig Corps arrived in Quebec in June 1776. The next summer the Braunschweig units under the overall command of General Friedrich zu Riedesel were placed under British General John Burgoyne's command for a campaign with Albany, New York, as its objective. From Melsheimer's letters written nearly two years later we learn that at some point during the campaign of 1777 Melsheimer came to be plagued in his conscience by the irreconcilable demands of Jesus Christ on the one hand and of military life on the other.[7]

His personal struggle likely did not occur in the early stages of the campaign, which saw rapid movement down Lake Champlain by boat and a sweep of victories to capture Ticonderoga and the chain of forts along Lake Champlain's length. These engagements had only limited impact on non-combatants. However during the grueling march from Fort Edward through the dense woods, operations were conducted along the flanks by Loyalists and Native Nations auxiliaries that renewed the terror of frontier war among New York's rural civilians. Patriots found their *cause celebre* in the murder of Jane McRae, engaged to a loyalist officer, who was scalped by a warrior for the trophy of her long red hair.[8]

Shortly afterward Burgoyne detached the Dragoons to raid the countryside for draught animals, mounts, and livestock. Melsheimer rode with the expedition, which set out on August 11.[9] The raiding started out successfully, meaning that civilians were being plundered.[10] It is doubtful, however, that even with a plagued conscience Melsheimer considered desertion as he continued on the move with the regiment. The Dragoons and their allies were confronted on August 14 by superior numbers and on August 15 dug in to a defensive position while Baum sent for reinforcements.[11]

In the conventions of the eighteenth century, a chaplain's place was with his regiment, even under live fire. What became known as the Battle of Bennington (Vermont) took place on the afternoon of August 16. Melsheimer was shot in the arm and captured, along with most of the regiment.[12] Baum, mortally wounded, died that night.

The Convention Army

Captivity behind patriot lines caused the regiment to be scattered, making it impossible for Melsheimer to perform his ministry. This new reality was not obvious at first. Being both wounded and marched from place to place as a paroled prisoner occupied his first couple of months in captivity. As a paroled prisoner he was an unguarded captive who pledged on his honor neither to attempt escape nor to discuss the war with civilians. Paroled captives were paid by their own armies, the wages passing through lines under truce, to provide for their billets in private homes. In Brimfield, Massachusetts, Melsheimer was eventually billeted in the home of Joseph Hitchcock, father of fifteen,[13] and he preached occasionally in the Congregationalist Church.[14]

Melsheimer's wound took eight weeks to heal.[15] On October 16, after two days of an uneasy cease-fire, Burgoyne surrendered the main army, which had suffered heavy losses in two battles near Saratoga. According to the terms of the Convention of Saratoga, the royalists were to march to Boston, board ships, and return to Europe, never again to participate in the war in North America. The convention explicitly covered the prisoners taken at Bennington. In the anticipation of going home, the state of Melsheimer's ministry was a non-issue for several months. Melsheimer traveled to the corps' headquarters in January 1778 and received news from General Riedesel that the ships to take them would arrive in February, and payroll guineas had arrived.[16]

The Convention of Saratoga, however, required the ratification of both the King of England and Congress. In March Congress refused to allow the Convention Army to board the ships waiting under truce in

Boston Harbor. Riedesel's biographer, Max von Eelking, suggests the problem was the tacit refusal of the king to acknowledge the authority of Congress to negotiate.[17] Catch-22.

Melsheimer's roommate, Dragoons surgeon Julius Wasmus, visited Riedesel's headquarters in April. He received money for all the officers billeted in the Brimfield area except Melsheimer, who "had not written to the general asking for money as the other gentlemen had done and therefore he did not get anything." Wasmus also records that headquarters had lost their mail, putting him in "low spirits."[18] Heller's descriptions of military ineptitude fit the armies of early modern Europe.

In late September 1778 Melsheimer was ordered to Newport, Rhode Island, with several other Dragoons officers to await a promising exchange.[19] They were paroled in the garrison of active-duty royalist auxiliaries from Ansbach-Bayreuth. At the same time General Sir Henry Clinton (1730-1795), commander of the royalist forces, wrote to George Washington on September 19, 1778, that, since Congress insisted Burgoyne's men were prisoners of war, the Convention Army was now their captors' responsibility and would no longer be supplied by the British. One month later Riedesel and most Braunschweig troops were ordered to barracks in Virginia. The Dragoons officers remained in Newport.

The deal for their exchange collapsed just as winter turned severe, and the garrison was struggling with resupply.[20] The parolees came under Clinton's policy. The Dragoons were returned to patriot lines on March 3, 1779, and they then were marched to the vicinity of Bethlehem, Pennsylvania.

Melsheimer's status as of March 3 is a mystery.[21] According to *The Dictionary of American Biography* he was "exchanged for W. Cardelle," chaplain of the 11th Virginia Regiment, and given "freedom to travel" in order to cross lines to the royalists; the article cites a document dated January 19, 1779.[22] By that date most of Riedesel's command was in Virginia. It may be that the exchange order never caught up to Melsheimer, or that when it did he had already resigned.

Resigning or Deserting

Bethlehem was a church-run community of the Unity of the Brethren, commonly known as "Moravians" even though they had become mostly German by the early eighteenth century. In a letter to Bethlehem's director Johann Ettwein dated April 26, 1779, Melsheimer wrote: "As soon as we arrived in Newport I wrote to . . . consistorial Chief Knittel in Wolfenbüttel, and pleaded for a change in my call. . . ."[23] This shows that by the time he had arrived in Rhode Island he had made up his mind to resign. The letter to Ettwein declares that his letter to the Wolfenbüttel Consistory is his resignation from his chaplaincy. In his *Selbst-biografie* he states that he resigned because of differences with his brother officers,[24] while in his letter to Ettwein he describes that his decision to resign caused the falling out.

While he had experienced a crisis of conscience that began during the campaign, he was now experiencing a crisis of vocation. According to Article XIV of the *Augsburg Confession,* a pastor without a "proper call" is not a genuine pastor. The call to the Dragoons Regiment had been properly issued through the Wolfenbüttel Consistory and included the ministries of preaching, teaching, and administering the sacraments specified in the article. When those ministries could no longer be performed, the ministry ceased to function and it was no longer a "proper" call. Yet Melsheimer could not legitimately conduct these ministries in other venues, such as in American parishes, of his own volition; "vagabonds" and "imposters" emigrating from Germany without proper credentials or calls had plagued the Pennsylvania Ministerium for decades.[25] He needed a call in the full Lutheran sense.

In the letter of April 26 Melsheimer asked, "Am I a deserter?" Such a smear on his honor struck him as unfair. He was a civilian, and the regiment he was supposed to serve was scattered across the colonies, making his call impossible to perform. Even so on May 6 the Dragoons officers in Bethlehem called in Melsheimer for a verbal "dressing-down," with threats, cursing, name-calling, and verbal shaming.[26] His alienation from the Braunschweig Dragoons was complete. The appendix to Eelking's biography of Riedesel notes that on May 11, 1779, Chaplain Melsheimer "deserted."[27]

With what was known in Bethlehem on May 6, Melsheimer had the stronger case that he had resigned. That Melsheimer had been exchanged, however, justifies the judgment that he deserted. Yet the Braunschweig command negotiated for his exchange in order to retain a chaplain without a ministry, an office that, for over a year had only existed on paper as a bureaucratic fiction.

Seeking Call

According to his April 26 letter Melsheimer had desired to leave his chaplaincy by the fall of 1778, when most of his parole had been in Brimfield, Massachusetts, to work at a church "in this land." In his third letter to Ettwein, Melsheimer notes that he had sent the copy of his resignation letter to *"Prediger Herr* Helmuth" in Lancaster.[28] Justus Heinrich Christian Helmuth (1745-1825) was a Halle missionary who arrived in 1769 and took the pulpit in Lancaster. It soon became clear that if Melsheimer's exit from the Dragoons had been rough, so would his entrance into parish ministry.

In a 1935 translation of his *Selbst-biografie,* Melsheimer notes that he preached his first sermon to a Lutheran congregation on May 13. This was at Hill Church in Lebanon, a congregation founded by Johann Caspar (J. C.) Stöver, Jr. (1707-1779). The church was in schism, with part of it served by Stöver.[29] Curiously Stöver died that day, in the parsonage, while preparing for a confirmation service.

May 13 was Ascension Day, a Thursday. While Melsheimer may have preached on Thursday to one party while Stöver readied himself for confirmation, it is probable that the 1935 English Recension of his *Selbstbiografie* is incorrect, and Melsheimer's first sermon was preached on Ascension *Sunday,* May 16, to the whole group. This fits reports that Melsheimer was more liked by Stöver's faction than by the "larger, complaining party."[30]

In any case Melsheimer stepped in to a split congregation with a checkered history of relations to the Pennsylvania Ministerium. While he was more popular with the Stöver camp, his interests lay with the larger, pro-synod faction. He attended the annual convention at his first opportunity, in October 1779.

That convention, in Tulpehocken, was poorly attended, with only nine of the Ministerium's twenty-six clergy present.[31] On receiving his application, the unanimous decision was to offer him friendship but not admit him into the synod until (1) they knew him better, and (2) he obtained his discharge from his chaplaincy.[32]

This action came second in the business. The third item concerned Tulpehocken's pastor Emmanuel Schultze, who would not accept a call to Lancaster because "his congregations strongly protested against it." This approbation for Schultze, the convention's host who happened to be the favorite of the synod party at Hill Church, followed immediately on Melsheimer's rejection. The fourth item resolved:

> (I)n the future no preacher shall leave his congregations unless he has well-founded reasons, and can also present them to the Ministerium when it has met; on the other hand, no one shall be permitted to accept a call from new important congregations without first having the consent of the President and at least four ordained preachers.[33]

While this policy was most likely enacted in response to events in Philadelphia,[34] the order of discussion implies criticism of both sides of Melsheimer's call in Lebanon: First, he could not provide a satisfactory resignation from his chaplaincy, and, second, he had candidated in Lebanon without pursuing synod channels.

The apparent harshness towards Melsheimer had three justifications: For one, the synod needed to protect its interest in Hill Church. Furthermore, a chaplaincy to a German auxiliary unit was a valid call regardless of politics. To receive Melsheimer risked alienating the Consistory of Wolfenbüttel and other German sources of Lutheran clergy such as Halle, Hamburg, and Württemberg. Finally, to receive a deserter from the royalists would violate the synod's neutrality, thus offending European benefactors who channeled support for the Pennsylvania Ministerium through the Halle Institutes.

Official Neutrality

The War of Independence in North America put at risk a lucrative base of support for the Halle Institutes, the London-based SPCK, not only for Halle's relatively small interests in North America, but also for other concerns, especially India. In 1777 there were approximately 800 mostly English subscribers to the SPCK.[35] During the Revolutionary War the global spirit of the society "wilted in the face of nationalist sentiment,"[36] and it chose to distribute 47,000 copies of Thomas Broughton's 1737 tract "Christian Soldiers" to British soldiers in 1780-81.[37] Anxiety among missionary Lutherans for their patronage was well-founded.

On June 1, 1776, Halle Institutes director Gottlieb Anastasius Freylinghausen (1719-1785) wrote a circular letter, addressed to Henry Melchior Mühlenberg, enjoining the Lutheran clergy of the Pennsylvania Ministerium to neutrality in the "civil unrest."[38] They were not to mix with politics, since that was not their office, but preach the pure gospel.[39]

The letter reached the United States in the care of German auxiliaries sailing to reinforce the Braunschweig Corps ahead of Burgoyne's campaign.[40] The letter then travelled to New York City and was taken into the custody of German officers marching with William Howe. During the royalist occupation of Philadelphia the letter was read aloud at various times, although according to Muhlenberg's several protests to Freylinghausen the letter seems to have never been actually delivered.[41]

Even so, its public reading got the message out effectively enough. The neutrality of the synod, thus enjoined, made it impossible for them to receive a German auxiliary chaplain accused of desertion. Melsheimer was at an impasse, a catch-22; the "synod party" in Lebanon insisted that Melsheimer had to produce his discharge before they would accept him.[42]

Acceptance

The impasse did not prevent Melsheimer from doing ministry in Lebanon and from cultivating friendships in the Pennsylvania Ministerium. On March 1, 1780, Melsheimer and two men from Lebanon stopped in Trappe to visit the elder H. M. Mühlenberg and his oldest son, the patriot brigadier general Peter Mühlenberg. They were on their way to Philadelphia to visit Friedrich, the synod founder's second son and a patriot assemblyman.[43] Although the only record of this visit comes from H. M. Mühlenberg's *Journals* and details are scant, it appears that the younger Mühlenbergs wanted to help Melsheimer resolve his status. It may have been at this time—a year after the fact—that Melsheimer finally learned of his "exchange" with Cardelle. His status as having been exchanged is included in Mühlenberg's account. On March 10 Melsheimer passed again through Trappe on his way back from Philadelphia and brought a letter for H. M. Mühlenberg from Friedrich.[44]

Whatever efforts the Mühlenbergs might have taken on Melsheimer's behalf were not fruitful inasmuch as his official status was concerned. One gets the sense, however, that this networking helped his standing among Pennsylvania's pastors. Even in Melsheimer's absence from the annual convention in 1781, the synod ruled on a request by the church in Reading to invite him into call:

> Resolved, to inform the congregation that Mr. Melsheimer was not yet received as a member of the Ministerium, and therefore nothing could be decided concerning him; but as we regard him as a friend, whose merits we appreciate, we

will not consider it a rupture of the union between the Reading congregation and us, if they call him to be their pastor.[45]

For reasons that are not known the call to Reading did not materialize,
yet the incident shows that the Pennsylvania Ministerium thought highly of Melsheimer and acted in good faith toward him—at least as much as
their official neutrality would allow. Their ruling was *de facto* a synodal
endorsement of Melsheimer, couched in protective language. This also
shows that after two years at Hill Church Melsheimer was accruing a
reputation as a preacher to be sought after.

Finally in September 1783 the Treaty of Paris was ratified, officially
ending the war with the recognition of the independence of the United
States. The royalist forces left New York City, their final stronghold in the
new nation, on November 25, 1783. Melsheimer did not attend the annual convention that followed, in June 1784, even though its location in
Lancaster was fairly close. It is likely that in the Hill Church schism, the
synod party's insistence that he receive a discharge had now, rather than
become moot, become irreconcilable to his detractors. The *Selbst-biografie* states that on November 12, 1784, he took the call to Manheim. The
Manheim call involved several associated parishes in conflict and the
result had been a rapid succession of pastors. Melsheimer was no exception. The minutes to the annual conference in Philadelphia in May 1785
show Melsheimer present and, for that year only, Manheim as his call.[46]

Melsheimer's appeal for acceptance was received as the fifteenth of
sixteen items of business, but was taken up first. The royalist evacua-
tion was decisive for the Ministerium's reversal. Neutrality in a civil war
was no longer germane; loyalty to the new sovereign power enjoined
the Lutheran clergy. In the new nation German auxiliary deserters were
embraced as examples of how erstwhile enemies could be won over by
the patriotic vision and promise of liberty.

It was "unanimously resolved, that Mr. Melzheimer (*sic*) be received
into the United Ministerium."[47] Melsheimer went on to serve in New Hol-
land, at Franklin College in Lancaster, as Ministerium secretary, and then
in Hanover, Pennsylvania from 1789 until his death in 1814.[48]

Conclusion

Was Melsheimer a deserter?

In the spirit and duty of a chaplain identifying with his unit,
Melsheimer remained on the march with the Dragoons even at the per-

sonal cost of being shot and captured. He remained dutiful even after his conscience troubled him concerning the chasm between the commands of Jesus and the demands of military life. Convinced that the dispersal of the captured Dragoons made his ministry to them impossible, he experienced a crisis of vocation at some time after the Convention of Saratoga was reneged and the prospect of returning home receded to an indefinite and uncertain future. With his chaplaincy voided by circumstances, his sense of call inspired his desire to help meet the needs of Pennsylvania's enormous, underserved population of German Lutherans.

From the military's point of view, the Braunschweig Corps should be commended for assuming responsibility for their civilian contractors. In 1781 the surgeon Julius Wasmus was given a passport to cross through lines and join exchanged officers from the Braunschweig Corps in Quebec; he eventually returned to Germany with the corps.[49] Braunschweig's officers evidently presumed Melsheimer would view himself in a similar vein and with a similar motivation when it secured his exchange for a captured patriot chaplain in the early months of 1779.

As a medical professional, Wasmus could be useful and appreciated in any place, and he was.[50] The pastoral office is more complex: The Lutheran call is tied to a specific community. Wandering preachers were suspect and considered "vagabonds," including several who had made their way across the ocean in the decades preceding the American Revolution and caused problems for the Pennsylvania Ministerium.[51]

The Braunschweig Corps simply needed to admit that the Dragoons chaplaincy no longer existed and release Melsheimer to pursue a call to another Lutheran community. That this was never admitted is, finally, the failure of the military apparatus—a failure Joseph Heller would have found unsurprising. At war's end other Braunschweig auxiliaries received permission to remain in the United States; failing to extend this to Melsheimer was sour grapes.[52]

The bureaucracy of the church fostered the impasse for several years. The pastors of the synod had to maintain their public neutrality, so they approved an untenable but convenient resolution: Melsheimer would not be accepted until he could produce his discharge. This requirement damaged his effort to unify Hill Church; his foes staked their opposition on the synod's catch-22, the demand for a discharge from a regiment that called him a deserter.

In Heller's *Catch-22* the pilots of an American Air Corps base in Italy had flown their full complement of missions but their commanding officer kept extending their duty, and each extension thinned their margins for surviving the war. They could not finally wait for the war to end; they had to find some way to end the war for themselves, even if it meant "deserting." For Melsheimer and his vocation the war had to end before doors could open that the military bureaucracy had closed. Even then the doors did not open immediately; he first had to escape the schism at Hill Church. Once he was in place at Manheim, the Pennsylvania Ministerium finally did what the army of Braunschweig-Wolfenbüttel ultimately had not done: the right thing.

Endnotes

1 Joseph Heller, *Catch-22* (New York: Simon and Schuster, 1961).

2 F. V. Melsheimer to John Ettwein, April 29, 1779 (Letters Received by John Ettwein, John Ettwein Papers, no. 400, Moravian Archives, Bethlehem, Pennsylvania).

3 F. V. Melsheimer to John Ettwein, May 11, 1779 (Letters Received by John Ettwein, John Ettwein Papers, no. 401, Moravian Archives, Bethlehem, Pennsylvania).

4 A. Spaeth, H. E. Jacobs, and G. F. Spieker, eds. and trans., *Documentary History of the Evangelical Lutheran Ministerium of Pennsylvania, 1748 to 1821* (Philadelphia: Board of Publication of the General Council of the Evangelical Lutheran Church in North America, 1898), 157.

5 This article abridges and recasts material and references found in chapters two through four of my dissertation. Jonathan M. Wilson, "Switching Sides: A Hessian Chaplain in the Pennsylvania Ministerium" (unpublished Ph.D. dissertation, Lutheran School of Theology at Chicago, 2015), 53-153.

6 F. V. Melsheimer, *Selbstbiografie* (1935 English-language recension), 1. Dragoons were "mounted infantry," armed with carbines (a shouldered fire-arm with a shorter barrel than a musket) and broadswords.

7 Robert Ketchum, *Saratoga: Turning Point of America's Revolutionary War* (New York: Holt, 1997), 147-244.

8 Ketchum, 274. cf. Julius Wasmus, *An Eye-Witness Account of the American Revolution and New England Life: The Journal of J. F. Wasmus, German Company Surgeon, 1776-1783*, trans. Helga Doblin, ed. Mary C. Lynn (Westport, Connecticut: Greenwood Publishing Group, 1990) 66.

9 Ketchum, 296.

10 Wasmus, 69.

11 Ketchum, 302-303.

12 Wasmus, 73.

13 Ibid, 77.

14 Wasmus notes that Melsheimer wore "a white vest and trousers underneath his black coat when he climbed into the pulpit to preach" (ibid., 112).

15 Ibid., 88.

16 Ibid., 106.

17 Max von Eelking, *Memoirs, and Letters and Journals of Major General Riedesel During His Residence in America*, vol.2, trans. William Leete Stone (Albany, New York: J. Munsell, 1868. Reprint, Forgotten Books, 2012), 46.

18 Wasmus, 110.

19 Melsheimer, *Selbstbiografie*, 1-2.

20 Walter K. Schroder, *The Hessian Occupation of Newport and Rhode Island, 1776-1779* (Westminster, Maryland: Heritage Books, 2009).

21 They may have left Rhode Island in time to avoid a scurvy epidemic. Stephan Popp, *A Hessian Soldier in the American Revolution: The Diary of Stephan Popp*, trans. Reinhart J. Popp (published by Reinhart Pope, U.S.A., 1953), 14.

22 "Frederick Valentine Melsheimer," *The Dictionary of American Biography*, vol. 12 (1933), 519.

23 *"So bald wir in Neuport angekommen waren: so schreib ich, an unseren geistlichen Consistorial-Rath Knittel in Wolfenbüttel, und bath um meine zurückberufung. . . ,"* F. V. Melsheimer to John Ettwein, April 26, 1779, Moravian Archives.

24 Melsheimer, *Selbstbiografie*, 1.

25 Henry Melchior Mühlenberg, *The Journals of Henry Melchior Muhlenberg* vol. 1, Theodore G. Tappert and John W. Doberstein, eds. (Philadelphia: Muhlenberg Press, 1942), 83-86.

26 F. V. Melsheimer letter to Johann Ettwein, May 11, 1779, letters received from Johann Ettwein no. 401, Johann Ettwein Papers, Moravian Archives, Bethlehem, Pennsylvania.

27 Eelking, 266.

28 Ibid.

29 Ibid.

30 Mühlenberg, *Journals,* vol 3, 377.

31 *Documentary History*, 156-157; Mühlenberg, vol. 3, 265-266.

32 *Documentary History*, 157; Mühlenberg, vol. 3, 266.

33 Ibid.

34 Mühlenberg, vol. 3, 235.

35 Katherine Carte Engel, "The SPCK and the American Revolution: The Limits of International Protestantism," *Church History,* Vol. 81, No. 1 (March 2012): 87.

36 Ibid., 91.

37 Ibid.

38 "G. A. Freylinghausen and H. Muhlenberg, June 1, 1776," *Die Korrespondenz Heinrich Melchior Mühlenbergs*, vol. 4, ed. Kurt Aland (Berlin: Walter der Gruyter, 1995), 730.

39 Ibid.

40 Letter from Wilhelm Pasche (Kensington) to Sebastian Fabricius (Halle), Archiv die Franckeschestiftungen, M4 C19:11.

41 Ibid., 101, 126; Pasche to Fabricius, M4 C19:11.

42 Mühlenberg, *Journals*, vol. 3, 377.

43 Ibid., 301.

44 Ibid., 303.

45 *Documentary History*, 178. Neither this event nor the actions concerning the constitution appear in Henry Melchior Mühlenberg's account of the meeting (Mühlenberg, *Journals*, vol. 3, 426ff).

46 *Documentary History*, 199.

47 Ibid.

48 Wilson, *Switching Sides,* 154-188.

49 Wasmus, preface.

50 Wasmus, 110.

51 Mühlenberg, *Journals,* vol.1, 106-108.

52 Eelking, 268 (Ensigns Langerjahn and Kolte); 273 (Ensign Specht).

CHAPTER FIFTEEN

Lutheranism's Finest Hour

James A. Scherer

Martin Luther and his cohorts at the Imperial Diet of Worms (1521), facing the undivided might of the Roman Catholic Church and the Holy Roman Empire, quickly learned that promoting reformation in the church was not a tea party. Diplomatic gestures, polite exchanges, and positive expectations were not enough to accomplish the task. Lutherans and other supporters of reform unanimously supported the learned monk in his cry of desperation, "Here I stand. I can do no other. God help me." Given the Catholic rejection of Lutheran proposals, the road to reformation was heavily burdened by negative stereotypes of the opposition. A hallmark of Lutheran identity was stalwart resistance.

Each group had its polemical theologians whose assigned task was to point out and denounce the heresies and deficiencies of others. Luther himself, as we now recognize in a more ecumenical age, was given to highly vituperative remarks condemning Papists, Jews, Anabaptists, and Zwinglians. Through 500 years of history, with brief but happy exceptions, Lutherans have often presented an angry or quarrelsome face in defending their own understanding of "truth" against the heresies of opponents. Conflicts and confrontations between and among Lutherans themselves have been nearly as frequent. The apostolic exhortation to "speak the truth in love" calls us to reflect on the appropriateness of such behavior as we engage in dialogue toward closer unity with Christian brothers and sisters of various confessions.

Happily, the person whom we honor in this *Festschrift*, Kurt Hendel, devoted many years in scholarly exposition of Johannes Bugenhagen, a Lutheran who presented a friendlier face, even to those with whom he disagreed. A town preacher in Wittenberg rather than an academic theologian, Bugenhagen spoke with a pastoral heart. His approach to ministry was holistic, incorporating music, liturgy, and sound catechetics into worship. With instinctive missionary consciousness, he laid the groundwork for the spread of Lutheranism into North German cities, Denmark, and Norway. He designed church orders for Wittenberg and many other cities. As a pastor concerned for the health and welfare of his people, he remained in Wittenberg during the plague of 1527, when many abandoned the city, and later refused to forsake his post when imperial troops occupied the city. He made special contributions to the sacramental piety of Lutheranism, guarding its distinctive emphasis on Real Presence. Johannes Bugenhagen, *Doctor Pomeranus,* showed Lutheranism at its best in a very troubled age.

Lutheranism's Finest Hour

Lutheranism in its later historical development did in fact enjoy many periods when its dominant image was one of kindness, generosity, caring, and sacrifice. These were associated with the period of Pietism, the rise of voluntary missionary societies, the rescue of missions and churches threatened by war, and the loving outreach of diaconic aid organizations in periods of disaster relief. Some of these prefigure the rise of the modern ecumenical movement and embody efforts by Lutherans, working together with Christians of other confessional backgrounds, for the saving of lost and dying peoples, cultures, and nations. Here we see seeds planted by Johannes Bugenhagen springing up and bearing a witness to the kingdom that transcends the goals of the Reformation.

One of the most inspirational but least well-known of these efforts, which demonstrates the amazing sacrifice and generosity of world Lutherans during both World Wars I and II, goes by the name of "Orphaned Missions."[1] Orphaned Missions refers to missions and missionaries cut off from their home bases of support during two world wars, thus becoming "orphaned." The majority were German evangelical missions, but others were Finnish and Norwegian. Most were in Africa, but some were in India, other parts of Asia, and the Pacific Islands. German Protestant missionaries captured by Allied forces during wartime were repatriated, leaving their fledgling "native church" communities without missionary leadership or funding. Mission properties belonging to German societies were subject to confiscation as wartime booty.

During World War I an emergency situation developed, calling for the immediate rescue of German and other orphaned missions. To pre-

SUBJECT TO NONE, SERVANT OF ALL

serve these orphaned young churches from confiscation or possible extinction, American and Swedish Lutheran mission agencies swung into action, sending experienced missionary administrators to provide leadership. During the Versailles Treaty negotiations (1919), thanks to timely intervention by the Edinburgh Continuation Committee of the World Missionary Conference of 1910, later to become the International Missionary Council (1921), it was agreed that German orphaned missions would be placed under a special trusteeship arrangement. Orphaned missions (Lutheran and other) would be temporarily administered by mission boards of the same confessional background, but from the Allied side, and helped to reach autonomy and eventual independence.

Participating American and Swedish mission boards strictly observed these trusteeship provisions as they guided their wards toward full autonomy. U.S. Lutherans after World War I came together to form cooperative agencies for the relief of Lutheran orphaned missions, soldier's and sailor's welfare, European relief, and other causes. One of these new agencies was the National Lutheran Council (1918), which worked closely with an inter-Lutheran mission committee known as the Commission on Younger Churches and Orphaned Missions (CYCOM).

In short order this international Lutheran rescue activity gave rise to the Lutheran World Federation Commission on World Mission (LWF CWM), often regarded as a kind of international parliament on world mission. Without question, it played a crucial role in the emergence of international Lutheran fellowship and communion, embodied in the founding of the Lutheran World Convention (1935) and The Lutheran World Federation (1947). German Lutheran missionary societies were pathetically grateful to their Lutheran mission counterparts on the Allied side.[3]

The North American Lutheran role in global mission was greatly enhanced and accelerated through participation in orphaned mission agreements. In the former German East African Territory (Tanganyika/ Tanzania) American missionaries became crucial trusteeship administrators and later acquired their own field of work. In India, Americans and Swedes provided trusteeship assistance to the Tamil Evangelical Lutheran church while American missionaries aided the Gossner Church. The South Andhra Lutheran Church was literally sold to an American Lutheran mission board. In China, the Berlin Mission offered to transfer its holdings in Shantung province to an American Lutheran board. In

Sumatra, Indonesia, the very large Batak folk church (HKBP), orphaned from the Rhenish Mission, became self-administered under its own tribal leaders and admitted into membership in the LWF. And in Papua New Guinea, American and Australian Lutherans became trustees for that fledgling island church body that had been the work of two German mission societies.

Prof. Kurt Hendel's two-volume English translation of the writings of Johannes Bugenhagen provides eloquent evidence for the way in which the work of this Pomeranian pastor helped to provide a foundation for Lutheran participation in the modern ecumenical movement.[5] We are in Kurt Hendel's debt for his life of scholarly service to the church, telling its whole story, including its finest hour.

Endnotes

1 W. Richey Hogg, "Orphaned Missions," *Concise Dictionary of the Christian World Mission* (Nashville: Abingdon, 1971), 456-7.

2 See James A. Scherer, *Mission and Unity in Lutheranism* (Philadelphia: Fortress Press, 1969), 62-72.

3 *Johannes Bugenhagen: Selected Writings*, ed. and trans. Kurt Hendel, 2 vols. (Minneapolis: Fortress Press, 2015).

CHAPTER SIXTEEN

A "Radical Incarnational Perspective" and the Poetry of the Mystery of Christ

Fragments for Kurt Hendel

Mark Swanson

He was ... carried in the womb by Mary,
   and clothed with his Father;
treading the earth
   and filling heaven ... ;
wanting food ... ,
   and not ceasing to nourish the world. ...
He stood before Pilate,
   and sat with the Father;
he was fastened to the tree,
   and held the universe.

                              Melito of Sardis (2nd c.)[1]

Holy God, holy and beautiful, beauty unsurpassed,
   you are despised, rejected;
   scorned, you hold us fast,
and we behold your beauty.

                              Susan R. Briehl (2002)[2]

From the early days of the Christian church to the present, Christians have gloried in the confession that the fully human Jesus Christ—born of a woman, living a human life, subjected to cruel treatment and executed—

is, just as fully, Immanuel, God-with-us. The Nicene Creed summarizes thus: The one who was "born of the Virgin Mary, suffered under Pontius Pilate, was crucified, died, and was buried" *is the same one* who is "God from God, light from light, true God from true God." While the creed is hardly devoid of rhetorical power, its affirmations about Christ's divine attributes and those about Christ's human history are largely grouped in separate blocks of text. However, we can also point to a remarkable "poetry of the Incarnation" that *matches* Christ's human deeds and attributes with divine deeds and attributes in an imaginative and deliberately provocative way. Thus, the second-century teacher Melito of Sardis (d. c. 190 CE) could match details of Christ's human history with statements of divine power, so as to preach: "He was fastened to the tree, *and held the universe*." And twenty-first century ELCA Lutherans have been learning to sing Susan Briehl's remarkable verses that match divine attributes with biblical descriptions of Christ's humility, crucifixion, and death: "*beauty unsurpassed*, you are despised, rejected," and later, "*life that never ends*, you show your love by dying."[3] Such statements seem designed to elicit cries of "Hallelujah!" from those who believe (and have sometimes elicited cries of "Nonsense!" from those who don't).

Even among Christians, not all theologians have been fully comfortable with such poetry of the Incarnation, although many have accepted it as consisting in vivid figures of speech—within which some intermediate distinguishing-and-sorting step must be understood.[4] But many significant Christian teachers have insisted, in effect, that the poetry of the Incarnation is not merely a set of striking juxtapositions but rather true statements enabled by a "radical incarnational perspective" (to use a phrase from Kurt Hendel).[5] One of the clearest teachers of this "radical incarnational perspective" in the early church was St. Cyril of Alexandria (d. 441 CE), whose fundamental insight was that, in the Incarnation, *the Word of God* takes on *as God's own* a human life, a human history.[6] This insight is the basis for a particular grammar for speaking of the Incarnation: One may predicate of *God the Word* any of the deeds and attributes of Jesus Christ to which the Gospels bear witness. Thus, one may rightly say that *God* was born of the Virgin Mary (and thus that the Virgin Mary is *Theotokos*), or that *the Word of God* suffered in the flesh, was crucified, and died.[7]

Throughout his career, Kurt Hendel has trained students in the "radical incarnational perspective" that came to powerful gospel-word in the Christian West in the preaching and teaching of Martin Luther and his colleagues.[8] Luther in fact adopted and developed the Cyrillian grammar of the Incarnation just mentioned, and he came regularly (especially in his later writings) to use the technical term *communicatio idiomatum* for the incarnational grammar that is a consequence of the unity of humanity and divinity in Christ:—"namely," as Luther explained in a set of theses for a disputation, that "those things that are attributed to the human being may rightly be asserted with respect to God; and, on the other hand, those things that are attributed to God may rightly be asserted with respect to the human being."[9] He goes on: "So it is true to say: this human being *created the world*; and *this God* has suffered, died, was buried, etc."[10]

The examples of the last sentence are grammatically (if not conceptually) simple: If we imagine a chart in two columns, divine titles and attributes in one, human titles and attributes in the other, these sentences pair a title from one column ("human being" and "God," respectively) with an attribute from the other ("created the world" and "suffered, died, and was buried," respectively). But one senses Luther's delight in taking such simple sentences and elaborating either subject or predicate or both for rhetorical effect. For example (from Luther's explanation of the fifth-century ecumenical councils in *On the Councils and the Church*),[11] one may say with regard to Christ: "There goes God down the street, fetching water and bread so that he might eat and drink with his mother;"[12] and also "[T]his man Christ, the flesh and blood of Mary, *is creator of heaven and earth, has vanquished death, abolished sin, broken hell.* . . ."[13] Or (from a set of theses for an academic disputation), "*God who is from all eternity* died; the boy who nurses at the breast of the Virgin Mary *is the creator of all things.*"[14] Luther's "radical incarnational perspective" not only imposes a grammar of the Incarnation, it flowers into a poetry of the Incarnation.

I will give one more example before leaving Luther. In an important article about Luther's "radical incarnational perspective," Kurt Hendel quotes Luther's response to the claim of Huldrych Zwingli (1484-1531) and others that it was "not fitting that Christ's body and blood should be in the bread and wine":

> To this first point I might say equally well that it is not reasonable that God should descend from heaven and enter into the womb; that he who nourishes, sustains, and encompasses all the world should allow himself to be nourished and encompassed by the Virgin. Likewise, that Christ, a king of glory [Ps. 24:10], at whose feet all angels must fall and before whom all

creatures must tremble, should thus humble himself below all men and allow himself to be suspended upon the cross as a most notorious evil-doer and that by the most wicked and desperate of men. And I might conclude from this that God did not become man, or that the crucified Christ is not God.[15]

The rhetoric of the passage, it is clear, depends fully on the fact that Luther *does* believe—and implies that the Swiss reformers should readily acknowledge as well—that it *is* right and fitting to confess that *God* descended from heaven and entered into the womb; *God* became human; the crucified Christ is *God*. We recognize here Luther's commitment to the grammar of the Incarnation, according to which one may predicate of *God* items from the Gospels' story of Jesus Christ: conception, gestation, birth, humanity, suffering, crucifixion. But we can also extract from the above paragraph some striking lines of incarnational poetry:

> [the One] who nourishes, sustains, and encompasses all the world
> [was] nourished and encompassed by the Virgin;
> a king of glory,
> at whose feet all angels must fall and before whom all creatures must tremble,
> [was] suspended upon the cross as a most notorious evil-doer. . . .[16]

My purpose in this extended introduction is, in the first place, to express my deep appreciation to Kurt Hendel for his witness to the "radical incarnational perspective" of the Lutheran tradition. There is nothing new in what I have written so far, which I submit to my dear colleague for critical review and correction! But in the second place, I want to set the stage so as to introduce *another* poet of the Incarnation, one who may not be so familiar to Kurt Hendel or to other readers of this book. His name was Eustathius—in the manuscript tradition he is referred to simply as "Eustathius, the monk"[17]—and he may have lived in Syria or Iraq in about the ninth century of the Common Era.[18] We know little about him besides two facts that, for Western Christians, have no doubt contributed to his obscurity: He was a *non*-Chalcedonian Christian, an adherent of what has customarily been called the "monophysite" christology, and he wrote in the Arabic language.[19]

We only have one theological work from Eustathius' hand, preserved in a handful of manuscripts and not yet published.[20] It appears to have lost its original title (although a good guess is that it was called

The Exposition [of the Faith]), and today it is simply known as *The Book of Eustathius the Monk.*[21] But if the book is practically unknown to us today, it was known to a number of Christian theologians who wrote in Arabic between the tenth and fourteenth centuries, especially in Egypt; indeed, the extant manuscripts of the book were produced in and/or preserved by Coptic Orthodox monasteries in Egypt.[22]

Eustathius' book is rather long and rambling (or so it seems), but full of interesting material. Like other Christian theologians of his time who wrote from within the lands of the Islamic Abbasid empire, in a language shared with the holy book of Muslims (the Qur'an), he devoted much space to defending specifically Christian doctrines: the triunity of God (against the background of the Qur'an's passionate monotheism), the divinity of Christ (explicitly denied in the Qur'an), and the crucifixion of Christ for the redemption of the world (where the Qur'an appears to call even the historicity of the crucifixion into question).[23]

It is the question about the divinity of Christ that concerns us here. One lengthy passage in the book begins with Eustathius's presumably Muslim interlocutor asking about Christians' worship of Jesus Christ:

> [A]re you not returning to [the worship of] a god who was born, nursed, hungered, thirsted, ate, drank, excreted, tired, fled, was frightened, was beaten, was crucified, cried out for help, and died?[24]

The question builds on passages from the Qur'an, e.g.:

> The Messiah, son of Mary, was only a messenger; other messengers had come and gone before him; his mother was a virtuous woman; *both ate food* [like other mortals].[25]

That is: how can you claim divinity for one who ate food? The list was easily extended by later writers: "How can you claim divinity for one who . . . "—and here one can add *any* of Christ's deeds of human weakness. Such lists were common in the early "refutation of the Christians" literature,[26] and we find yet another witness here in Eustathius's book.

Eustathius will address several of the items in his interlocutor's list individually. But first, he gives a global response which does not so much *explain* the simultaneous divinity and humanity of Christ as to *assert* it in a provocative way, matching Christ's deeds of human weakness (from his interlocutor's list) with Christ's deeds of divine power, *as borne witness to in the Gospels*, so as to provide a rich and memorable summary of the Gospels' witness to the person of Jesus Christ. Eustathius writes:[27]

If the time of his birth and the number of his years
    were understood,
  he is the one who said to the Jews,
    "Truly, truly I say to you, I am before Abraham."[28]

If he hungered,
  he is the one who satisfied nine thousand people
  from twelve loaves
    (apart from the women and children).
  The remnants were gathered after all were satisfied,
    and they filled nineteen baskets. . . .[29]

Next, he thirsted;
  and he is the one who provided exceptional wine to
  drink to the people at the wedding of Cana of Galilee
  after their wine ran out,
    without a word or touch of a hand. . . .[30]

Next, he became tired from walking;
  and he is the one who walked upon the water
    and caused Peter to walk with him.[31]

He tired from carrying his cross;
  and he is the one who commanded the one paralyzed
    for thirty-eight years
  to pick up his bed,
    and he got up, picked it up, and departed.[32]

He feared and was anxious about those who sought him,
  and fled to the land of Egypt from Herod;
    and he is the one who said to them,
    "I am Jesus whom you seek,"
      and they retreated and fell backwards out of fright
      and anxiety,
        until he had mercy on them after that and
        took away their fear.[33]
  And when Satan heard his voice saying,
    "Depart from me, Satan,"
he fled from him in terror, unable to stand before him.
  And the angels came to serve him.[34]

He died as all people die, as sight has borne witness;
    and he is the one who raised the dead
    by his saying "Rise!"
        and the dead one arose.[35]

He was buried like all who are buried;
    and he is the one on whose account the graves were
    opened
        and the saints who were in them came out,
        and they entered the holy city.[36]

He was counted among those who had perished,
    and the opening of the grave was sealed
    so that he would not decompose;
        and he is the one who came to the grave of Lazarus
        on the fourth day,
            after he had begun to smell, and cried out
            "Lazarus, rise and come out!"
And he came out in his own form without lack,
    while in his graveclothes.
His body had not decomposed,
    and he lived for some years after that.[37]

For the moment, I hope that this passage from an Oriental (non-Chalcedonian) Orthodox theologian who wrote from the heart of medieval Christian–Muslim controversy will be enough to suggest that, when it comes to a "radical incarnational perspective" and the poetry of the Incarnation, Lutherans might appreciate and learn something from the work of their distant Cyrillian cousins. There are plenty of issues to discuss in Eustathius's chapter, as he turns from the global response reproduced above to explanations of particular acts of human weakness, but it may well be fruitful to discuss these alongside issues in Luther's christology and its reception. The heirs of Cyril of Alexandria have always faced the question of whether their paradoxical speech about Jesus Christ is coherent and whether in the end it sufficiently safeguards the true humanity of Jesus. Some modern Luther scholars, troubled by the predication of divine attributes to what we might call a synoptic Jesus, have asked such questions of Luther's christology.[38] There certainly are questions that we can ask of Eustathius, who appears to have been troubled by the predication of certain human attributes to a more Johannine Jesus.[39]

But that will be another essay. Here I am content to give thanks for a cloud of witnesses to "God in flesh made manifest," to point to the existence of such witnesses outside the usual Lutheran curriculum, and most of all to express my gratitude to Kurt Hendel, who has trained thousands in the "radical incarnational perspective" of Luther and his colleagues within the larger Christian tradition.

Endnotes

1 Melito of Sardis, Fragment 14; ed. and trans. Stuart George Hall, *Melito of Sardis: On Pascha and Fragments* (Oxford: Clarendon Press, 1979), 81-82. Formatting mine.

2 Susan R. Briehl, "Holy God, Holy and Glorious," stanza 3, in *Evangelical Lutheran Worship* (Minneapolis: Augsburg Fortress, 2006), no. 637. Formatting mine.

3 Briehl, "Holy God," stanza 5, italics added

4 E.g., so that the divinity performs what is proper to divinity, and the humanity what is proper to humanity, as presented in the *Tome of Leo* (Epistle 28) [Letter to Flavian, Patriarch of Constantinople, 13 June 449]. Republished in J. P. Migne, PL 54, cols. 755-782.

5 See Kurt Hendel, "*Finitum capax infiniti*: Luther's Radical Incarnational Perspective," *Currents in Theology and Mission* 35 no. 6 (December 2008): 420-33.

6 See, e.g., Cyril of Alexandria, *Second Letter to Nestorius* (in *Cyril of Alexandria: Select Letters*, ed. and trans. Lionel R. Wickham (Oxford: Clarendon Press, 1983), 2-11, where (in Wickham's translation) the Word makes "the birth of his flesh *his very own*" (par. 4), "he *himself* suffered death for our sake," "*in his own body*" (par. 5), that the Word "is one in union *with his own flesh*" (par. 6); emphasis added.

7 Cyril of Alexandria, *Third Letter to Nestorius* 12, in *Cyril of Alexandria: Select Letters*, ed. Wickham, 28-33, here par. 12, anathemas 1 and 12.

8 James M. Estes, "Johannes Brenz and the German Reformation," *Lutheran Quarterly* 16 (2002): 373-414, raises the question of who should have the honor of being number three on "the list of the most important Lutheran reformers in Germany" after Luther and Melanchthon (373). While he opts for Johannes Brenz (who could certainly be mentioned here for his "radical incarnational perspective"!), he mentions as serious "competition for that honour" (409, n. 5) Luther's colleague and pastor Johannes Bugenhagen, to whom Kurt Hendel has devoted so much energy. It is a joy to be able to cite *Johannes Bugenhagen: Selected Writings*, ed. and trans. Kurt Hendel, 2 vols. (Minneapolis: Fortress Press, 2015).

9 Martin Luther, *Disputation Concerning the Divinity and Humanity of Christ* 2 (1540), translated in Mitchell Tolpingrud, "Luther's Disputation Concerning the Divinity and the Humanity of Christ," *Lutheran Quarterly* 10 (1996): 151-78, here 153.

10 Martin Luther, *Disputation Concerning the Divinity and Humanity of Christ* 3, translated in Tolpingrud, "Luther's Disputation," 153. Semicolon and italics added.

11 Martin Luther, *On the Councils and the Church* (1539), LW 41, 3-178; for the Councils of Ephesus and Chalcedon, 93-119.

12 Ibid., 101. Italics added.

13 Ibid., 110. Italics added.

14 *Die Promotionsdisputation von Theodor Fabricius und Stanislaus Rapagelanus* 35, WA 39, 280, translated in Paul Althaus, *The Theology of Martin Luther*, trans. Robert C. Schultz (Philadelphia: Fortress Press, 1966), 194. Italics added.

15 LW 36:388 (From *The Sacrament of the Body and Blood of Christ—Against the Fanatics* of 1526), quoted in Kurt Hendel, *"Finitum capax infiniti,"* 425-26.

16 Ibid., stating Luther's presuppositions in positive terms in the past tense. Italics added.

17 In Arabic, *Ustath al-rahib.*

18 For what we know about Eustathius, see Eid Salah and Mark N. Swanson, "Ustath al-Rahib," in *Christian-Muslim Relations: A Bibliographical History*, vol. 1 (600-900), ed. David Thomas, Barbara Roggema, et al. (Leiden: Brill, 2009), 907-10.

19 The term "monophysite" is widely heard today as pejorative (especially by those whose christological position it is meant to describe) and is best avoided. I have used alternative labels (for theologies, not people) such as "miaphysite," but have come to think that it is quite possible to speak precisely about the one-nature christology and its adherents without recourse to "-physite" labels.

20 It may be that this theologian Eustathius is to be identified with other Eustathii who are reported to have translated Greek philosophical works into Arabic in the ninth century.

21 In Arabic, *Kitab al-bayan* and *Kitab Ustath al-rahib*, respectively.

22 Eid Salah and Swanson, "Ustath al-Rahib," 909.

23 Our best introduction to Arabic-language apologetic theology from within the Dar al-Islam is Sidney H. Griffith, *The Church in the Shadow of the Mosque: Christians and Muslims in the World of Islam* (Princeton: Princeton University Press, 2008).

24 My translation from the early fourteenth-century manuscript Aleppo, Fondation Salem, arabe 209 (Sbath 1011), ff. 162b-163a. The passage or chapter under consideration here extends to f. 179a. [Readers of these words: please pause and pray for the peace of Aleppo.]

25 Q 5:75; English interpretation of M.A.S. Abdel Haleem, *The Qur'an: A New Translation* (Oxford: Oxford University Press, 2004). Emphasis added. Cf. Q 21:8 and 23:33.

26 My favorite introduction to this literature is Abdelmajid Charfi, "La function historique de la polémique islamochrétienne à l'époque abbasside," in *Christian Arabic Apologetics during the Abbasid Period (750-1258)*, ed. Samir Khalil Samir and Jørgen S. Nielsen (Leiden and New York: E.J. Brill, 1994), 44-56.

27 MS Aleppo, Salem ar. 209, ff. 163b-165a; my translation. In another paper I discuss how this and other passages were used by the great Coptic Orthodox theologian, Sawirus ibn al-Muqaffa': Mark N. Swanson, "A Copto-Arabic Debt to Syriac-Arabic Literature: Sawirus ibn al-Muqaffa' and Ustath al-Rahib on Christ's Human Deeds," to appear in *Parole de l'Orient* (Kaslik, Lebanon).

28 John 8:58.

29 Mark 6:30-44; 8:1-10; Matthew 14:13-21; 15:32-39.

30 John 2:1-11.

31 Matthew 14:22-33.

32 John 5:2-9.

33 John 18:1-12.

34 Matthew 4:10-11.

35 E.g., Luke 7:14-15; Mark 5:41-42; John 11:43-44.

36 Matthew 27:52-53.

37 John 11:38-44.

38 Paul Althaus asked "whether Luther's presupposition that the man Jesus had the attributes of the divine majesty available to him can be reconciled with the biblical picture of the historical Christ," and concluded the chapter ("God in Jesus Christ") as follows: "Luther's basic christological confession (that the Father's heart and will are present in Christ) will always be significant. However, his dogmatic theory which describes Christ as true God and true man is not unified within itself but displays contradictions. Theology had to go beyond it." Paul Althaus, *The Theology of Martin Luther* (Minneapolis: Fortress Press, 1966), 196 and 198.

39 Eustathius's interlocutor thought that human digestive processes obviously disqualified Jesus from being considered divine. Eustathius is clearly troubled about attributing unseemliness to Jesus Christ and suggested in response that Jesus' eating was like that of Abraham's guests (Genesis 18:8) or of the Archangel Raphael (Tobit 6:6 in the shorter Greek version; see the RSV rather than the NRSV).

CHAPTER SEVENTEEN

Luther on Copernicus and Models for Faith and Science Dialogue

Roger E. Timm

I appreciate the opportunity to contribute to this *Festschrift* for Kurt K. Hendel for both personal and professional reasons. On a personal level we have known each other since we both entered high school at Concordia College in Milwaukee, Wisconsin, in 1958, and we have been friends and colleagues in ministry for nearly sixty years. We shared twelve years of preparation for ministry in the Lutheran Church–Missouri Synod "system," and then refreshed our friendship during the last twenty years of my ministry when I was a parish pastor in the Metropolitan Chicago Synod of the ELCA and served on its candidacy committee.

On a professional level I have "sat at his feet" and benefitted from his great knowledge of Martin Luther and Reformation theology. I remember especially his series of presentations on Luther's theology for a program for lay education at Grace Lutheran Church in LaGrange, Illinois, and I participated in one of his tours of Luther sites in Germany that included both visiting historic places and hearing in-depth historical and theological presentations over dinner and during bus rides in the German countryside.

In particular I remember Kurt's keynote address for the June 2010 Metropolitan Chicago Synod Assembly, "You Will Be My Witnesses," which was a revision of his earlier *Currents in Theology and Mission* article, "'No Salvation Outside the Church' in Light of Luther's Dialectic of the Hidden and Revealed God."[1] What impressed me about this presentation was how Kurt applied his deep knowledge and understanding of Luther's theology in faithful, careful, yet creative ways to a contemporary discussion of missiology and interreligious dialogue. His approach in that keynote address has inspired my intention for this article: to explore how Luther's thought and theology may provide guidance for how we approach dialogue between faith and science today.

Models for the Relationship of Religion and Science

In current discussion of the relationship of religion and science several models have been suggested for characterizing that relationship. The late Ian Barbour (1923-2013), a founder of the contemporary study of faith and science dialogue, proposed four models of the relationship.[2]

The first model is CONFLICT, which sees religion and science as inescapably in opposition to each other. People of faith, especially those who interpret the Bible literally, view science as an opponent of what they believe the Bible teaches, particularly in the conflict they see between the theory of evolution and biblical teaching of creation. Some scientists share this view as well, especially those who insist that only those phenomena that can be confirmed by naturalistic causes are legitimately held to be true. Scientists are appropriately "epistemologically materialistic," for the scientific enterprise focuses on collecting, analyzing, and experimenting with observable data. Some scientists slip into "ontological materialism," a philosophical position claiming that only observable entities or those explainable by materialistic causes are genuinely real. Such a belief system is sometimes referred to as "scientism."

Another model is INDEPENDENCE, which views religion and science as essentially distinct enterprises that have different purposes, methods, and languages. Those who hold this view argue that science examines the physical characteristics of our universe while religion seeks to understand its spiritual foundation and meaning. Science deals with facts and the theories to explain them, and religion deals with meaning and values. Or as Galileo put it, quoting someone else, "The intention of the Holy Ghost is to teach us how one goes to heaven, not how heaven goes."[3] The various scientific methods are different than theological methods, and each has its own language. Those who hold this view see religion and science as representing different "language games" or distinct communities of discourse. Puzzling over some statements about science, evolution, and Roman Catholic faith by Popes Pius XII (1876-1958) and John Paul II (1920-2005) and noticing references to the "magisterium"

SUBJECT TO NONE, SERVANT OF ALL

or teaching authority, of the Roman Catholic Church, Stephen Jay Gould (1941-2002) suggested that religion and science constitute "Non-Overlapping Magisteria," NOMA for short.[4]

A third model is DIALOGUE. Those who hold this view acknowledge the differences between religion and science, but they deny that those differences are so absolute that no communication is possible between them. There are overlapping issues of interest to both religion and science, ranging from the origins of the universe and of life to its path in the future. Medical ethics, environmental issues, climate change, relation of mind and brain are among the issues that concern people of both science and religion. In addition methods in both science and religion overlap. In both religion and science, experience of various sorts is used to support beliefs, and in both various forms of models and metaphors are used to express positions. As the evangelical theologian Palmer Joss said to the press to explain his support of astronomer and SETI explorer Ellie Arroway in the movie *Contact,* "We're both seeking the truth." In contrast to Stephen Jay Gould's NOMA, William Brown suggests a model he labels TOMA—"Tangentially Overlapping Magisteria."[5]

A fourth model is INTEGRATION. Those who advocate this model view science and religion as partners and construct theology in conversation with experience of nature or theories common in science. Examples of using experience of nature to construct theology include Aquinas' five arguments for the existence of God and those today who use the "anthropic principle" to argue for the necessity of a Creator. Those who use scientific theories to construct their theology include Teilhard de Chardin's (1881-1955) use of evolutionary theory and the followers of Alfred North Whitehead (1861-1947) who share his process view of God that is strongly shaped by current biology and physics, especially the world of quantum mechanics. The Institute on Religion in an Age of Science, an ancestor of the Zygon Center housed at LSTC, was founded to integrate religion and science and to foster the construction of theology shaped by and compatible with contemporary science.[6]

Guidance from Luther for Religion and Science Dialogue Today

Which of these models might Luther or his theology support?

Is it the CONFLICT model? Luther's supposed attitude toward Nicolaus Copernicus has been cited to support a claim that he was an opponent of science, at least of the heliocentric system of Copernicus.

People who hold this view quote a portion of Luther's *Table Talk*, record-ed by Anthony Lauterbach on June 4, 1539:

> There was mention of a certain astrologer who wanted to prove that the earth moves and not the sky, the sun, and the moon. This would be as if somebody were riding on a cart or in a ship and imagined that he was standing still while the earth and the trees were moving. [Luther remarked] "So it goes now. Whoever wants to be clever must agree with nothing that others esteem. He must do something of his own. This is what that fellow does who wishes to turn the whole of astronomy upside down. Even in these things that are thrown into disorder I believe the Holy Scriptures, for Joshua commanded the sun to stand still and not the earth" (Joshua 10:12).[7]

Johannes Aurifaber (1519-1575), Luther's secretary in the last year of Luther's life and the first to publish a collection of Luther's *Table Talk*, quotes Luther as referring not to "that fellow" but to "that fool."[8] Those who consider Luther to be an opponent of science often use Aurifaber's version of Luther's comment. Does this remark from *Table Talk* support that judgment?

First, since Luther's *Table Talk* is based on collections of notes taken by various students and house guests of Luther, it is not considered as reliable a source for Luther's opinions as are the works he wrote and published himself. Secondly, Aurifaber's edition of Luther's *Table Talk* has been shown to be less reliable than other collectors of the Reformer's sayings, including Anthony Lauterbach.[9]

But even if this quotation is accurate, does it reflect an opposition to Copernicus? The quotation does not mention Copernicus by name, but there is no doubt that Luther was referring to him. Several factors are im-portant to consider: The *Table Talk* quotation was recorded in 1539, four years *before* Copernicus' book, *On the Revolutions of the Heavenly Spheres,* was published. Most people at that time, scientists and theologians, ac-cepted the Ptolemaic geocentric system. Copernicus' heliocentric system was not based on any new observations that contradicted the Ptolemaic system; rather Copernicus offered his position as a way to simplify the mathematical calculations that were necessary to square the geocentric system with the observations of the actual orbits of planets and stars that could be made in his day. New observations that supported Copernicus' position had to wait for Johannes Kepler (1571-1630) and Galileo Galilei (1564-1642) a century later. Moreover, two professors at Wittenberg who were associates of Luther—Georg Joachim Rheticus (1514-1574) and Andreas Osiander (1498-1552)—were instrumental in encouraging Copernicus to publish his book, and then they arranged for its printing.[10] Judging Luther to stand in conflict with science because of his comment about "this fellow who wishes to turn the whole of astronomy upside down" is neither fair nor accurate.[11]

Does Luther or his theology reflect the INDEPENDENCE model? Would Luther agree that science and religion exemplify distinct language games from different communities of discourse, or that they represent "non-overlapping magisteria"? Luther's reference to Copernicus quoted above seems to suggest this approach, for Luther forms his response with reference to Scripture. The language of the Bible, particularly the verse from Joshua, supports one view apparently in contrast to the scientific view attributed to Copernicus. Luther himself does seem to support this view. In chapter one of his *Lectures on Genesis* (1535), he argues that "one must accustom oneself to the Holy Spirit's way of expression. . . . Therefore just as a philosopher employs his own terms, so the Holy Spirit, too, employs His. An astronomer, therefore, does right when he uses the terms 'spheres,' 'apsides,' and 'epicycles'; they belong to his profession. . . . By way of contrast, the Holy Spirit and Holy Scripture know nothing about those designations."[12]

Luther's doctrine of the "two kingdoms" may support this view as well. In his 1523 treatise, *Temporal Authority: To What Extent It Should Be Obeyed*, Luther argues that there are two "kingdoms," the kingdom of God and the kingdom of the world. The kingdom of God consists of genuine Christians for whom Christ is king and within whom the Holy Spirit is at work, guiding and directing them. The kingdom of the world is the world of temporal authority and is ruled by those with power to enforce laws and regulations. The kingdom of God is essentially spiritual, whose members are motivated by the internal rule of the spirit of Christ's love; the kingdom of the world is secular, whose members are kept in check by the external rule of leaders with temporal authority.[13] Perhaps one might extend this "two kingdom" imagery to the relationship of science and religion and argue that they constitute two distinct "kingdoms," each with their own authorities and guiding principles. Science and religion function independently, operating in separate realms.

Would Luther agree, then, with Gould in designating science and religion as NOMA, "non-overlapping magisteria"? I think not. As similar as some of Luther's comments are to the INDEPENDENCE model of their relationship, Luther's overall position does not support a view that science and religion are completely distinct from each other, functioning in hermetically sealed separate realms of practice and discourse. Luther would agree that believers are members of both God's kingdom and the kingdom of this world, so his "two kingdoms" metaphor does not support a view of two realms totally independent of each other. Luther's theology and practice are more akin to the DIALOGUE model. In his writings, especially in his sermons, he frequently makes references to the natural world.[14] As a faculty member of the University of Wittenberg he was a colleague and supporter of professors of mathematics, which in those days included astronomy, such as Georg Rheticus who encouraged Copernicus to publish the book describing his heliocentric system.[15] In his *Lectures on Genesis* Luther speaks favorably of astronomy and recognizes astronomers as experts in their field.[16] Contrary to Philipp Melanchthon (1497-1560), Luther contends that astrology is a "pseudo-science" and mocks Melanchthon for using it.[17] Luther's apparently critical remark about Copernicus does not set him off in a separate "theological kingdom," distinct from some sort of "scientific kingdom," for in the early sixteenth century both theologians and scientists accepted the Ptolemaic system. Luther exemplifies the DIALOGUE model—not NOMA, but TOMA, William Brown's "tangentially-overlapping magisteria."

Perhaps the best example of Luther's positive relationship with science is his attitude toward medicine. The University of Wittenberg included a faculty of medicine in Luther's day, and he supported that medical faculty as important members of the university. His family displayed a sign of that attitude, for Luther's son Paul became a doctor and taught medicine at the University of Leipzig. Luther valued medicine highly especially because of the need to provide medical care for the poor. The *Gemeindekassen* (Community Chest) initiated by Luther and his colleague and pastor, Johannes Bugenhagen (1485-1558), was used to support such medical aid for people in need. Because of his valuing of medicine Luther could say that medicine is a gift of God and definitely a science.[18]

Might Luther's approach to science be characterized by the fourth approach, INTEGRATION? Here the answer is clearly "No." Perhaps Melanchthon and other reformers remained Thomistic in their theology and would affirm that the existence of God can be demonstrated by arguments from nature, but not Luther. As Kurt Hendel wrote in the article referenced at the beginning of this essay, Luther believed that in nature one can find only *deus absconditus,* the hidden God. In his *The Bondage of the Will,* Luther opposes Erasmus by insisting that God's will is revealed in scripture but otherwise hidden and secret.[19] Luther uses God's refusal in Exodus 33:23 to grant Moses' request to see God's face, agreeing only to show him God's backside, to argue against constructing a view of God from nature: "For this inquisitiveness is original sin itself, by which we are impelled to strive for a way to God through natural speculation. But this is a great sin and a useless and futile attempt . . . ."[20] Perhaps the hiddenness of God shows us, as Hendel argues, that we can not know the fullness of God, but it also prevents us from using nature to construct positive, theological descriptions of God.

Luther's use of reason in his theology was at best ambiguous. At the Diet of Worms (1521) Luther said that he would not recant unless he could be shown by scripture and reason that he was in error, but he could also reject reason as a "whore."[21] Surely labelling reason as a prostitute is no basis for the integration of scientific reasoning with theology!

I would like to suggest a fifth approach to the relationship of faith and science, FAITH AND SCIENCE IN PARADOX. This understanding of how religion and science relate to each other is influenced by H. Richard Niebuhr's book, *Christ and Culture,* and his description of the "Lutheran" option, "Christ and Culture in Paradox."[22] This approach suggests that the relationship between faith and science is not one-dimensional. At times scientific evidence and experience supports or reinforces religious affirmations. Luther surely used his experience of nature to reinforce his theological views. The beauties of nature added reasons for his praise of God's grace and mercy. Whether through his support of the study of the sciences at the University of Wittenberg or through his enjoyment of the wonders of God's creation, especially in his garden, Luther viewed nature and its scientific study quite positively.[23] At other times science and religion follow separate and distinct paths. Luther's focus was on finding a gracious God through faith in Christ. Luther was convinced that the gracious God could be found only through revelation; nature could lead only to the hidden God—a God according to Luther who demanded righteousness and who was anything but gracious. At still other times science and religion may be in conflict. Luther's *Table Talk* comment about Copernicus might seem to suggest a conflict between faith and science. My discussion of this incident above, however, shows that it is wrongheaded to infer from this reference that Luther opposes science. Nonetheless, there are indeed times when faith and science conflict with each other —or at least, times when differences between religion and science need careful examination. The phrases "religious experience" and "scientific evidence" may suggest important similarities in the importance of data of some sort for both enterprises, but careful analysis will also show how different are the data accepted in each sphere. Perhaps by now a number of resolutions to the supposed conflict between evolution and creation have been proposed, but whether purpose can be seen in the evolutionary process and what the relationship is between the brain and the mind or soul are two questions that still engender conflict between scientists and people of faith.

This fifth approach, then, FAITH AND SCIENCE IN PARADOX, may be the most accurate way to describe the relation between science and faith, for that relationship is diverse and complex and cannot adequately be captured in a one-dimensional way. The paradox is that these two dialogue partners can also be in harsh conflict and that these adamant opponents can find themselves in utter agreement and that times also occur when they are like two ships passing in the night—or as Stephen Jay Gould would say, like "non-overlapping magisteria."

Luther has one more, and perhaps most important, contribution to make to the dialogue between faith and science. One of the fundamental tenets of Luther's theology was the "priesthood of all believers." In his questioning the status of ordination as a sacrament in *On the Babylonian Captivity of the Church* Luther proclaims, ". . . all of us that have been baptized are equally priests" and "therefore we are all priests, as many of us as are Christians."[24] Luther did not mean that all believers are priests but that all believers have equally important ministries in the eyes of God. Monks and nuns, priests and bishops are not higher than other believers in some hierarchy of Christian virtue or status before God. Moreover, as priests we serve one another. We are called to enact Luther's famous summary of the Christian life in *The Freedom of the Christian*: "A Christian is a perfectly free lord of all, subject to none; a Christian is a perfectly dutiful servant of all, subject to all."[25] Another way of putting this is that all believers have a ministry to carry out whatever their status or position in life. This translates into the sense that all Christians have a "vocation," a calling from God to live out their Christian life in whatever they do and through whatever relationships they have. Therefore scientists too have a vocation, a calling to use their scientific talents and positions in ways that serve God's will. I believe we can say this of any scientist, but at least it is true of scientists who are Christian. Christian scientists have a vocation to use their scientific gifts to "love their neighbors," a typical emphasis of Luther based on the command of Jesus that believers are to love God with all their heart, soul, and mind and to love their neighbors as themselves.[26]

I believe that an important corollary of this sense of vocation for scientists who are Christian is that the church should recognize and affirm their calling as scientists. Rather than seeing scientists in their midst as dangerous or indifferent to faith, congregations would do well to affirm their vocations as scientists and give them opportunities to share their work and express how their vocation is important to them as part of their life of faith. As medicine is a gift from God, so are scientists gifts from God to the church. The church has an important responsibility to acknowledge the scientists in its midst and to support the ministry they carry out through their scientific endeavors. This may be the most important dialogue between faith and science of all.

I would argue that it is a mistake to cast Luther as an enemy of science because of his off-handed comment about Copernicus. Better to see him as valuing the work of scientists as they engage in their baptismal calling of honoring God and serving neighbors.

Endnotes

1 Kurt K. Hendel, "'No Salvation Outside the Church' in Light of Luther's Dialectic of the Hidden and Revealed God," *Currents in Theology and Mission*, vol. 35, no. 4 (August 2008): 248-257.

2 Cf. Ian G. Barbour, *Religion in an Age of Science: The Gifford Lectures, Volume One* (San Francisco: Harper and Row, 1990), 3-30.

3 Galileo Galilei's letter of 1615 to Christine of Lorraine, Grand Duchess of Tuscany, available in translation in Stillman Drake, *Discoveries and Opinions of Galileo* (New York: Anchor-Doubleday, 1957), 173-216.

4 Stephen Jay Gould, "Nonoverlapping Magisteria," *Natural History* 106 (March 1997): 16-22.

5 William P. Brown, *The Seven Pillars of Creation: The Bible, Science, and the Ecology of Wonder* (New York: Oxford University Press, 2010), 17.

6 In his recent book, *Science and Faith*, John Haught proposes a set of three models for the relation of religion and science: *Conflict, Contrast,* and *Convergence.* "Contrast" compares

with "Independence" as described above. "Convergence" bears characteristics of both "Dialogue" and "Integration," although his Teilhardian sympathies skew it more toward "Integration." See John F. Haught, *Science and Faith: A New Introduction* (Mahwah, New Jersey: Paulist Press, 2012), 3-5.

7 Martin Luther, *Table Talk;* Vol. 54, *Luther's Works,* ed. and trans. Theodore G. Tappert; (Philadelphia, Fortress Press, 1967), 358-359.

8 Donald H. Kobe, "Copernicus and Martin Luther: an encounter between science and religion, " *American Journal of Physics* 66 (March 1998): 192.

9 See the introduction to Luther's *Table Talk.*

10 Werner Elert, *The Structure of Lutheranism,* vol. 1, trans. Walter A. Hansen (St. Louis: Concordia Publishing House, 1962), 421f.

11 See Kobe, "Copernicus and Luther," 190-196, for a most helpful and thorough discussion of Luther's comment about Copernicus in particular and his attitude toward science in general.

12 Martin Luther, *Lectures on Genesis: Chapters 1-5;*Vol. 1, *Luther's Works,* ed. Jaroslav Pelikan, trans. George Schick (St. Louis: Concordia Publishing House, 1958),47.

13 Martin Luther, *Temporal Authority: To What Extent It Should Be Obeyed; Luther's Works* Vol. 45, ed. and rev. Walther I. Brandt, trans. J. J. Schindel (Philadelphia: Fortress Press, 1962), 88-96.

14 Cf. Heinrich Bornkamm, *Luther's World of Thought*, trans. Martin H. Bertram (St. Louis: Concordia Publishing House, 1958), 176-194.

15 For a thorough account of Luther's attitude toward natural science in general and the "Copernicus affair" in particular see Werner Elert, *The Structure of Lutheranism* (St. Louis: Concordia Publishing House, 20013), 414-431.

16 Martin Luther, *Lectures on Genesis: Chapters 1-5* d. Jaroslav Pelikan, trans. George V. Schick and Paul D. Pahl (St. Louis: Concordia Publishing House, 1958), 41.

17 Ibid., 41-45. See also *Table Talk,* 172-173.

18 Wolfgang Böhner und Ronny Kabus, *Zur Geschichte des Wittenberger Gesundheits- und Sozialwesens, Teil 1: Von der Stadtfrühzeit bis zum Ende des 17. Jahrhunderts* (Stadtgeschichtlichen Museum Lutherstadt Wittenberg, 1981), 23-28.

19 Martin Luther, *The Bondage of the Will,* trans. Philip S. Watson, *Luther's Works* Vol. 33, ed. Philip S. Watson (Philadelphia: Fortress Press, 1972), 138-147.

20 Martin Luther, *Lectures on Genesis, Chapters 26-30, Luther's Works* Vol. 5, ed. Jaroslav Pelikan, trans. George V. Schick and Paul D. Pahl (St. Louis: Concordia Publishing House, 1968), 44.

21 Martin Luther, "Luther at the Diet of Worms, 1521," trans. Roger A. Hornsby, *Luther's Works* Vol. 32, ed. George W. Forell (Philadelphia: Muhlenberg Press, 1958), 112. "The Last Sermon in Wittenberg," Vol. 51, *Luther's Works,* ed. and trans. John W. Doberstein (Philadelphia: Muhlenberg Press, 1959), 377 and 379.

22 H. Richard Niebuhr, *Christ and Culture* (New York: Harper and Row, 1951).This approach was suggested to me by Pastor George Koch, a pastoral colleague and fellow supporter of faith and science dialogue, in our conversations about the relationship between religion and science.

23 See especially *"Beschäftigung mit der Schöpfung"* in Elke Strauchenbruch, *Luthers Paradiesgarten* (Leipzig: Evangelische Verlagsanstalt, 2015), 53-60.

24 Martin Luther, *The Babylonian Captivity of the Church*, trans. A. T. W. Steinhäuser, rev. Frederick C. Ahrens and Abdel Ross Wentz, Vol. 36, *Luther's Works*, ed. Abdel Ross Wentz (Philadelphia, Muhlenberg Press, 1959), 112-13.

25 Martin Luther, *The Freedom of a Christian*, trans. W. A. Lambert, rev. Harold J. Grimm, *Luther's Works* Vol. 31, ed. Harold J. Grimm (Philadelphia: Muhlenberg Press, 1957), 344. Cf. also 355.

26 Matthew 22: 34-40 and Mark 12: 28-34.

CHAPTER EIGHTEEN

They Can Do No Better Work

Luther on the Gift and Task of Parenting

Timothy Hiller

One of the important insights of hermeneutical philosophy is that an author does not control the meaning or reception of his or her text. This fact was brought home to me as Kurt Hendel worked on his great Johannes Bugenhagen translations. During this time, Kurt's wife, Jobey Hendel, graciously watched and helped raise our firstborn son, John. One day, when John was around two and just starting to speak, he spent the day at the Hendel's while Papa Kurt, as John affectionately called him, worked away in his study. That night, when I put John to bed, he mumbled, "Bugenhagen . . . Bugenhagen . . . Bugenhagen . . ." as he drifted off to sleep. Whatever other achievements it will receive, the Bugenhagen translations were a marvelous success for our household that night.

Because of the great gift Kurt and Jobey were to our family in helping raise our children, this essay concerns Luther's reflection on parenting. This question of parenting, however, occupies a strange space in contemporary theology. In more conservative denominations, parenting is a central, if not *the* central topic, of theological reflection—Christians are instructed to focus on the family, to be promise keepers, and to be good Christian mothers and fathers in order to raise godly children. Conservative Christian talk shows spend a large part of their programming on family roles, often blending reified traditional gender roles with practical advice to their listeners.[1] In more mainline and academic theological discussions, the issue of parenting is rarely addressed.[2] Perhaps this reticence arises as a corrective from the overemphasis family life receives in more conservative denominations; perhaps it is rooted in the academic study of theology's divorce from the church—even where theologians are active in the local parish, their conversations are rarely born out of pastoral considerations; or perhaps, academic theologians just think they do not have much to add. This negligence is unfortunate for the mission of the church, as the home is the primary place for the transmission of faith.

In this essay, I suggest that Martin Luther's reflections provide a framework for helping Christians understand the nature and task of parenting. Luther's reflections are important as they avoid many of the dangers in contemporary discourses on parenting and provide a structure for understanding one's duties and tasks in this role. I will first very briefly discuss the nature of contemporary discourses on parenting. I will then turn to Luther's own reflections as a compelling alternative to these pictures.

Contemporary Parenting

The question of how to best raise a child is a source of deep existential anxiety for most parents. Parents have at least some recognition of the importance of their own upbringing in the formation of their own identity, and, at the same time, they have a deep yearning for their own children to be successful and happy. Together, this leads to a deep vulnerability—the question that constantly confronts parents is How can I best raise my children? To help parents answer this question, there is a vast literature with many different voices, aims, and purposes. What this body of literature lacks in uniformity and coherence, it makes up for in bulk. I think there are at least two noteworthy trends in the literature.

First, there is a strong emphasis on parenting as technique. In an important book, *The Technological Society,* Jacques Ellul argues that the modern era is marked by the dominance of technology, by which he means a pervasive view that all questions, anxieties, and human problems can be solved through the application of rational techniques.[3] Applying this paradigm to family life, children are viewed as a project that can be manipulated, formed, and shaped through certain activities of the parents. If you want your child to be successful in life, the parent must adopt an appropriate method and technique. The appeal of such applications is obvious: While actual parenting is a fraught activity that is hard, confusing, and wrapped in uncertainty, parenting as technique provides clarity and security—if you do X, your child will turn out well.

In *The Mystery of the Child,* Martin Marty argues that this approach to childhood, which occurs everywhere from developmental psychologists to conservative writers like James Dobson, operates with "the implicit claim that the child can be understood, explained, and somehow cut to size, and thus will turn out in ways that will please adults with their various cultural preconceptions."[4] The problem, however, is that treating children as a project fails to honor the mystery and joy of each child. Instead of solely a project to manage, manipulate, and form, each child is gift to be loved.

Second, in both Christian and non-Christian discourses, the family has been elevated, idealized, and often treated as the center of one's life. Parents are encouraged through media depictions, social pressure, and their own internal desires to make the child the center of their universe. Parents are pressured to be at every game, to shield their child from disappointment and losses, and to make sure the child's life is as happy as possible. From the early emphasis on attachment parenting to the aggression some parents display at youth sporting events or the problem of helicopter parenting in college, the child easy becomes the source of value for the parent. Luther's celebrated description of the subjective meaning of God in the Large Catechism—"A 'god' is the term for that to which we are to look for all good and in which we are to find refuge in all need. . . . As I have often said, it is the faith and trust of the heart alone that make both God and an idol"—applies to much of the way parents elevate their children to be the source of value and meaning in their life.[5] The child is not simply loved, but idolized. Instead of a good creation, the child is loved as a Creator. While it is undoubtedly good to love the child, love has barriers and limits, and these limits are infringed upon in much contemporary life.[6]

The Child as Gift and Parenting as a Task

Luther's reflections on parenting are deeply theological.[7] Parenting does not occur in a secular sphere apart from God or God's Word, but its aim, joys, and tasks are grounded in the abundant goodness of God. To investigate Luther's understanding of parenting requires us first to investigate his understanding of the God who lavishes good gifts upon all the creation.

Luther's fundamental understanding of God is that God is the one who gives good gifts freely and abundantly. In his commentary on Psalm

118, Luther notes that God is the fount of all blessings, the one who always gives good gifts to all people. God is nothing except "goodness in action."[8] To understand God is to see that God gives good gifts continually and copiously and always and everywhere does concrete acts of goodness. Whereas humans exist in relationships of reciprocity, in which one expects acknowledgment in return for good gifts, God gifts categorically: "God is good, but not a human being is good; from the very bottom of His heart He is inclined to help and do good continually. . . . God abundantly and convincingly proves His friendly and gracious favor by His daily and everlasting goodness, as the psalmist writes: 'His steadfast loves endures forever'; that is, He unceasingly showers the best upon us."[9]

For Luther, this vision of God as the fount of all goodness entails that creation itself is a gift. All of creation is a great gift of God and these gifts are directly experienced in all facets of life. Because creation is a gift of God, Luther's understanding of God's gifts are comprehensive: our body, the cosmos, the forces that sustain life, our daily necessities, as well as the substance of human life (economy, home, marriage, land) are all created and given to us by God:

> He is the Creator of our bodies and souls, our Protector by day and by night, and the Preserver of our lives. He causes the sun and the moon to shine on us, fire, air, water, and the heavens to serve us. He causes the earth to give food, fodder, wine, grain, clothes, wood, and all necessities. He provides us with gold and silver, house and home, wife and child, cattle, birds, and fish. In short, who can count it all? And all this is bountifully showered upon us every year, every day, every hour, and every minute. Who could measure even this one goodness of God, that He gives and preserves a healthy eye or hand?[10]

In this economy of grace, in which God gives gifts freely to the created order, Luther locates the child. The first and most important fact of the child is that he or she is a gift given by God freely and without human merit to the parents. In his commentary on Psalm 147, Luther underlines this point by appealing to the power of God: while God does not need to use human means to act, God nevertheless appoints humans to fulfill God's purposes. Just as God could have defeated Israel's enemies by God's own power, so too, God could create the child spontaneously without human aid. Yet God does not do this; rather, God works through the parents to give the good gift of children. God did not need us, but gives us the great joy of having children to serve.[11] The first task incumbent upon parents, then, is to rejoice and give thanks for the gift of children.

This point, while perhaps obvious from Luther's perspective, counters a lot of contemporary parenting discourse. Before one treats the child as a project and problem, before one attempts to impose one's will on the child, parents must remember that the child is fundamentally a gift graciously bestowed upon us by God.

Luther, however, is not naïve. Children, like everything else in the created order, are infected by original sin. Christian parenting occurs, not in some dreamland, but under the burdens and strains of this fallen life.[12] Parenting is a joy and gift, but it is also a daily challenge. Not only can children be obstinate, throw fits, refuse to eat their dinner, stay up all night, and destroy all the nice things a parent owns, but, at a personal level, children can take away the parent's freedom and peace. Instead of spending a night relaxed, one ends up changing diapers, doing laundry, tending to sick children, and struggling to get just a few hours of sleep. This realism, Luther claims, leads natural reason to despise the task of parenting. In "The Estate of Marriage," he writes:

> Now observe that when that clever harlot, our natural reason (which the pagans follow in trying to be most clever), takes a look at married life, she turns up her nose and says, "Alas, must I rock the baby, wash its diapers, make its bed, smell its stench, stay up nights with it, take care of it when it cries, heal its rashes and sores, and on top of that care for my wife, provide for her, labor at my trade, take care of this and take care of that, do this and do that, endure this and endure that, and whatever else of bitterness and drudgery married life involves? What, should I make such a prisoner of myself? O you poor, wretched fellow, have you taken a wife? Fie, fie upon such wretchedness and bitterness! It is better to remain free and lead a peaceful, carefree life; I will become a priest or a nun and compel my children to do likewise."[13]

For Luther, the natural self feels burdened by parenting and yearns for the freedom of the monastery.

Luther's acknowledgment of the struggles of parenting is a reminder against the idolatry of parenting that centers one's own joy in the success of the child. The child is a gift and can bring joy, but the child is not the ultimate good for the individual. To place one's trust here is to replace God with something that is most certainly not God.

Nevertheless, Luther argues, the burden of parenting is not the final word; in light of God's Word, these tedious tasks take on a different hue. Drawing on God's command to all creatures to be fruitful and multiply in Genesis 1:28, Luther claims that the task of parenting, far from being a mere burden, is actually an activity that brings God great joy. The Word of God enacts a transformation of vision: what appears to be menial labor under the eyes of the world appears, in the eyes of faith, to be a holy, wonderful action in which God rejoices. Because God instituted the station of parenting as a means of preserving life and gives the gift of the child to the parents, God takes pleasure in the parent's labor. Because God has created, blessed, and given us children, all we do on behalf of the child pleases God. To have the knowledge and security that our actions cause God to rejoice is among the richest treasures in all of life. Luther writes:

> What then does the Christian faith say to this? It opens its eyes, looks upon all these insignificant, distasteful, and despised duties in the Spirit, and is aware that they are all adorned with divine approval as with the costliest gold and jewels. It says, 'O God, because I am certain that thou hast created me as a man and hast from my body begotten this child, I also know for a certainty that it meets with thy perfect pleasure. I confess to thee that I am not worthy to rock the little babe or wash its diapers, or to be entrusted with the care of the child and its mother. How is it that I, without any merit, have come to this distinction being certain that I am serving thy creature and thy most precious will? O how gladly will I do so, though the duties should be even more insignificant and despised. Neither frost nor heat, neither drudgery nor labor, will distress or dissuade me, for I am certain that it is thus pleasing in thy sight.'[14]

To find joy in parenting, thus, is dependent on the Word of God. Without the promise we are either left with parenting as a burden, which leads to resentment, or to investing our joy in the child, which leads to idolatry. By locating the good of parenting in God's Word, however, Luther helps frame parenting as a task whose joy comes not simply by the child's success, but in the God who loves and gives to us.

For Luther, the fact that God entrusted children into the care of parents places special duties, tasks, and limits on parents. In an occasional piece from 1524, "That Parents Should Neither Compel nor Hinder the Marriage of Their Children and that Children Should not Become Engaged without Their Parents' Consent," Luther details the duty and aim of the parents. At the most fundamental level, like all persons in positions of authority, the parent's task is to build up the child. "Now Paul says in 1 Corinthians 16 that even the very highest authority namely, to preach the gospel and govern souls, was granted by God for building up and not for destroying. How much less, then, should the authority of parents, or any other authority, have been given for destroying rather than exclusively for building up."[15] This emphasis on building up demarcates the limits of parenting: A parent is not a parent if he or she destroys or harms the child. To use a child for one's economic advancement or for one's own pleasure, to abuse one's authority, or to force a child to conform to one's own will is to renege on the trust God has granted the individual. While parents have authority over the child, the aim of this power is towards upbuilding and edification. Luther continues:

> It is quite certain therefore that parental authority is strictly limited; it does not extend to the point where it can wreak damage and destruction to the child, especially to its soul. If then a father forces his child into a marriage without love, he oversteps and exceeds his authority. He ceases to be a father and becomes a tyrant who uses his authority not for building up—which is why God gave it to him—but for destroying. He is taking authority into his own hands without God, indeed, against God.[16]

To be a good Christian parent is thus to seek the child's welfare; to seek the self over the child is to misappropriate God's gift.

What does it mean to build up the child? For Luther, the fundamental duty of the parent is to train children to love, worship, and serve God. Gottfried Maron argues that in his rejection of monasticism, Luther placed the Christian household as the primary place in which persons live out their faith. In Luther's reordering of the world, the parents function like a monastic abbot; their primary duty is to look after the spiritual health of their children.[17] Both mothers and fathers are to be apostles and priests to their children and to share the good news of the gospel with them. This is a great joy and pleasure of parenting. In a famous passage, Luther writes,

> The greatest good in married life, that which makes all suffering and labor worthwhile, is that God grants offspring and commands that they be brought up to worship and serve him. In all the world this is the noblest and most precious work, because to God there can be nothing dearer than the salvation of souls. Now since we are all duty bound to suffer death, if need be, that we might bring a single soul to God, you can see how rich the estate of marriage is in good works. God has entrusted to its bosom souls begotten of its own body, on whom it can lavish all manner of Christian works.

It is important to see here that Luther affirms that both mother and father are to be priests to the children. The task of preaching the gospel is mutual and the tasks are to be shared: just as the father is to wash diapers, so too both the mother is tasked with preaching and training her children in Christian faith.[18]

While the duty to raise a child in faith is by far the most important role a parent plays, Luther fears that most parents neglect this role. Instead of viewing the child as entrusted to their care for the glory and worship of God, parents see the good of the child either in terms of a future economic gain, and thus train them solely for a prosperous vocation, or as a source of joy in themselves. While a parent must work to provide for the physical well-being of a child, economics must always be secondary to faith formation. Precisely because God gives parents the child, parents must be obedient to God and bring their children up in faith. In the Large Catechism, Luther writes,

> Instead, parents should keep in mind that they owe obedience to God, and that, above all, they should earnestly and faithfully discharge the duties of the office, not only to provide for the material support of their children, servants, subject, etc., but especially to bring them up to the praise and honor of God. Therefore do not imagine that the parental office is a matter of your pleasure and whim. It is a strict commandment and injunction of God, who holds you accountable for it.[19]

The injunction to raise children well is serious; if you fail to raise your children well, Luther claims that you can earn hell for yourself, no matter what the rest of your life is like.[20]

Because faith formation is so central, Luther vigorously defends the importance of educating youth. In numerous essays, Luther argues that we must educate the young so that they can be leaders in the church and grow in spiritual knowledge. To put a child into a trade before he or she can read and study the Scripture is to treat them as a means for future economic gain and not to attend to their spiritual health. Education is necessary, precisely for the spiritual health of children and the church.[21]

The task of preaching to the young requires the parent to accommodate the good news to their child's understanding. Luther illustrates this beautifully in a letter he wrote to his first son, Hans Luther, on his fourth birthday. In this letter, Luther encourages his son to grow in faith through committing himself faithfully to his studies. This letter displays the heart, warmth, kindness and encouragement a parent should display in teaching faith. Luther writes,

> I know of a pretty, gay, and beautiful garden where there are many children wearing golden robes. They pick up fine apples, pears, cherries, and plums under the trees, and they sing, jump, and are happy all the time. They also have nice ponies with golden reins and silver saddles. I asked the owner of the garden who the children were. He replied: "These are children who love to pray, learn their lessons, and be good." Then I said: "Dear sir, I also have a son. His name is Hans Luther. May he too enter the garden, eat of the fine apples and pears, ride on these pretty ponies, and play with the other children?" The man answered: "If he likes to pray and study and is good, he may enter the garden, and also Lippus and Jost. And when they are all together there, they shall get whistles, drums, lutes, and other musical instruments, and they shall dance and shoot with little crossbows.". . . Therefore, dear Hans, continue to learn your lessons and pray, and tell Lippus and Jost to pray too, so that all of you may get into the garden together.[22]

Luther's exhortations are creative, appealing, and encouraging. To show God's love, to encourage faith in children, parents must employ imagination and kindness and warmth.

So far I have argued that Luther provides a framework for understanding the role and task of faithful parenting. Parents are to view their child as a gift, to treat them in line with God's command, and to rear them in

SUBJECT TO NONE, SERVANT OF ALL

the faith. The final point that Luther experienced, more than explicitly reflected upon, concerns the vulnerability of parenting. For Luther, living under the reign of sin entails that Christians, like everyone else, will suffer tragedy and experience deep loss. All human beings are vulnerable to the evil forces of sin, death, and the devil.[23] From 1526 to 1534, Luther and Katharina welcomed six children: John (1526), Elizabeth (1527), Magdalena (1529), Martin (1531), Paul (1533), and Margaret (1534). Tragically, two of Luther's daughters died young: Elizabeth as an eight month old, probably infected with the plague, and the deeply beloved Magdalena, who died in Luther's arms at the age of 14.[24] The loss of these two children caused Luther enormous grief and sorrow. Concerning Magdalena, he wrote to Justus Jonas:

> You will have heard of the new birth into the kingdom of Christ of my daughter Magdalena. Though my wife and I ought in reality to have no other feeling than one of profound gratitude for her happy escape from the power of the flesh, the world, the Turk and the devil, yet the force of natural affection is so great that we cannot support our loss without constant weeping and bitter sorrow—a thorough death of the heart so to speak. We have ever before us her features, her words, her gestures, her every action in life and death—my darling, my all-dutiful, all-obedient daughter. Even the death of Christ (and what are all other deaths in comparison with that?) cannot tear her from my thought, as it ought.[25]

To be a parent is to open oneself up to a profound vulnerability. Parents naturally love their child deeply; to lose a child is to enter a space where even the greatest comfort of the Word of God cannot always provide consolation. The sorrow of a lost child is a deep wound that stands beyond much grief. Even as one can acknowledge the joyful welcome of the child in heaven, to be a parent in the flesh is to mourn and grieve in life. Luther's sorrow was not limited or brief. In a letter of consolation written to Andrew Osiander in 1545, Luther acknowledges that his sadness abided and remained years later:

> I know from the death of my own dearest child how great must be your grief. It may appear strange, but I am still mourning the death of my dear Magdalena, and I am not able to forget her. Yet I know surely that she is in heaven,

that she has eternal life, and that God has thereby given me a true token of his love in having, even while I live, taken my flesh and blood to his Fatherly heart.[26]

Christian hope offers some consolation, but the grief over the loss of a child does not go away while we are in the flesh. To be a parent is to love deeply and to open oneself to all the vulnerabilities this entails.

Even as parenting can lead to deep sorrow and pain, Luther is confident that parenting is a great gift of God. While parenting is stressful, unglamorous, and leads to great vulnerability, Christians can rejoice in it, as it is a work that pleases God. In "A Sermon on the Estate of Marriage," Luther offers this assurance: "But this at least all married people know. They can do no better work and do nothing more valuable for God, for Christendom, for all the world, and for their children than to bring up their children well."[27] For the joy, task, and gift of parenting, we owe it to God to thank and praise, serve and obey. We can do no better work.

Endnotes

1 Sirius XM Radio, for example, has a full channel devoted fully to Christian family talk.

2 An exception to this is Bromleigh McCleneghen and Lee Hull Moses, *Hopes and Fears: Everyday Theology for New Parents and Other Tired, Anxious People* (Herndon, Virginia: Alban Institute, 2012).

3 Jacques Ellul, *The Technological Society*, trans. John Wilkinson (New York: Vintage Books, 1964).

4 Martin Marty, *The Mystery of the Child* (Grand Rapids: William B. Eerdmans Publishing Co., 2007), 49.

5 Martin Luther, "The Large Catechism," in *The Book of Concord: The Confessions of the Evangelical Lutheran church*, eds. Robert Kolb and Timothy Wengert (Minneapolis: Fortress Press, 2000), 386.

6 Anecdotally, over-parenting seems to be delaying the maturation of children. I was recently at an academic discussion on teaching incoming first-year students. The speakers repeated that most college freshman display the emotional independence from their parents of what fourteen year olds displayed in the early 2000s.

7 For background on this question, see Steven E. Ozment, *When Fathers Ruled: Family Life in Reformation Europe* (Cambridge, Massachusetts: Harvard University Press, 1983); Merry E Wiesner, *Women and Gender in Early Modern Europe* (Cambridge: Cambridge University Press, 1993); Scott H. Hendrix, "Luther on Marriage," *Lutheran Quarterly* 14 (2000): 335-350; Mickey L. Mattox "Luther on Eve, Women, and the church," *Lutheran Quarterly* 17 (2003): 456-474.

8 LW 14:50; WA 31-1, 7425-27.

9 LW 14:47; WA 31-1, 69.24-30.

10 LW 14:46-47, WA 31-I. 69.31-70.5.

11 "God uses us to give gifts. Children are God's gifts to us and for them we should be thankful. They happen by God for us. God could give children without using men and women. But God does not want to do this. Instead, God joins man and woman so that it appears to be a work of man and woman, and yet God does it under the cover of such masks. We have the saying: 'God gives every good thing, but not just by waving a wand.' God gives all good gifts; but you must lend a hand and take the bull by the horns; that is, you must work and thus give God good cause and a mask." LW 14: 114-115; WA 31:436.

12 Paul Althaus, *The Ethics of Martin Luther,* trans. Robert Schultz (Minneapolis: Fortress Press, 2007), 83-100.

13 LW, 45:39.

14 LW, 14:39-40.

15 LW 45:386.

16 LW 45:386.

17 Gottfried Maron, "*Vom Hindernis zur Hilfe: Die Frau in der Sicht Martin Luthers*," *Theologische Zeitschrift* 39, no. 5 (1983): 280.

18 Mickey L. Mattox, "Luther on Eve, Women, and the church," *Lutheran Quarterly* 17 (2003): 456-474.

19 Martin Luther, "The Large Catechism," in *The Book of Concord*, 409.

20 "Think what deadly harm you do when you are negligent and fail to bring up your children to be useful and godly. You bring upon yourself sin and wrath, thus earning hell by the way you have reared your own children, no matter how holy and upright you may be otherwise." Martin Luther, The Large Catechism, 410.

21 See, for example, the 1524 *To the Councilmen of All Cities in Germany that They Establish and Maintain Christian Schools*, LW 45:339-378.

22 Martin Luther, "Luther to Son John Luther June 19, 1530," in *Luther: Letters of Spiritual Counsel*, trans. and ed. Theodore G. Tappert (Vancouver: Regent College Publishing, 1960), 144-145.

23 In *Fourteen Consolations* from 1520, he writes, "No man is safe from the evils that befall any other, for what one has suffered another may also suffer." LW 42: 127; WA VI: 108, 16-24.

24 Tappert, *Luther: Letters of Spiritual Counsel*, 51: "When his daughter was in the agony of death, he fell upon his knees before the bed and, weeping bitterly, prayed that God might save her if it be his will. Thus she gave up the ghost in the arms of her father. Her mother was in the same room but was farther from the bed on account of her grief. "

25 Quoted in John Shaw Banks, *Martin Luther: the Prophet of Germany* (London: Hayman Brothers and Lilly, 1887), 79.

26 Martin Luther "To Andrew Osiander June 3, 1545" in *Luther: Letters of Spiritual Counsel*, 80-81.

27 LW 44:12.

CHAPTER NINETEEN

Reading the Bible as "Lutherans" in the Twenty-First Century

Ralph W. Klein

The quotation marks on the word "Lutherans" are part of the dilemma. The professors who teach exegesis to future pastors at our ELCA seminaries study at the same graduate schools as their Roman Catholic and Reformed counterparts, publish in the same journals, belong to the same scholarly societies, and employ the same methods. In what ways do we read the Bible as Lutherans?

While there are still major theological and liturgical differences among the major Christian church bodies, the ecumenical movement in general and the ELCA's ecumenical decisions in particular have reduced polemics and recognized more than a little unity amid our diversity. The ELCA has six "full communion" partners.

Reading the Bible as Lutherans should not lead to any triumphalist claims about the superiority of our exegesis, and many of our ecumenical partners might recognize commonalities in their and our biblical interpretation even when we claim distinctiveness. In this brief essay I will lift up characteristic emphases which I expect to find in Lutheran exegesis.

The Basis of the Bible's Authority

My theological stance, like that of my dear colleague and friend Kurt K. Hendel himself, has been dramatically shaped by the Seminex experience. Our critics back in the 1960s and 1970s located the Bible's authority in its inspiration and inerrancy. We too recognized the Spirit's central role in the composition and preservation of the scriptures, but we knew that Moses did not write the Pentateuch or Isaiah all sixty-six chapters and that the Bible contained historical, geographical, and other "errors." The Bible is not a perfect book. What gives the Bible its authority is its central, saving message, that is, the gospel. By the word gospel we referred to what was accomplished in the life, death, and resurrection of Jesus. That central, saving message is expressed somewhat differently in the Old Testament, but the God of the two testaments is emphatically identical. The Old Testament proclaims a gracious, promising, covenant-making God, who calls people together into the community of faith and transforms them into doers of justice and righteousness.

Neither the Bible's inerrancy nor even its canonicity is at the center of the authority question. When Luther translated all twenty-seven books of the New Testament in 1522, he created a table of contents that gave numbers only to the first twenty-three, omitting numbers for the books of Hebrews, James, Jude, and Revelation, whose place in the canon was by no means clear to Luther. Most of us Lutherans do not share Luther's critique of these books, but his main point was that what gives the words of Scripture their authority is the way they announce the central message of salvation. In the 660-page *Book of Concord* of 1580, there is no listing of the books that belong to the canon. Contrast that to the Westminster Confession and the Council of Trent! Lutherans have a kind of canon within the canon—the Bible's central saving message—and this emphasis persists in the twenty-first century.

Reading the Bible Critically

We have already mentioned the modern findings about the authorship and dating of biblical books. Even during my career, the scholarly dating of Old Testament books has gotten later and later. The present form of Daniel is at least four centuries later than pre-critical scholars believed. Mark is probably the first Gospel, later than all of Paul's seven authentic letters. In addition to these standard introductory conclusions, we also criticize the content of the biblical books. Patriarchy is a common blight in both testaments. Both testaments in large part condone slavery, and the New Testament in far too many verses is anti-Judaistic. The theology of Holy War tried to show the futility of trusting in military armaments and emphasized the insignificance of human numbers in military victory, but its justification for offering up the enemy as a sacrifice to God is scandalous. In other words, God's Word comes to us in words of human authors. These authors were people of their time, with the presuppositions of their time. Does the origin of the earth go back about 4,000 years or four and a half billion years? It is all too evident that we who count ourselves theologians are also creatures of our time. We try to recognize our own presuppositions, not always successfully. The recent debates about homosexuality in the ELCA often failed to recognize how culturally conditioned the few biblical passages dealing with this subject are and how notions like sexual orientation, which many of us take for granted, was totally unknown by the biblical authors.

We customarily talk today about the social location of the biblical interpreter—his or her gender, ethnicity, and social class. And what about the social location of the biblical writers? They were probably almost all male. They could read and write, an achievement separating themselves from at least 97 percent of the population. Inter-faith appreciations of the religion of the other characterize neither testament.

We read the Bible inevitably from a critical perspective, but we recognize that the biblical authors' testimony to their experience of God often puts our feeble testimony to shame. We recognize that the challenges of their times were daunting indeed, and that their testimony to the faith could lead to martyrdom. Christian sisters and brothers over the years have rightly acknowledged the powerful testimony of the Bible's authors. We also recognize that the Bible is critical of our attitudes and idolatries, our complacency with evil.

What it Meant and What it Might Mean

This famous distinction of Krister Stendahl (1921-2008), the late Lutheran biblical scholar, has a fair number of critics. Stendahl was too optimistic that scholarship eventually could come to a common understanding of what the text meant. What we exegetes bring to the table does not easily allow us to decide objectively exactly what the text meant. But Stendahl had his point in that through the dialogue and debate of scholarship we do eventually come to common understandings of the original meaning or at least understandable disagreements.

Stendahl recognized more importantly that after describing what the text might have meant comes the bilingualism of the biblical scholar: What might that ancient text mean today? Two millennia have flown by since the New Testament was written, and hundreds of additional years since the Old Testament was finalized. Just think of the things that have changed: the age of the earth and its roundness; the "discovery" of North and South America; the development of the church from the few gathered around Jesus to the billions who have identified themselves as Christ's disciples; the Catholic/Orthodox split of the eleventh century and the Roman Catholic/Protestant split of the sixteenth century; the lengthening of lifespan from the 40s in biblical times to the 70s and 80s today; the invention of airplanes and nuclear weapons capable of destroying much of human life; the overpopulation of the earth; the environmental crisis; the divisions in church and society caused by ethnicity, race, and class; the continuous development of other great religions; the rise of capitalism; the secularization of the West—the list could go on, but my point is surely clear. Once biblical interpreters think they understand what the text of the Bible said, they have to ask themselves what that text might mean today.

Tradition—creeds and confessions, liturgy, hymns, the great theological thinkers of the last 2,000 years, everyday witness to the meaning of the faith—helps, but also hinders. Once the congregation has heard readings from the Old Testament, the epistles, and the gospels, preachers try to indicate the significance of those texts for the diverse set of listeners sitting before them. In the biblical world people married in their teens to partners whom their parents had chosen. In the small scale agriculture of the Old Testament, the gender roles were less hierarchical than in modern life, whereas both men and women now work outside the home and at unequal wages. Questions about the beginning of life (e.g., in vitro fertilization) and the ending of life (e.g., removal of life support) are far different and far more complex today. Let's not forget the elephant in the room: A high percentage of Christians today have a very thin understanding of what the Bible says or does not say. The translation from what the Bible meant back then to what it might mean today also involves the whole community. Defining what the text might mean is an assignment for Lutherans and for the whole Christian movement.

The Lutheran Interpreter and Martin Luther

I have already indicated my deep debt to Luther for his clear identification of the source of the Bible's authority, and I have spent many riveting hours reading his exegetical works. Luther lived five centuries ago, before the Enlightenment and the rise of biblical criticism, before the discoveries of modern archaeology and the recovery of the Ancient Near East, and obviously before 500 years of subsequent biblical study.

As an Old Testament scholar I am often puzzled, and sometimes quite perplexed, by his interpretation of the Hebrew Bible. For Luther Genesis 3:15 was one of the most important texts of the Bible. In his biblical translations he noted marginally: "This is the first gospel and promise of Christ on earth, to the effect that he will overcome sin, death, and hell and save us from the power of the Serpent."[1] While this reading goes back ultimately to Irenaeus (ca. 125-202) in the second century, it is almost universally rejected in critical scholarship. Luther's scandalous attacks on the Jews in his later life have now shown to be quite characteristic of his writings throughout his life. For Luther the true Jew has always been a *de facto* Christian. What's more, "The historical accounts of the kings and of the judges and finally that frightful crime when they crucified the Son of God and their Messiah [are designed to show what the fallen human is by nature]."[2]

A Lutheran reading of the Old Testament can often find an approach to the deity that is echoed in the New Testament. Luther never tired of talking about the righteousness of God and how this means that God's wrath is trumped by God's grace. Lexical study of the term "righteousness" in the Old Testament demonstrates that righteousness involves living up to the requirements of a relationship. That definition of righteousness works with God's actions and with human actions. Take Genesis 15:6: "He [Abram] believed in the LORD; and he [the LORD] reckoned it to him [Abram] as righteousness." When Abram and Sarai worried about God's promises to give them an heir, God increased the promise: You will have as many children as the stars. In this translation of the text, Abram did what was expected in such a promissory relationship: He trusted in the promise.

Many scholars today would propose an alternate translation of Genesis 15:6: "Abram believed the LORD; and he [Abram] reckoned it to him [the LORD] as righteousness." In this reading of the text, Abram recognized that the LORD's doubling down on the promise is typical divine activity: The LORD lived up to the expectations that Abram had of the relationship. In either translation of the verse, righteousness means living up to the expectations of a relationship. A Christian would recognize that the New Testament confesses that God doubled down on his relationship with humanity by sending his Son. And the Christian recognizes that God expects humanity to live up to the demands of the relationship inaugurated by God in ways that go far being "keeping the rules." In the ambiguities of human life, the believer asks, "How can I love God and the neighbor in this particular circumstance?"

Or take another favorite Old Testament passage: Hosea 11:1-9. Pre-critical scholarship focused on verse 1: "When Israel was a child, I loved him, and out of Egypt I called my son." Matthew interpreted this as fulfilled in the return of Joseph, Mary, and Jesus from the flight into Egypt (Matthew 2:15). Matthew was using a type of first-century exegesis attested also at Qumran: All Scripture deals with the end time; we live in the end time; all Scripture is directly about us. Matthew and other New Testament writers were intent to show that their experience of Jesus was in continuity with their Bible, what we call the Old Testament or the Hebrew Bible. Modern readers are trained to read passages in context: If Hosea 11:1-2 is taken literally and if verse 1 applies to Jesus, verse 2 would seem to make him a devotee of Baal.

A modern critical reader would interpret Hosea as speaking to his contemporaries rather than predicting the distant future. Despite the LORD rescuing Israel from Egypt in the Exodus, many Israelites became followers of Baal. The following verses demonstrate God's parental, even maternal love. God taught Israel how to walk (v. 3) and lifted them lovingly to God's cheeks and fed them (v. 4). Despite all this, God's people are bent on turning away from God (v. 7). What one might expect is an outbreak of divine anger, as God did at Sodom and Gomorrah.[3] Instead God contradicts divine wrath with divine love because "I am God and no mortal" (v. 9). This contradiction of divine wrath by divine love is also central throughout the New Testament.

I believe these examples of modern critical readings of passages from Genesis and Hosea demonstrate clearly the continuity in the character of God through both testaments. Christian readers find that their understanding of the New Testament story agrees with understandings of the God of the Old Testament. This, of course, does not mean that the believers in the Old Testament were Christians, but they were faithful.

Conclusion

In this essay I have explored themes that I expect to find in Lutheran readings of the Bible: the basis for biblical authority, a critical reading of the biblical text, a struggle to translate what the Bible meant into what it might mean today. Other Christian interpreters may well recognize continuities with their own understanding of Scripture. As Lutherans we are deeply indebted to the contributions of the great Reformer. But we can also see where a modern reading of the Old Testament can transcend the limits of Luther's own exegesis and lend support to some of his central affirmations about the righteousness of God and the ethics of the Christian life, and how in both testaments God's wrath is finally contradicted by God's love.

Endnotes

1 All editions of Luther's translation of the Hebrew Bible/Old Testament contain this marginal comment at Gen 3:15. For the German original see LW DB 8:45.

2 For evaluation of Luther's anti-Judaistic tendencies see Brooks Schramm and Kirsi I. Sterna, eds., *Martin Luther, the Bible, and the Jewish People: A Reader* (Minneapolis: Fortress Press, 2012). Brooks Schramm has also studied these tendencies in *"Populus Dei:* Luther on Jacob and the Election of Israel (Genesis 25)" in *The Call of Abraham: Essays on the Election of Israel in Honor of Jon D. Levenson,* ed. Gary A. Anderson and Joel S. Kaminsky (Notre Dame: University of Notre Dame Press, 2013), 280-305.

3 Admah and Zeboiim are cities related to Sodom and Gomorrah (Deuteronomy 29:23).

CHAPTER TWENTY

"As Though Not"

A Wittenberg Sermon with a Preamble

Vítor Westhelle

On Sunday, October 21, 2012, I stepped into the pulpit of All Saints, the Castle Church in Wittenberg, to deliver the sermon for that Sunday's service. It was 495 years earlier (minus ten days), so the legend goes, a monk nailed to the door of that very church some theses for disputation, provoking a revolutionary movement called the Reformation. But significant also was the assigned text for that Sunday's homily, 1 Corinthians 7: 29-31. The reason of its importance follows here as a preamble to the actual sermon preached on that occasion.[1] The rendering into print of that sermon and this added preamble is dedicated to Kurt Hendel.

"What's Love Got to Do With It?"

Kurt K. Hendel, my colleague and friend, is a theologian whose commitment to Reformation studies has made him at home with Martin Luther (1483-1546), Johannes Bugenhagen (1488-1558), Philipp Melanchthon (1497 – 1560), etc. He lived as if sharing the main concerns that affected the homestead of the Wittenberg reformers. Yet he knows the rules of being a guest. Even while having so much provided by gracious hosts, he knows that nothing belongs to him. After his visitations, all in turn became Kurt's guests: in the classroom, in the pews, in office 316 at LSTC, or in the pages of his writings. One must learn to be a guest in order to become a good host.

Looking at the Reformation movement as a whole, Hendel did it from the privileged perspective of one of the closest associates of Luther, his pastor, and the one whose main mission was to implement the Reformation in many regions and cities: Johannes Bugenhagen.[2] If this was the perspective, the lenses through which the Reformation was read, what it brought to sight were some particular topics. Justification was at the center as the liberating gift of God to humans living under the tyranny of sin. If through faith this gift is received, then what? This left Hendel with two basic tasks in his agenda. The first was to explicate the incarnation as a testimony "that the material is a vehicle of the divine" through which by grace faith is obtained.[3] This in turn led him to the core of both the incarnation and the sacraments as expressed ultimately by the cross. The cross, as we learn, "constitutes the very heart of the Reformer's theology and informs all of his theological constructs," which indeed also "points to the very heart of the scriptural message."[4] However, while this core is addressed, and the reception of the gift through faith is truly passive, what about human works? Are they just "mortal sins" as Luther repeatedly claimed?[5] The second task, then, was to elucidate the relationship between grace and works, faith and love.[6] If faith must be kept clean from the pretentions of any work, Tina Turner's song takes a dazzling theological significance: "What's Love Got to Do with It?" What is love all about? Prompted by this question, the second task was placed in Hendel's lap.

Paul the Theologian and the Pastor: Luther and Bugenhagen

For both the above mentioned tasks, Paul's theology is "formative" for shaping the confessional program and the pastoral practice of the Wittenberg reformers. The doctrine of justification lies at its core and is its unerring focus, as it was expressed by Luther's reading of Paul the *theologian*. Yet this core cannot subsist but in the neighborly love as Bugenhagen saw elucidated by the *pastoral* Paul.[7] The Apostle to the Gentiles is the hub from which flow both streams that warrant the Reformation: the theology that grounds it and the pastoral-ethical practice that follows. Luther and Bugenhagen are the names that personify both, the theological-doctrinal and the ethical-pastoral pursuits, respectively. Using one or the other for accentuating either of the tasks certainly does not mean that the pastoral aspect is lacking in Luther or that the doctrinal aspect is deficient in Bugenhagen. The pastor and the theologian are certainly found in both, but each stand for a different emphasis.

Luther and Bugenhagen can be seen as epitomizing the two dimensions of Paul's thought as they were conceptualized by the reformers, and these two dimensions became the springboard for Kurt Hendel's teaching and writing. The reformers were opposed to the use of Paul in support of the use of good works as meritorious, for it implied the abandonment of the doctrinal aspect. Therefore the geographical areas in which the Reformation had a formative impact kept both dimensions of the Apostle. The use of Paul in social programs for the care of the poor was different in Roman Catholic regions, where he "remained primarily as a biblical example and authority cited in support of the care of the poor . . . rather than serving as a formative theological resource."[8] For Protestantism Paul remained both the theologian and the pastor.

The issue at stake is how to relate these two quests when faith and love are distinct and discrete dimensions of human existence and not stages in a continuous scale or quantities that can be added to each other. To explicate this duplex dimensionality Luther resorted precisely to Paul. "Concerning the verse in Galatians (5:6), 'faith working through love,' we also say that faith doesn't exist without works. However, Paul's view is this: Faith is active in love, that is, that faith justifies which expresses itself in acts. Faith comes first and then love follows."[9] The decisive point, however, is that there is no causality between the two; one does not attest to the other. On the contrary, in the very moment good works insinuate themselves as even an indication of faithfulness the opposite is the case: "The works of the righteous would be mortal sins if they would not be feared as mortal sins by the righteous themselves out of pious fear of God."[10] As far as faith is concerned, love has nothing to do with it, and yet wherever there is faith, there too must be love.

What remains at the core of Luther's theology as far as its relationship to ethics is concerned is expressed in its most concise form in *The Freedom of a Christian*. In this text, one of the three foundational essays of the Reformation published in 1520, Luther states with succinct clarity that a "Christian lives in Christ through faith and in the neighbor through love."[11] This counterposing of faith and love corresponds to Luther's affirmation that "being holy [*heilig sein*] and being saved [blessed—*selig sein*] are entirely different things." And he adds: "We are saved [*selig*] through Christ alone; but we become holy through this faith and these divine foundations and orders."[12] Here love is spelled out as that which takes place in what Luther defined as the *coram mundo* relation. *Coram deo* is a relation defined by faith alone; love is a term reserved for the human and institutional relations which take place in this world that is passing away.

In this respect the reformer is following the Pauline reduction of the double commandment of love to the love of the neighbor alone. Since Jacob Taubes' Heidelberg Seminar on "Paul's Political Theology" (1987), [13] this insight into Pauline theology took on central significance and generated an astonishing renaissance of Pauline studies even beyond theological circles. [14] This radical commandment of love of the neighbor is reserved precisely for this world that is passing. In this passing the love is uncompromisingly radical precisely because this passing renders vain any investment toward making it permanent, or extending it indefinitely. This constitutes idolatry and is the reason why works do not merit grace. They can only merit love—the love of the neighbor, the uncompromising love for those who are in this passing world, but awake for the "yet-time" (*ho nun kairos*) of messianic presence (*parousia*). [15]

Love the World—Trust the Shabbat

One particular text, 1 Corinthians 7: 29-31, of Paul has been regarded "a remarkable passage that may be his [Paul's] most rigorous definition of messianic life." [16] In it all turns around the expression *hos mē*, "as not" (or "as though not"), which is repeated five times in these three verses. Luther refers to this passage several times in his writings. [17] In the Genesis Commentary he uses it to explain how Abraham, being well off in affairs of the house and of the state, was still in exile, having means at his disposal, but not possessing them as ends. [18] But it is in his commentary on Psalm 68 that brings this passage to a sharp resolution interpreting the conditions of this world to which the "as-not" applies as boundaries that the faithful "peers with the awaking eyes of faith over . . . to the life beyond . . . and to celebrate the Sabbath." [19] Within these boundaries, however love is all that matters. Following Paul's reduction of love, this is how his argument goes: "For the sum and substance of the entire Gospel is faith in God and love of neighbor. . . . Faith points away from us toward God; love bears all things and points us toward our body, that is, toward our neighbor." [20]

Luther reads the sheepfolds of Psalm 68:13 as the transitory confines or boundaries of what constitutes this world that passes and the staying within those frontiers as a state of sleeping. [21] This is then juxtaposed to peering "with the awaken eyes of faith over these boundaries." As such, the comparison leads naturally to Paul's own summons to being awake for the messianic *kairos* in the very midst of this world, in its passing, in its utter transience, in its being bound to *chronos*. The boundaries are

SUBJECT TO NONE, SERVANT OF ALL

the ones Luther defined in teachings about the institutional spheres of the transient world, about the constitution of the three worldly publics (*ecclesia, oeconomia, politia*). Within those publics, love finds its most sublime expression precisely because it calls for a detachment in dealing with this world for the sake of the other instead of taking it as a means of commerce to attain permanence. And this love is no sentimentality; it demands reason and efficacy for the sake of justice and equity. Reason and equity are the yardsticks that gauge love's efficacy in the affairs of this transient world. This is the reason why the legend, attributed to Luther, that he would plant today an apple tree if he knew the world would end tomorrow, is not at all a preposterous attribution. The legend suggests the purest act of love, the one that is done without the expectation of retribution, of reciprocation. In this regard Søren Kierkegaard (1813-1855) was faithful to Luther is saying that the love shown for a deceased one is the purest gesture of love because it invests in no return, entails no commerce. To love the world is not done in spite of its transience, but precisely because of it. Only by virtue of this transience, its passing away, can love be genuine.

Paul, and Luther following him, submits the love commandment to the reduction of loving the neighbor because love can only be shown toward transience, toward the world. To use the same word "love" in the human relationship toward God is an unsuitable choice of words. For Paul and those who followed his lead, as did Luther and the reformers, God is to be trusted and feared; the world is to be loved.

The Homily

Text: 1 Corinthians 7:29-31

> I mean, brothers and sisters, the appointed time has grown short; from now on, let even those who have wives be as though they had none, and those who mourn as though they were not mourning, and those who rejoice as though they were not rejoicing, and those who buy as though they had no possessions, and those who deal with the world as though they had no dealings with it. For the present form of this world is passing away.

Dear sisters and brothers, beloved community,

The text for today's homily is indeed appropriate to be delivered in this place and time. The verses from 1 Corinthians are fitting and timely for today's reflection here in this town, in this church. We are gathered here just ten days to the 495th anniversary of the symbolic event when Luther's 95 Theses were made public at the door of this church for town folk and the academic community, or so the legend goes. October 31 has since been regarded and celebrated as the launching day of the Reformation movement, even if people at the time barely grasped the dimension and far-reaching consequences of a not so uncommon gesture of a young monk, not even twenty-nine years old, making public display of his thoughts about the situation of the church and of society.

I say this because embedded in just these three verses are two of the central themes of Luther's theology: the ever coming presence of Christ and how we should live in a world into which the Messiah indeed comes. The first theme, as Paul phrases it, serves as a frame. It begins with verse 29 and closes at verse 31: "The appointed time (*kairos*) has grown short . . . the system of this world (or *das Wesen dieser Welt* as Luther correctly translates *schēma tou kosmou* in this context) is passing away." Translation of these words needs to be made clear. *Kairos*, the appointed time, is not ordinary time; it is not clock time, which is *chronos* in Greek. *Kairos* is an immeasurable moment pregnant with promises and assailed by trials that only one who is there in that packed instant and situation may attest to and experience its reality. It is not a time we spend in waiting, constantly consulting the watch; it is rather a time of hope and tribulation as if we were near a friend, a beloved one, or an enemy, an adversary. It is when and where life is lived in all its splendor and squalor. It is not just about beginning and end, but equally about the muddy middle. The city of Corinth was a classic example of this muddy middle where peril and promise, despair and hope held hands. It is thus a setting that begs a decision: To whom are we going to turn? A time of decision is at hand, soon to come, impending, adjacent to us, and coming to us. This is, for Paul, the time and space of the Christian community; the time and place of Christ himself. *Kairos* is a messianic time. Hence it is the time and the place of promise. But the time of promise is always haunted by risks and dangers, assailed by demons of torment. Friedrich Hölderlin has phrased it poetically: "Near and hard to grasp the god. But where danger lies, grows also that which saves."Or even sharper stated are the words of Walter Benjamin: "The Messiah comes not only as the redeemer, he comes as the subduer of the Antichrist. Only the historian will have the gift of fanning the spark of hope in the past who is firmly convinced that even the dead will not be safe from the enemy if he wins. And this enemy has not ceased to be victorious."[22]

The messianic reality that opens a window to another world is always in the closest proximity to perils that threaten. Liberation and condemnation rub each other. But by the same logic, when danger is averted, when trials are administered and kept at bay, promise seems to move the farthest and hope fades and no longer is the Abrahamic hope against hope. Hope that refuses to be audacious is dislodged to the category of waiting that belongs to the order of clock time, of *chronos*. So listen to what Paul is implying: To the same extend that we are safe and risks are administered and controlled, hope becomes anemic. These are hard words for societies with high levels of development and social services, health care, pension plans, insurance policies, and so forth. If perils are administered, where then is the hope? Benjamin points to the most fundamental and stubborn belief that even the dead will be rescued from the power of the enemy when they are remembered, and their sacrifice not surrendered to oblivion. But is that it? What about us, the living? What about those of us who can afford to keep perils at bay and know how to administer most dangers and fare pretty well in face of risks? Is hope left for the last battle with the enemy? Paul most definitely did not think so. In the text for today he is speaking about the living, even those who like himself enjoyed some privileges (after all he had Roman citizenship, and he used it). He knew that an insurance policy is not the same as liberation, that safety is not salvation. Paul is speaking about resurrection now, pocketed in the *kairotic* event! But resurrection does not come without dying. Hope grows and blossoms in a dirty soil.

And this is the second theme that needs to be lifted in this passage. If the *kairos* fleeting with messianic presence forms the frame of this text, its content, that which is framed, the "picture" in the frame ought not to be missed. In this short text, the content of which is on how to live in the world whose essence is passing away, one particular expression is repeated five times (which is not maintained in Luther's translation probably for stylistic reasons). The repeated expression is the Greek *hōs mē* ("as though not"). Paul was a master rhetorician. He knew how to use pleonasms to underscore a point he was making, without falling into boring redundancies. And what is he saying with the *hōs mē*? And why does this *hōs mē* entail a promise?

But first we have to see what Paul is not saying. He is not saying what two other groups of his time were preaching. We may call them the "apocalyptics" and the "spiritualists." For those with apocalyptic tendencies the world was a wastebasket because it was passing anyway and a future rule of God would bring a new reality. So anything goes. "Let's abuse the world" was their outlook. It is the sort of attitude for whom the worse it got the better it was. Such abuse of the world and its institutions, so goes the argument, will hasten the coming rule of God. To them Paul says to live and be in the world but not to misuse it as it were an instrument to be used and abused to hustle in the coming reign of God.

Spiritualists are the other group that Paul is addressing (and this is particularly true for the Corinthian community where spiritualists abounded). Contrary to the apocalyptic, they did not want to have any dealings with the world and its institutions. They would opt out of marriage, of property, and of dealings with the world in general, and instead boast and rejoice for being already above the world, or mourning and crying for the poor souls entangled in the dealings of the world. To this group the Apostle says: Live in the world and live responsibly, but not as if it were your own precious treasure; be in the world as a guest is received by a host. Indeed "to be a guest" is what Luther's suggests as the reading of this passage: "This is a common lesson for all Christians, that they . . . should rather behave like guests in the world, using everything for a short time because of need and not for pleasure."[23]

As guests we are at every moment painfully aware that at best it is for us a home and yet not our home. For guests the house is not of what matters most; it is neither a property that defines who we are and our belonging, nor is it a jail that fetters us, holds us captive, and does not set us free to leave. What matters is the hope and promise that it holds. But what Luther meant by being a guest could be better expressed these days by another image—the one of being an immigrant. Immigrants live through the experiences of loss, and every loss comes with the sting of death. A home is left behind; beloved ones are not around; friends are faraway; costumes and legislation are not friendly; expatriation, deportation, or prison terms lurk at every *kairotic* moment.

But the phenomenon of migration does not describe only the crossings of geo-political borders. There are also sorts of "migration" that all of us eventually experience. From health to a lengthy illness or other psychosomatic disorders implies an experience akin to migration, and even more so if it results in hospitalization or institutionalization. Akin to migration is the loss of a beloved whose life was entangled with ours. The loss of a job, a sudden change of career—many are the examples that describe such experiences of "migration." The common denominator is the loss of a familiar context of a place by which we were recognized. Thus a new context, a novel niche must be carved, but it remains always, for the migrant, as though not home, not a place of belonging. But why? Because life matters, matter matters! And it is in this matter, through the dirty soil where tears were shed, laughter echoed, dread and fear were borne, and joys shared that the shoot of stubborn hope emerges and takes bloom. Life shines in the shadows of danger; resurrections happen.

Rudolf Bultmann interpreted the *hōs mē* to mean "participation by inner distance." The great New Testament scholar was a bit too close to the spirtualists for whom liberation meant an inner spiritual disposition. "As though not" must here be understood as living participation with outer manifestation, dwelling as immigrants, sojourners, having the means to meet ends "as though not." And if we live so, we will see a crack, a small slit, in the gates of a shrinking *kairos.* Through this slit the spark of hope shines. Through this breach the Messiah, the Christ, might pass through any time, even now in the midst of this world whose systems and powers are always passing away and for which hope is an unintelligible word. But not so for the tribe of Jesus, who "have the gift of fanning the spark of hope" amidst ashes.

Endnotes

1 For the German text as delivered, go to: http://www.vitorw.com/category/sermons/

2 Hendel's work on translating and interpreting Johannes Bugenhagen is now available for the benefit of all. Kurt Hendel, *Johannes Bugenhagen: Selected Writings,* 2 vols. (Minneapolis: Fortress, 2015).

3 Kurt K. Hendel, "The Material as a Vehicle of the Divine," *Currents in Theology and Mission* 28, no. 3-4 (June-August 2001): 332.

4 Kurt K. Hendel, "Theology of the Cross," *Currents in Theology and Mission* 24, no.3 (1997): 223, 231.

5 LW 31: 39f.

6 Hendel taught for many years a popular advanced-level course on Luther's theology and social thought, "Luther and Social Reform," framing the question of the relationship between faith and love.

7 Kurt K. Hendel, "Paul and the Care of the Poor during the Sixteenth Century: A Case Study," in *A Companion to Paul in the Reformation*, R. Ward Holder, ed. (Leiden: Brill, 2009), 541-51, see particularly 569f.

8 Ibid., 570.

9 LW 54: 74.

10 LW 31: 40.

11 LW 31: 371.

12 LW 37: 65.

13 Jacob Taubes, *The Political Theology of Paul* (Stanford: Stanford University Press, 2004), 52f., 55f., and 92.

14 Current Pauline studies need to deal with philosophers as Jacob Taubes, Alain Badiou, Giorgio Agamben, Slavoj Žižek, Kenneth Reinhard, Eric Santner, and before all of them Walter Benjamin—none of them claiming confessional allegiance.

15 For a critical appraisal of the recent literature on the issue, see L. L. Welborn, *Paul's Summons to Messianic Life: Political Theology and the Coming Awakening* (New York: Columbia University Press, 2015).

16 Giorgio Agamben, *The Time that Remains: A Commentary on the Letter to the Romans* (Stanford: Stanford University Press, 2005), 23.

17 E.g. LW 2: 252 f.; 13: 15; 35: 280-83.

18 LW 2: 252f.

19 LW 13:15.

20 LW 13:14.

21 The original expression for "sleeping within these boundaries" (LW 13: 15) is *"Schlaffen zwischen den Grenzen"* (WA 8, 14).

22 Walter Benjamin, *Illuminations*, Hannah Arendt, ed. (New York: Schoken Books, 1969), 255.

23 LW 28:52.

SECTION THREE

Concluding Essays

CHAPTER TWENTY-ONE

Church History

Millstone of Anguish or Milestones to Cherish?

Peter Vethanayagamony

Church history as a discipline within theological curricula does not always receive a ceremonial red-carpet welcome. Many seminarians greet their courses in church history with a yawn, while running to courses in biblical studies, theology, pastoral care, and so on.[1] Perhaps they do so because somewhere in their background they have been taught that history is only about places, names, and dates; that it is irrelevant to "real ministry"; and, worse yet, that it is boring. So, how can we regain, and gain recruits for, what I believe is the lively, risky, and sometimes subversive enterprise of church history?

To regard church history simply as a chronicle of events in the history of the church, without taking into account the *faith* by which the church has lived, the *worship* by which its life has been sustained, the *piety* which has flowered within it, and the *witness* to which it has been committed, would be to give an entirely false picture of the discipline. Church history is at once interested in everything that has influenced the church, and in one thing in particular: the proclamation of the gospel. For only by trying to understand the total impact of the church upon the world, and of the world upon the church, can the mission entrusted to the church in our days be carried out truthfully.

It is heartening to know that Martin Luther had a great appreciation for history. He lamented the fact that he had not read more of it: "How

I regret now that I did not read more poets and the historians, and that no one taught me them!"[2] After all, history for him was "the mother of truth." Luther also thought of history as being a very pragmatic discipline. As Lewis W. Spitz rightly concludes, for Luther "[h]istory is important for moral philosophy, for it is philosophy teaching by examples."[3]

From church history we learn as much about ourselves as we do about others. Edward C. Zaragoza made a distinction between millstones and milestones, commenting: "Church history is not the millstone we often make it out to be; rather it is made up of milestones that mark times of transition, times of renewal, times of faith, that root us, hold us accountable, and give us a vision for the future."[4] A society unaware of its history is a society suffering amnesia; it has lost its identity. I recently heard someone refer to the U.S. as the "United States of Amnesia"! For me, as Zaragoza has put it, church history is all about making connections on multiple levels with "living voices of people who just happen to be dead."[5] By connecting with these voices, by engaging in dialogue with the "cloud of witnesses," we not only know about the past; we may also learn how to live more faithfully in the present.

What do I mean by "church history"? The term has come to be contested in our time. For the last couple of decades, some historians have come to be uncomfortable with the "church" part of church history and have adopted names for the discipline and practitioners of it that seemed more academically respectable.[6] For example, they could be "religious historians," in effect secular historians who choose to study churches as their topical focus. Mark Noll, a prominent voice in the interpretation of American Christianity in our time, has observed that "Christian historians took their place in the modern academy by treating history not so much as a subdivision of theology but as an empirical science. This choice meant that they have constructed their historical accounts primarily from facts ascertained through documentary or material evidence and explained in terms of natural human relationships."[7] The implications for the discipline are enormous, because this choice calls into question whether church history by its very nature has much to do with a Christian community's self-understanding, or with reflection on the divine relationship to human beings and the world of nature, or with whether the church can be an instrument for sharing the gospel.

Historians are faced with the question about the nature, meaning, purpose, use, and best method of doing church history. At issue is how the story of the church is to be told. This can be done either from a theological perspective or by viewing the church as a social tradition. We all profit from the current debate in historiography, since the conflict offers useful insights on how to do church history.

Historiography from von Ranke to Carr

Varieties of history exist because historians have regularly perceived the character of their discipline either from the dominant epistemology of their time or from some privileged ideological concerns. For instance, the nineteenth-century historian Leopold von Ranke (1795-1888), himself a Lutheran, famously declared that history is a record of "what really happened" in the past. This "past" could be recovered by rigorous, scientific, archival research, whose results could be laid out for all to see and be convinced. Von Ranke privileged an epistemology that had an ideological concern precisely because his was a voice boasting the optimism of his time.

By 1961 the world had changed. Edward Hallet Carr (1892-1982) stripped away these ideological and epistemological idiosyncrasies and presented a relativist agenda. Carr argued that "history" is the past as reconstructed by the historian from fragments of evidence. Facts do not come pure; all historians transform the facts of the past into historical facts by their interpretations. A fact in history becomes a "fact" only when the historian uses it to interpret the past; bias is everywhere present and the historian's perspective always intrudes. Therefore, we must always understand who wrote, for whom, and to what end.[8] All history, argued Carr, masks hidden agendas: political, economic, and ideological. All history is interpretation. Thus, in complete contrast to von Ranke, Carr rejected objectivity in history. However, he added that historians have certain obligations such as respect, accuracy, inclusiveness, and balance. The historian employs empathy and imaginative understanding of the minds of the subjects of research, employs rules of evidence, and uses a conceptual scheme or discourse to lay bare the perspective. It may be the case that the vice of bias can become a virtue, if properly controlled.

The great movements of liberation from the 1960s forward have freed us all (including historians) from telling the same old lies to one another and helped us learn fuller truths from once silenced peoples. The deconstructionist paradigm in history enables many suppressed voices to be heard, such as those of women, marginalized and colonized people. Deconstructionists went further by attacking the limits of scientific knowledge and the myth of the intellectual purity of science; science too was a social construct. The deconstructionists dismantled a number of absolutes. The power and the bias of the historian turn the enterprise into an interpretation. The ideological dimension is so real that history can be used to dominate or liberate. As Alan Munslow succinctly puts it:

> Deconstructionist history treats the past as a text to be examined for its possibilities of meaning, and above all exposes the spurious methodological aims and assumptions of modernist historians which incline them towards the ultimate viability of correspondence between evidence and interpretation, resulting in enough transparency in representation so as to make possible their aims of moral detachment, disinterestedness, objectivity, authenticity (if not absolute truthfulness) and the objective constitution of historical facts—allowing the sources to speak for themselves. . . . [T]here are only possible narrative representations in, and of, the past, and none can claim to know the past as it actually was.[9]

It seems clear that the implications of recent historiographical debates for church history are immense at (at least) four levels: definition, ideological underpinnings, mode of representation, and method. Church history becomes an interpretation by the people of God as they search their memories. Writing and studying church history are opportunities to remember how the gospel encountered the people and how they responded and were transformed. In other words, in our writing and study of church history the focus and emphasis is more on people in their encounter with the gospel in their socio-cultural and religious context than on the church's institutional history. That is, church history is the story of the presence of the kingdom of God in communities around the world. As Ogbu Kalu states, "[t]he church is the called-out people who in their being, saying, and doing serve as signs, witnesses, and representatives of the presence of the Kingdom of God among communities. They are the church because they are engaged in mission, the only reason for the existence of the people of God." Kalu continues, "Mission is not the task that the church undertakes, but what the church is."[10] Church history should be at the interface of history and theology because both reflect and talk about God's relationship to all creatures. Beyond this self-understanding and ideology is the mode of representation of church history. The fortunes of the gospel in a community are often affected by the socio-economic and political milieu, and this secular profile must be carefully analyzed. Church historians should endeavor to tell the story. We must constantly reevaluate our biases, our parochialism and our penchant for special pleading in order to avoid any self-serving distortions of historical knowledge, remembering that some historians have privileged the story of European Americans vis-à-vis those, say, of Native Americans or African Americans, or the wider global church.

So, Why Should One Study Church History?

In the past, the study of church history has been justified for reasons we likely no longer accept. For instance, one reason that church history holds its current place in a seminary education is because earlier leaders believed that its study is useful for the indoctrination of their future ministers. Such a use can encourage mindless memorization—a real but not very appealing aspect of the discipline. It is crucial to remember, however, that *mindlessness* is the problem, not memorization! In the ecumenical age in which we live, a strong grounding in one's own tradition helps one to bring the richness of that tradition to the ecumenical table; this is not the same as bigotry, which is certainly detrimental to Christian witness. Without a sustained attempt to understand both others and ourselves, we can too easily identify one particular trajectory through history as exemplifying the *correct* or *only* gospel-centered Christianity. We then exaggerate the strengths of our own traditions and downplay the strengths of others. Doing history from a global as well as an ecumenical perspective is therefore the need of the hour, given the fact that the church of our time is increasingly being challenged by the practical realities of Christian pluralism brought about by intermarriage and other dimensions of social mobility, as well as by methodological, theological, and ideological considerations. Federated churches may be found throughout the United States. A number of struggling churches belonging to diverse confessional families have come together as multi-point parishes. Adequate information about various church traditions can go a long way to help a minister called to serve in such parishes.

Church history studied from an ecumenical and global perspective can also provide a much-needed link to various disciplines taught within the seminary curriculum and makes provision for cross-referencing. Indeed, in a theological curriculum the study of history possesses not only a distinct and ordered character of its own, it also integrates various disciplines. For example, a study of Pietism, an eighteenth-century renewal movement among German Lutherans, includes not only a consideration of significant events and the interpretations of the period—religious renewal, social activism, the beginning of Protestant missionary work—but also a consideration of how the Bible was studied, interpreted, and expounded in the early eighteenth century; how religious changes affected the society; how various changes revolutionized the way people understood "spirituality"; how religious education was done; how pastoral care was provided; even how preaching was attempted. Pietism continues to instruct us, if only we are attentive. The voices that are stirred up from such a topic will echo through biblical studies, ethics, systematic and pastoral theology, and other disciplines, giving a different perspective to the work being done in those areas of the curriculum. One may even say that no field of study can be complete without a look to the past to discover the foundations on which its principles and present achievements rest.[11] Each discipline of study has its beginning, pioneers, milestones, and achievements, and it is desirable for students of theology to be acquainted with them, if they are to have an adequate grasp of each field's development and its significance for the church today.

The purpose of teaching church history is to give each generation a fuller identity and a deepened sense of belonging. Developing historical sensitivity and knowledge helps them to fathom Christianity's heritage. For those who take great pride in their heritage, "[t]he question 'Who am I?' does not refer only on a horizontal level to the relationship of the self to others immediately present. Men [sic] are begotten, not manufactured, and genes link each generation to the previous one."[12] This is unquestionably one of the reasons all seminaries encourage history teaching in some form or other. Historical data include evidence about the colonial beginnings, immigrant experiences, oppression and liberation, ethnic and linguistic identity, social quietism and activism, fine theological controversies and conflicts, attempts to Americanize, the formation and evolution (and coherence or dissolution) of congregations, synods, and denominations. We need to tell the story to know our identity and to understand how the past has shaped our present.

Histories that tell the specifically ecclesiastical story, emphasizing distinctive features of the church's experience, are meant to drive home an understanding of identity, values, and confessional loyalty. Clergy are inevitably the conveyors and purveyors of denominational identity, the interpreters of the practices in which their church is engaged in the mission of proclaiming the gospel. Pastors should deeply know the congregation and the ecclesiastical tradition within which they function. This is especially important for somebody who considers or receives a call to pastoral ministry. A candidate for a call to a North American Lutheran congregation should know whether it was founded by colonial Germans, "American Lutherans," Scandinavian immigrants, etc., or whether it was a post-Civil War mission development. It is important to note whether a major controversy—the language of worship, slavery, predestination, etc.—ever ripped through the congregation's life. It is significant to remember that North American Lutheranism was defined in terms of ethnic identity right up to the Second World War. Knowledge of North American Lutheran history will aid today's pastors in understanding the experience through which the local congregations has passed and the trends in the ongoing development and transformation of the Lutheran church. The same could be said of any other congregation in other confessional families.

Facing the Past: Telling the Truth

History is more than just trying to tell true stories about what happened in the past; history is also about the present and future. Therefore, church history does not rest with knowing what happened and what that says about us, but also considers the ethical, that is, how we are called to account for our actions in the past and the present, while looking forward to a more loving and just community. This way of doing church history holds us accountable for who we have been, who we are, and who will be as we seek first the reign of God.

In other words, the purpose of remembering the past is not to reinforce patterns—"We do it because they (our ancestors) did it"—but to throw light on the present situation through reflection on what has happened in the past. While history does not give blueprints for solving problems, it does illumine their roots, indicate some of the factors involved, and reveal past attempts at solutions, whether adequate or inadequate. This reminds me of the poet Maya Angelou, who wrote,

> History, despite its wrenching pain,
> Cannot be unlived, and if faced with courage,
> Need not be lived again.[13]

Attention to the struggle of African-Americans within North American Lutheranism illustrates this clearly.

The history of the Lutheran church is intertwined with the history of African-Americans from the earliest days of the United States of America. In many ways, it is a shameful history, which reveals how the North American Lutheran Churches as institutions perpetuated racist social structures. Perhaps because of a myopic view of Lutheranism as a Midwestern phenomenon, American Lutheranism's involvement in slavery has largely been ignored. In actuality, Lutherans were implicated in slavery from the earliest colonial days. As Johnson notes, for Lutherans as well as other Christians, "for almost two and a half centuries, from 1623 to 1825, slavery and colonialism were the primary context for contact, conversion, and Christian brotherhood, if indeed those labels can be used."[14] Lutherans welcomed African slaves in the urban settlement of New Amsterdam (later to become New York City) as early as 1669, when Jacob Fabritius (d. 1693) baptized a slave named Emmanuel in New York. Other baptisms of slaves followed in quick succession in the Hudson Valley. Justus Falckner (1672-1723), the first Lutheran pastor ordained in the United States, baptized a number of African-Americans in Albany and northern New Jersey. Most African-Americans who received baptism from Lutheran pastors in the early years were slaves of Lutheran masters.[15] It is significant to note here that the baptismal vows stressed slave–master relation, as the baptized person "solemnly promised before the omnipotent Lord and this Christian congregation that he would, after he was received into the church, continue to serve his worldly master and mistress as faithfully and truly as if he were yet in his benighted state."[16] This promise underscored the fear of many slaveholders that "Christianity would undermine the legal basis of slavery."[17] During this time period, Christian scriptures such as "neither slave nor free in Christ" rubbed uneasily against the prevailing social order.[18] To mitigate the radical tendencies of Christianity, instruction and baptismal vows emphasized that this freedom was not for this world, but rather for the next.[19] As such, "[i]n addition to its emphasis on the humane treatment of their slave charges, the church also emphasized the obligation of the slave to accept the conditions in which he existed."[20] Nevertheless, the promise of freedom in the gospel, even when not realized in this life, remained a powerful source of hope for many enslaved persons joining the Lutheran church.[21] The emphasis on freedom-not-yet-realized would become a powerful force to shape the emerging African-American Lutheran church identity and theology.

As an increasing number of African-Americans were baptized in the Lutheran church, free African-American leaders emerged who had the potential to begin significant Lutheran strongholds within their communities. Unfortunately, despite the passion and tenacity of these emerging leaders, the support and encouragement of the Lutheran church was half-hearted at best. One of the clearest examples of such a missed opportunity is in the ministry of Daniel Alexander Payne (1811-1893), the sixth bishop of the American Methodist Episcopal Church (AME) and the most influential African-American Christian in the nineteenth century. In his teens, Payne experienced a religious conversion in which he heard a voice saying, "I have set thee apart to educate thyself and in order that thou mayest be an educator to thy people."[22] With very few resources, Payne opened a school the following year, quickly gathering students and a reputation as an educator of note. John Bachman (1790-1874), the South Carolina Synod president who carried on a ministry to African Americans in the cities in South Carolina, identified the gifts in Payne and introduced him to Lutheran clergy in Philadelphia and New York. [23] After quietly tutoring Payne for some time, Bachman facilitated Payne's attendance at Gettysburg Seminary. Payne was supported and encouraged by Samuel Simon Schmucker (1793-1876), with whom he developed a close relationship during his time as a student at Gettysburg Seminary.

Nevertheless, when Payne graduated in 1823 and the time came for him to seek a church, the Lutherans had no position for him, and Payne was encouraged by his mentor to seek out a placement in the AME.[24] Payne was licensed by the Lutherans [Franckean Synod], but only received calls from black parishes in the Presbyterian and Episcopal churches.[25] After pursuing a successful career with the AME, Payne wrote to the Lutheran leader, William A. Passavant (1821-1894) as follows: "Tens of thousands . . . could be led into the bosom of your denomination . . . if the right kind of missionaries were sent to win them for the Savior. . . . Luther ought to be as widely known among the colored Christians of the South as Calvin, Knox, or Wesley."[26] In 1878, the Franckean Synod's historian H. L Dox lamented the Lutheran church's mistake:

> He left it not because he did not love it. He left it because it had no place for him, because he felt he had no right to ex-

pect . . . cooperation from the denomination at large, in any movement he might make on behalf of the colored people. Were he with us now, it is hoped he would find it otherwise.[27]

Payne was one of many African-Americans who sought to offer their gifts to the Lutheran church. Unfortunately, the Lutheran church would continue to squander their time and talent in the new era following the American Civil War. The historical lesson is that, in order for Lutheran churches to become a truly welcoming community, awareness of the past is essential. Today, we have an opportunity for a much-needed process of truth-telling and healing. An important step towards healing the hurt created by slavery is to let the painful story be told from the perspective of the victims and oppressed. We need to overcome defensiveness and create openness and space to receive the critique. African-Americans have much to say, many stories to tell, much pain to reveal. Our relationships will not mature into mutuality until we walk through this needed process of truth-telling and reconciliation.

Modern church history also provides terrain for moral contemplation. Studying the stories of individuals, communities, and situations in the past allows a student of history to test his or her own moral sense, to test it against some of the real complexities individuals have faced in difficult settings. People who have weathered adversity not just in some work of fiction, but in real, historical circumstances can provide inspiration. "History teaching by example" is one phrase that describes this use of a study of the past—a study not only of certifiable heroes, the great men and women of history who successfully worked through moral dilemmas, but also of more ordinary people who provide lessons in courage, diligence, or constructive protest. Readings about the crises the church has faced and its faithful witness to the gospel provides motivation for the current generation to fight for justice and to bear witness to the gospel. One thinks of 1936, when the Confessing Church in Germany, the network of those who resisted the anti-Semitic legislation of the Third Reich, bound itself to the Barmen Declaration[28] and affirmed the sovereignty of God in Christ over all other claims to authority; or South Africa in the 1980s, when the Kairos Document[29] declared the church's judgment against apartheid and made the theological case for defining apartheid as heresy. These stories of confession and resistance continue to inspire and motivate students to commit themselves with seriousness and courage to the cause of justice.

In addition to the advantages to be had from attending to the "voices of the people who happened to be dead," the skills one acquires while doing history come in handy for those training to be leaders in church and society. The study of history provides experience of dealing with and assessing various kinds of evidence—public statements, private records, numerical data, visual materials—and in making coherent arguments based on such evidence. These skills can also be applied to information encountered in everyday life. Experience in assessing past examples of change is vital to understanding change in society today—something essential in what we are regularly told is our "ever-changing world." Analysis of change means developing some capacity for determining the magnitude and significance of change, for some changes are more fundamental than others. Comparing particular changes to relevant examples from the past helps students of history develop this capacity. The ability to identify the continuities that always accompany even the most dramatic changes also comes from studying history, as does the skill of determining probable causes of change. It is significant to note that many congregations are looking for someone who will lead them to bring about needed change.

Though the seminary's primary objective is to produce able pastors and church leaders, the task of producing professional church historians cannot be overlooked. One of the notable characteristics of American Lutheranism, Mark Noll points out, is that "some secret elixir devised to develop special muscles for historical scholarship is regularly dispensed to young Lutherans, for how else can one account for the fact that Lutherans are the country's most distinguished church historians—Sydney Ahlstrom, Jaroslav Pelikan, and Martin Marty being at the top of the list and a host of only slightly lesser lights following close behind."[30] Other notable names that come to mind are H. George Anderson, Eric W. Gritsch, John F. Bachman, Eugene L. Fevold, Leigh David Jordahl, Paul P. Kuenning, Frederick K. Wentz, Abdel Ross Wentz, Edmond Jacob Wolf, Franz Hildebrandt, Robert W. Jenson, E. Clifford Nelson, Magnus Nodtvedt, Harry Julius Kreider, G. H. Gerberding, Robert H. Fisher, Schneider, Theodore G. Tappert, James A. Scherer, Gunther Gassmann, Timothy Wengert, L. DeAne Lagerquist, Carter Lindberg, Robert B. Fisher, Maria Elizabeth Erling, Kurt Hendel, Mark Swanson, James Echols, Mark Alan Granquist, and Jeff G. Johnson.[31] Yet, as Mark Noll observes,[32] while there are scores of Lutheran church historians, there is no truly great monograph about American Lutheranism[33] to compare, for example, with George Marsden's *Fundamentalism and American Culture*,[34] Donald G. Mathews' interpretation of antebellum Southern evangelicalism,[35] Grant Wacker's interpretation of early Pentecostals,[36] Dee Andrews' interpretative history of Methodists,[37] or Harry Stout's work on the American Puritans.[38] Though not every seminarian is destined to fill this vacuum, given the curious Lutheran capacity to produce great modern church historians like Martin E. Marty (who has been called the "foremost interpreter of American religion today"), let us not deprive bright seminarians the opportunity of making their own mark on the field.

Finally, for new generations of ministers called to serve locally as well as globally, adequate awareness of the changes happening in global Christianity is of utmost importance for effective ministry. For several centuries and until very recently, Christianity has been identified almost exclusively with Euro-American civilization. European and North American thinking about Christianity also has been a prisoner of this mentality of the Euro-American centrality and superiority. Paul Spickard is probably right when he concludes that Euro-Americans are still susceptible to the colonialist condescension Rudyard Kipling expressed in "The White Man's Burden."[39] From the colonizer's condescension has come the common conviction that Christianity is a European and American religion. But it is not so! Not only does Christianity now appear vastly pluralistic and diverse, but its very future seems to lie not in the West but rather in the non-Western parts of the globe.[40] In Africa the number of Christians has increased at a staggering rate, from 10 million in 1900 to 360 million in 2000. This massive shift of the Christian population from the north (Europe and North America) to the south (Africa, Asia, and Latin America), a fact long known among missiologists, was brought to the attention of the larger public a few years ago by Philip Jenkins in his *The Next Christendom: The Coming of Global Christianity*.[41] In a crisp summary of current statistics, Jenkins stresses the increasingly global character of Christianity:

> According to the respected *World Christian Encyclopedia*, some 2 billion Christians are alive today, about one-third of the planetary total. The largest single bloc, some 560 million people, is still found in Europe. Latin America, though, is already close behind with 480 million. Africa has 360 million,

and 313 million Asians profess Christianity. North America
claims about 260 million believers. If we extrapolate these
figures to the year 2025, and assume no great gains or losses
through conversion, then there would be around 2.6 billion
Christians, of whom 633 million would live in Africa, 640 million in Latin America, and 460 million in Asia. Europe, with
555 million, would have slipped to third place. Africa and
Latin America would be in competition for the tile of most
Christian continent. . . . Soon, the phrase "a White Christian"
may sound like a curious oxymoron, as mildly surprising as
"a Swedish Buddhist."[42]

The numerical changes in Christianity have countless implications for
theology and religious practice. A number of global south-dominated
churches are likely to be assemblies of the poor, in marked contrast to
the Western/Northern church. For this reason, some Western Christians since the 1960s have expected that the religion of the "third world"
Christians would be fervently liberal, activist, and even revolutionary,
the model represented by liberation theology. Frequently, the liberation-
ist voices emanating from the "third world" proved to be derived from
clerics trained in Europe or North America, and their ideas won only
limited support. In general, Christians of the global South tend to be conservative in terms of both beliefs and moral teaching. They retain a very
strong supernatural orientation and are by and large far more interested
in personal salvation than in radical politics. In addition, rapid growth is
occurring in non-traditional denominations that adapt Christian belief
to local tradition, groups that are categorized by titles like "African indigenous churches."[43]

This demographic shift presents at least two formidable challenges.
First, how should the churches of the northern hemisphere and those of
the southern hemisphere relate to each other? While the latter used to
be called the "younger churches" or "daughter churches" with respect
to the former, on which they depended for material support as well as
personnel, this is no longer the case.[44] This reversal of relationships was
dramatically illustrated recently in Anglicanism. More than half of the
seventy-seven million Anglicans live in Africa, South America, and Asia.
There are more Anglicans in Kenya (about three million) than there
are Episcopalians in the United States (2.2 million). In Uganda, church

membership is nine million, and in Nigeria it is twenty million. What is more significant is that whereas in the Church of England, the "mother church," membership is much in decline and practice barely lukewarm, church life is booming and faith is vibrant in the African Anglican churches. Furthermore, though the Archbishop of Canterbury is officially the spiritual head of the world's Anglicans, the most powerful figure in Anglicanism currently is arguably Archbishop Peter Akinola, primate of the church of Nigeria.

This shift of power in church politics was demonstrated recently in the controversy caused by the ordination of an openly gay man, Gene Robinson, as Bishop of New Hampshire. Archbishop Akinola and his allies forced the Archbishop of Canterbury, Rowan Williams, to establish a church inquiry into the crisis, and the ensuing Windsor Report urged the Episcopal Church of the United States to express "regret" over the consecration of Gene Robinson and to refrain from further consecration of gay bishops.[45] Whether Anglicanism will or will not be split by this controversy, there is little doubt that the Christianity of the South is no longer taking what is done by the Christianity of the North for granted, much less as the norm, and it is not shy to force its own doctrines and practices on their wealthier northern colleagues.

The second, no less difficult, challenge of the demographic shift in Christian population concerns the church's evangelizing mission. If the membership of the church of the South will be more numerous than that of the church of the North, and if the faith life in the former is more vibrant than that in the latter, then who should evangelize whom? Who are the exporters and who are the importers? According to the Korean Research Institute for Missions, in the year 2006 there were 14,905 Korean missionaries sent by 175 mission organizations serving different regions of the world.[46] Churches in the North are being called to be accountable for the legacy of the modern missionary movement which lived within, benefited from, and was influenced by its historical context(s) of colonial expansion, the slave economy, the Enlightenment, and legalistic elements of Pietism. Today, we have the opportunity for a much-needed process of truth-telling and healing. Our relationships will not mature into mutuality until we walk through this needed process of truth-telling and reconciliation. Needless to say, greater knowledge of church history will aid us in our lives together in the world-wide church.

Conclusion

What do we hope from the study of church history? At a minimum, we hope for some habits of mind, some basic knowledge about the forces that affect our own lives, and an enhanced capacity for informed citizenship and effective pastoral leadership for change. Some, depending on personal taste and vocation, will delight in the search for beauty, the joy of discovery, and intellectual challenge. Between the hoped-for minimum and the pleasure of deep commitment comes the grasp of history that, through cumulative skill in interpreting the unfolding human record, provides a real sense of how the world works. The church, called to be God's instrument in God's mission for the world, can be richly equipped and inspired to accomplish this call, both locally and globally, when it takes its own story seriously.

Endnotes

1 This may be an over-generalization that does not hold from culture to culture. To be sure, we do have considerable number of students who show interest in church history and some even plan to make a career out of church history and research. Nonetheless, it is not uncommon to come across a majority of students who have little inclination to the subject, despite the seminary's conviction that the study of church history is an essential ingredient of a good theological education.

2 Martin Luther, "To the Councilmen of Germany," in *Luther's Works*, Vol. 45, *The Christian in Society*, ed. Walther I. Brandt (Philadelphia: Concordia Publishing House and Muhlenberg Press, 1962), 370.

3 Lewis W. Spitz, "Luther's View of History: A Theological Use of the Past," in *Light for our World: Essays commemorating the 150th Anniversary of Concordia Seminary, St. Louis, Missouri,* ed. John W. Klotz (St. Louis: Concordia Seminary, 1989), 150.

4 Edward C. Zaragoza, "Why Study Church History? For Students and Graduates Alike," *Journal of Theology* 104 (2005): 89.

5 Ibid., 89.

6 Ogbu U. Kalu, "Clio in a Sacred Garb," *Fides et Historia* 35, no. 1 (Winter/Spring 2003): 29.

7 Mark Noll, "The Potential of Missiology for the Crises of History," in *History and the Christian Historian*, ed. Ronald A. Wells (Grand Rapids: Wm. B. Eerdmans Publishing Co., 1998), 110.

8 Edward Hallet Carr, *What is History?* (New York: Random House, 1961), 22.

9 Alan Munslow, *Deconstructing History* (London and New York: Routledge, 1997), 16.

10 Kalu, "Clio in a Sacred Garb," 36.

11 Vincent Strudwick, "The Role of History in Theological Education," *Theology* 98 (1995): 358-364.

12 Iris V. Cully, "Teaching History in Church Curriculum," *Religious Education* 64 (1969): 133.

13 Maya Angelou, "On the Pulse of Morning," available online at "Gifts of Speech," http://gos.sbc.edu/a/angelou.html (accessed 13 January, 2010).

14 Jeff Johnson, *Black Christians: the Untold Lutheran Story* (St. Louis: Concordia Publishing House, 1977), 22.

15 Though Lutherans in general took an anti-slave stance, some Lutherans did own slaves during the eighteenth century.

16 Johnson, *Black Christians*, 30.

17 Ibid., 31.

18 Galatians 3:28.

19 James Kenneth Echols, "The Two Kingdoms: A Black American Lutheran Perspective" in *Theology and Black Experience*, ed. Albert Pero (Minneapolis: Augsburg, 1988), 118.

20 Thomas R. Noon, "Early Black Lutherans in the South," *Concordia Historical Institute Quarterly* 50 (1977):51.

21 Jeff Johnson, *Black Christians*, 30.

22 Daniel Alexander Payne, *Recollections of Seventy Years* (New York: Arno Press and the New York Times, 1968), 17.

23 John Bachman, who had helped found Newberry College and the Lutheran Theological Southern Seminary, as well as the South Carolina Lutheran Synod, was one of the first writers to argue scientifically that blacks and whites are the same species.

24 Paul P. Kuenning, "Daniel A. Payne: First Black Seminarian," *Lutheran Theological Seminary Bulletin, Gettysburg, Pennsylvania* 67, no. 4 (Fall 1987), 6.

25 Ibid., 8.

26 G. H. Gerberding, *Life and Letters of W. A. Passavant* (Greenville, Pennsylvania: The Young Lutheran Company, 1906), 531-32, cited in Kuenning, "Daniel A. Payne," 12.

27 *The Lutheran Observer*, 17 May, 1978, cited in Kuenning, "Daniel A. Payne," 12.

28 The full text of Barmen Declaration may be found online, e.g. at "Presbyterian Church of Aotearoa New Zealand—About us—Statements of Faith," http://www.presbyterian.org.nz/about/statements-of-faith/the-barmen-declaration-1934 (accessed 13 January, 2010).

29 The full text of Kairos Document may be found online, e.g. at "African Christianity: A History of the Christian Church in Africa," http://www.bethel.edu/~letnie/AfricanChristianity/SAKairos.html (accessed 13 January 2010).

30 Mark A. Noll, "The Lutheran Difference," *First Things* 20 (February 1992): 32.

31 This list is no way exhaustive!

32 Mark A. Noll, "American Lutherans Yesterday and Today," in *Lutherans Today: American Lutheran Identity in the Twenty-First Century*, ed. Richard Ciminio (Grand Rapids: Wm. B. Eerdmans Publishing Co., 2003), 19.

33 While Clifford Nelson, ed., *The Lutherans in North America*, revised ed. (Philadelphia: Fortress Press, 1980), L DeAne Lagerquist, *The Lutherans: Student Edition*, Denominations in America 9 (Westport, Connecticut: Praeger, 1999) and Mark Granquist, *Lutherans in America: A New History* (Minneapolis: Fortress Press, 2015) attempt a comprehensive history of Lutheranism in North America, each is a descriptive account of North American Lutherans.

34 George M. Marsden, *Fundamentalism and American Culture: The Shaping of Twentieth Century Evangelicalism, 1870-1925* (New York: Oxford University Press, 1980).

35 Donald G. Mathews, *Religion in the Old South* (Chicago: University of Chicago Press, 1977).

36 Grant Wacker, *Heaven Below: Early Pentecostals and American Culture* (Cambridge, Massachusetts: Harvard University Press, 2001).

37 Dee Andrews, *The Methodists and Revolutionary America, 1760-1800: The Shaping of an Evangelical Culture* (Princeton, New Jersey: Princeton University Press, 2000).

38 Harry S Stout, *The New England Soul: Preaching and Religious Culture in Colonial New England* (New York and Oxford: Oxford University Press, 1988).

39 Paul Spickard, "It's the World History: Decolonizing Historiography and the History of Christianity," *Fides et Historia* 31, no. 2 (Summer/Fall 1999): 19.

40 See David B Barrett, George T. Kurian, and Todd M. Johnson, *World Christian Encyclopedia*, 2nd ed. (New York: Oxford University Press, 2002).

41 Philip Jenkins, *The Next Christendom: The Coming of Global Christianity* (Oxford: Oxford University Press, 2002).

42 Jenkins, *The Next Christendom*, 2-3.

43 Ibid., 9.

44 While the dependency on the Western churches for personnel is no longer the case, the churches in the southern hemisphere are yet to achieve full economic sufficiency, though the patronizing attitude of the so-called "older churches" toward "younger churches" has been challenged from the Jerusalem World Missionary Conference (1928) onwards. At the same time, the churches in the global South have become more assertive in making their voices heard on matters of belief and practice.

45 For further details about this controversy refer to Peter Boyer, "A Church Asunder," *The New Yorker* (17 April 2006): 53-65.

46 This total makes Korea the second largest missionary-sending country in the world, ranking only after the United States in its number of overseas missionaries. For details, see Steve Sang-Cheol Moon, "The Protestant Missionary Movement in Korea: Current Growth and Development," *International Bulletin of Missionary Research* 32, no. 2 (April 2008): 59–62.

Works of Kurt Hendel

Translation, annotation, and illustration of "The Smalcald Articles," in Kirsi Stjerna, ed. *Word and Faith. Vol. 2 of The Annotated Luther.* Minneapolis: Fortress Press, 2015.

Johannes Bugenhagen: *Selected Writings.* 2 vols. Minneapolis: Fortress Press, 2015.

"Theology of the Cross: A Theology of Revelation" *The Lutheran* (October 2012).

Translation and editing of Luther, Martin. Preface to Ambrosius Moibanus, The Twenty-Ninth Psalm, On the Power of the Voice of God in the Air (1536) in Brown, Christopher Boyd, ed. *Luther's Works, vol. 60*, Preface. St. Louis: Concordia Publishing House, 2011.

Translation and editing of Luther, Martin. Preface to Ambrosius Moibanus, The Glorious Commission of Jesus Christ our Lord and Savior (Mark 16[:15]) (1537) in Brown, Christopher Boyd, ed. *Luther's Works, Vol. 60*, Prefaces. St. Louis: Concordia Publishing House, 2011.

Review of The Pastoral Luther. Essays on Martin Luther's Practical Theology by Timothy J. Wengert, ed. Lutheran Quarterly XXV, 25, 3 (Autumn 2011): 337-340.

Review of *Early Protestant Spirituality* by Scott H. Hendrix, ed. *Religious Studies Review* 37, 3 (Summer, 2011): 192.

"Paul and the Care of the Poor During the Sixteenth Century: A Case Study," in Holder, R. Ward, ed. *A Companion to Paul in the Reformation Brill's Companions to the Christian Tradition, 16.* Leiden: Brill, 2009, 543-573.

Review of *Fortress Introduction to Salvation and the Cross*, by David A. Brondos. *Interpretation: A Journal of Bible and Theology* 63, 4 (October 2009): 425-426.

Review of *Ordination in Wittenberg. Die Einsetzung des kirchlichen Amt in Kursachsen zu Zeit der Reformation* by Martin Krarup. *Journal of Ecclesiastical History* 60, 3 (July 2009): 597-598.

"Faithfulness: Luther's Vision of Excellence in Ministry." *Currents in Theology and Mission* 36, 3 (June 2009): 170-198.

"The Historical Context of the Barmen Declaration." *Currents in Theology and Mission* 36, 2 (April 2009): 133-136.

Articles on Johannes Bugenhagen, Johannes Brenz, Lefèvre d'Étaples, Moritz of Saxony, Thomas Murner, the Pack Affair, Urbanus Rhegius, Hans Sachs and Franz von Sickingen for: Benedetto, Robert, ed. *New Westminster Dictionary of Church History*, Vol. 1. Louisville: Westminster John Knox Press, 2008.

"*Finitum capax Infiniti*: Luther's Radical Incarnational Perspective," *Currents in Theology and Mission* 35, 6 (December, 2008): 420-433.

"*Finitum capax Infiniti*: Luther's Radical Incarnational Perspective." *Seminary Ridge Review* 10, 2 (June, 2008): 20-35.

"'No Salvation Outside the Church' in Light of Luther's Dialectic of the Hidden and Revealed God." *Currents in Theology and Mission* 35, 4 (April, 2008): 248-257.

Review of *Two Reformers. Martin Luther and Mary Daly as Political Theologians* by Caryn D. Riswold. *Currents in Theology and Mission* 35, 1 (February, 2008): 62.

Review of *Bound Choice, Election, and Wittenberg Method: From Martin Luther to the Formula of Concord*, by Robert Kolb. *The Catholic Historical Review* 62, 4 (October 2006).

"Johannes Bugenhagen, Organizer of the Lutheran Reformation." *Lutheran Quarterly* XVIII, 1 (Spring 2004):43-75.

"Three Women Watch Their Husbands' Back: Walpurga Bugenhagen, Anna Rhegius and [Anna] Margarethe Corvin." *Lutheran Quarterly* XVIII, 1 (Spring, 2004): 28-42. Translation of "*Drei Frauen halten ihren Männern den Rücken frei: Walpurga Bugenhagen, Anna Rhegius und [Anna] Margarethe Corvin*," by Inge Mager. *Jahrbuch der Gesellschaft für niedersächsische Kirchengeschichte*, XCVII (1999), 237-248.

"The Material as a Vehicle of the Divine." *Currents in Theology and Mission*, 28, 3-4 (June and August, 2001): 326-334.

Review of *Habsucht bei Martin Luther: Ökumenisches und theologisches Denken, Tradition und und Soziale Wirklichkeit im Zeitalter der Reformation* by Ricardo Rieth. *Lutheran Quarterly* XII, 2 (Summer 1999): 222-225.

Review of *Luther and the German Humanists*, by Lewis W. Spitz. *Lutheran Quarterly* XII, 3 (Autumn 1998):358-360.

Review of *The Catholicity of the Reformation*, by Carl E. Braaten and Robert W. Jenson. *The Christian Century* (October 15 1997): 918-921.

"Theology of the Cross." *Currents in Theology and Mission* 24, 3 (June 1997): 223-231.

Introduction to and translation of "A Christian Sermon over the Body and at the Funeral of the Venerable Dr. Martin Luther, Preached by Mr. Johann Bugenhagen Pomeranus, Doctor and Pastor of the Churches in Wittenberg." Atlanta: Pitts Theology Library, 1996.

Review of *The Decalogue and a Human Future*, by Paul Lehmann. Introduction by Nancy J. Duff. *Lutheran Quarterly* X, 3 (Autumn 1996): 345-348.

Review of *Antiklerikalismus und Reformation*, by Hans-Jürgen Goertz. *The Sixteenth Century Journal* XXVII, 2 (Summer 1996): 634-635.

Review of *Johannes Bugenhagens Rechtfertigungslehre und der Römische Katholizismus. Studien zum Sendbrief an die Hamburger (1525)*, by Ralf Kötter. *The Sixteenth Century Journal* XXVII, 1 (Spring 1996): 289-291.

Review of *The Catholic Roots of the Protestant Gospel: Encounter between the Middle Ages and the Reformation*, by Stephen Strehle. *The Sixteenth Century Journal* XXVI, 4 (Winter 1995): 1002-1003.

"Luther's Responsibility for the Theory and Practice of 16th-Century Lutheran Churches." Report on Seminar 3 of the Eighth International Congress for Luther Research. *Lutherjahrbuch* LXII (1995): 196-198.

Review of *The Fabricated Luther*, by Uwe Siemon-Netto. *Lutheran Quarterly* IX, 3 (Autumn 1995): 342-345.

Review of *Problems of Authority in the Reformation Debates*, by G. R. Evans. *The Thomist* LIX, 2 (April1995): 326-330.

Review of *Geschichte des Pietismus*, Vol. 1, by Martin Brecht, ed. *Lutheran Quarterly* IX, 1 (Spring 1995): 80-83.

"The Doctrine of the Ministry: The Reformation Heritage." *Luther Digest* II (1994): 75-76.

Review of *Luther's Approach to Scripture as Seen in his "Commentaries" on Galatians 1518-1538*, by Kenneth Hagen. *The Sixteenth Century Journal* XXV, 4 (Winter 1994): 946-948.

Review of *Martin Luther: His Road to Reformation 1483-1521*, by Martin Brecht. *The Sixteenth Century Journal* XXV, 2 (Summer 1994): 449-450.

Review of *Black Christians: The Untold Lutheran Story*, by Jeff G. Johnson. *Lutheran Quarterly* VIII, 2 (Summer 1994): 216-218.

Review of *Beyond Charity: Reformation Initiatives for the Poor*, by Carter Lindberg. *Lutheran Quarterly* VIII, 1 (Spring 1994): 71-73.

Review of *Outmoded Condemnations?*, by the Faculty of Theology of the University of Göttingen. *Lutheran Quarterly* VII, 4 (Winter 1993): 469-471.

Comparative review of *Martin Luther. Theology and Revolution*, by Gerhard Brendler and *Luther: Man Between God and the Devil*, by Heiko Oberman. *Modern Theology* VIII, 3 (July 1992): 312-315.

Review of *War Against the Idols*, by Carlos M. N. Eire. *Lutheran Quarterly* V, 1 (Spring 1991): 116-117.

Review of *The German People and the Reformation*, ed. by R. Po-chia Hsia. *Lutheran Quarterly* IV, 2 (Summer 1990): 234-236.

"The Doctrine of the Ministry: The Reformation Heritage." *Currents in Theology and Mission* 17, 1 (February 1990): 23-33.

"Luther and Sacramental Theology." Resource tape, Series 16, No. 10 (October 1989).

"The Care of the Poor: An Evangelical Perspective." *Currents in Theology and Mission* 15, 6 (December 1988): 526-532.

Review of *Martin Luther: An Introduction to His Life and Work*, by Bernhard Lohse. *Currents in Theology and Mission* 15, 5 (October, 1988): 453-454.

"The Word Must be Proclaimed: Luther on Ministry." *Currents in Theology and Mission* 15, 1 (February 1988): 112-119.

Review of *The Rise of Christianity*, by W. H. C. Frend. *Currents in Theology and Mission* 13, 4 (August 1986): 245-246.

"Johannes Bugenhagen: A Retrospect on His 500th Birthday." *Currents in Theology and Mission*, 12, 5 (October 1985): 277-289.

"Philip of Hesse: Militant Confessor." *Currents in Theology and Mission* 7, 6 (December 1980): 369-373.

"Elector John of Saxony: Steadfast Confessor." *Currents in Theology and Mission* 7, 5 (October, 1980): 297-300.

"John Bugenhagen: Confessor Behind the Scenes." *Currents in Theology and Mission* 7, 4 (August 1980): 243-245.

"Martin Luther: Impatient Confessor." *Currents in Theology and Mission* 7, 3 (June 1980): 176-179.

"Philip Melanchthon: Controversial Reformer." *Currents in Theology and Mission* 7,1 (February 1980): 53-55.

Articles on "Johannes Bugenhagen, Conciliarism, Martin Luther and Marsiglio of Padua" in *The Holy Roman Empire*. Edited by Jonathan W. Zophy. Westport, Connecticut: Greenwood Press, 1980.

Digest: "Christianity and Other Religions." *Theology Digest* XXVII (Summer 1979): 121-124.

Abstract: "Bridges between Christian and Buddhist Spirituality." *Theology Abstract*, XXVI, 2 (Summer 1978): 131-133.

Abstract: "Mark and Early Christian Theology." Theology Abstracts, XXVI, 1 (Spring 1978): 28-29.

Sections on "The Church of the Augsburg Confession and on the Radical Reformation." in: *Piepkorn, Arthur Carl. Profiles in Belief: The Religious Bodies of the United States and Canada*. Vol. II. New York: Harper & Row, 1978.

"Motives in the Quest for Religious Freedom." *Currents in Theology and Mission* 3, 4 (August 1976): 211-218.

Review of Confrontation at Worms, by DeLamar Jensen. *The Sixteenth Century Journal* V, 3 (Fall 1974): 133.

Translation: Liermann, Hans. "Protestant Endowment Law in the Franconian Church Ordinances of the Sixteenth Century." *The Social History of the Reformation*. Ed. by Lawrence P. Buck and Jonathan W. Zophy. Columbus, Ohio: The Ohio State University Press, 1972.

"Johannes Bugenhagen's Educational Contributions," unpublished Ph.D. Dissertation, The Ohio State University, 1974.

"Luther's Use of the Sermon for Teaching Purposes," unpublished M.A. Thesis, The Ohio State University, 1971.

EDITOR, *Currents in Theology and Mission* for the following issues: June, 2009 (36,3); August, 2009 (36,4); December, 2009 (36,6); December, 2010 (37,6); April, 2011 (38,2); June, 2012 (39,3); October, 2012 (39,5); consulted on February (37,1) and June (37,3), 2010 issues.

FORTHCOMING PUBLICATIONS:

Translation and editing of Luther, Martin, *A Sermon about Jesus Christ Preached at the Court in Torgau, Luther's Works*, vol. 57.

Review of *Unser Martin: Martin Luther aus der Sicht katholischer Sympathisanten* by Franz Posset, *Lutheran Quarterly*.

"Johannes Bugenhagen Pomeranus, Servant of the Gospel," *Lutheran Forum*

"*Finitum capax Infiniti*: Luther's Radical Incarnational Perspective," *Encounters with Luther: New Directions for Critical Studies*. Louisville: Westminster John Knox (to be published in 2016).

Theology of the Cross

Kurt K. Hendel

Introduction

The theology of the cross is a fascinating and multifaceted theme in Luther's thought. Indeed, it could easily be argued that it constitutes the very heart of the Reformer's theology and informs all of his theological constructs. It also illustrates Luther's tendency to think dialectically, i.e., to conceptualize reality in seemingly contradictory or paradoxical but in fact complementary terms.

While the diverse themes which constitute the theology of the cross are addressed repeatedly and widely in Luther's writings, the Heidelberg Theses are generally considered to be his most focused articulation of the theology of the cross; they will serve as the primary source for this discussion. The publication and dissemination of Luther's 95 Theses in 1517 very quickly brought him to the attention of the theological, ecclesiastical, and political worlds. Both eager support for and bitter criticism of Luther's message were voiced. The opponents of Luther, especially within the Dominican order, recognized the implications of his position for the theology, piety, and fiscal resources of the church, and they encouraged Pope Leo X to deal with the audacious monk from Wittenberg. The pope decided that it would be best to examine Luther and to discipline him, if necessary, through his own monastic order. Luther was therefore commanded to appear before the General Chapter of the Augustinian Hermits in Germany which met in Heidelberg in the spring of 1518. Johannes von Staupitz, Luther's own monastic superior and spiritual advisor as well as the vicar of the Augustinian Hermits in Germany, asked Luther to prepare theses which would be debated in Heidelberg. He encouraged Luther to avoid volatile issues, however, and to focus on the themes of sin, free will, and grace. Staupitz may have sought to avoid controversy, but these themes were in fact essential topics for Luther's emerging evangelical theology and his difficulties with the theology and practices of his contemporary church. Luther prepared the theses and traveled to Heidelberg. He did not debate the theses, however, but presided over the debate, held on April 26, 1518, while Leonhard Beier, a fellow Augustinian from Wittenberg, defended the theses. The content of the theses as well as Luther's comments greatly impressed some of the younger Augustinians assembled in Heidelberg, while the older brothers generally opposed Luther. No definitive decision regarding Luther and his theology was made in Heidelberg, but the theses were and have remained a relatively concise but extremely significant articulation of Luther's evangelical theology, especially of his theology of the cross.[1]

Scriptural sources

Martin Luther was a biblical theologian who attempted to explicate the Scriptures in his theological writings. The specific scriptural passages which particularly informed his theology of the cross are Romans 1:19-25, 1 Corinthians 1:18-31, and Exodus 33: 18-23. The formative impact of these passages will become apparent in the course of this discussion.

Theology of the Cross: Central Themes

1. The theology of the cross is foremost a theology of justification.

Luther's chief purpose in pointing to the cross and its meaning is to proclaim the gospel by articulating his doctrine of justification. He does so particularly by contrasting the theologian of glory and the theologian of the cross, by distinguishing between the alien and the proper work of God, and by presenting his law/gospel dialectic.

Luther offers a concise description of the theologian of glory and the theologian of the cross in Thesis 21 : "A theologian of glory calls evil good and good evil. A theologian of the cross calls the thing what it actually is."[2] What is it that a theologian of glory calls good? It is works, of course, particularly works done to earn merit so that one can bargain with God; works done to contribute to one's salvation, thereby usurping God's role as the sole Savior. The Reformer clarifies this point in his challenging explanation of Thesis 21:

> [The theologian of glory] prefers works to suffering, glory to the cross, strength to weakness, wisdom to folly, and, in general, good to evil. These are the people whom the apostle calls "enemies of the cross of Christ" [Phil. 3:18], for they hate the cross and suffering and love works and the glory of works. Thus they call the good of the cross evil and the evil of a deed good.[3]

The church of Luther's day maintained that humans retain their free will, in spite of the fall and of original sin, and that they can therefore do works pleasing to God. Luther responded in Thesis 13: "Free will, after the fall, exists in name only, and as long as it does what it is able to do, it commits a mortal sin."[4] The Nominalist theologians, by whom Luther was trained at the University of Erfurt, argued that even fallen human beings retained a spark of divinity and that they were expected to do what they could (*faceré quod in se est*). Only then would they receive the gifts of grace. Luther denied this inherent ability and asserted that the natural human being can only sin. "The person who believes that he can obtain grace by doing what is in him adds sin to sin so that he becomes doubly guilty."[5] The works which this person does are sinful because she is a sinner and because the trust she places in her works is sinful. Thus her sin and her guilt are compounded. While the theologian of glory preaches works and calls them good, such works are not good, no matter how positive their practical effects might be. Rather, they are evil, argues Luther, because they do not let God be God and because they lead people to trust in their own righteousness.

While the theologian of glory "calls evil good and good evil," the theologian of the cross "calls the thing what it actually is."[6] Thus, the theologian of the cross calls works evil, not because they might not be beneficial to another, but because they are done by sinful human beings and because they cannot accomplish what the theologian of glory expects of them. They cannot make a person righteous, merit grace, or earn salvation. Through them the theologian of glory seeks to usurp God's place and role. What, then, does the theologian of the cross call good? Precisely that which the theologian of glory calls evil, namely, humiliation, suffering, dying, the cross. They are called good because it is through them that God saves and that humans are saved. They are good because they are Christ's ways and therefore God's ways. Luther obviously remembers 1 Corinthians 1.

In addition to contrasting the theologian of glory and the theologian of the cross, Luther also points to God's alien and proper work. The point he seeks to make is that God alone saves and God alone justifies, not human beings through their good works. God does so in a dialectical fashion by means of God's dialectical Word—law and gospel. The alien work of God is God's judging and condemning, which God does through the law. Luther explains in his comments on Thesis 4:

> . . . the Lord humbles and frightens us by means of the law and the sight of our sins so that we seem in the eyes of men, as in our own, as nothing, foolish, and wicked, for we are in truth that. . . . And that it is which Isaiah 28 [:21] calls the alien work of God. . . .[7]

The radical effects of the law are clarified even more strikingly in Thesis 23: "The law brings the wrath of God, kills, reviles, accuses, judges, and condemns everything that is not in Christ [Romans 4:15]."[8]

God does God's alien work by means of the law in order to prepare us for God's proper work. Thus both God's alien and God's proper work are done for the same gracious purpose, namely, to save. Luther stresses this point in his explanation of Thesis 4: "[God] humbles us thoroughly, making us despair, so that he may exalt us in his mercy, giving us hope. . . ."[9] Of course, God exalts us through the precious good news of the gospel which proclaims Christ and his redemptive acts on our behalf. Through the gospel God rescues us from our despair, our desire to save ourselves, our state of rebellion, and shows us God's mercy, heals our brokenness, forgives our sins, makes us righteous, and transforms us from enemies of God into God's faithful people.

Luther's theology of the cross is, therefore, a theology of justification. That theology is a radical one because the Reformer considers it to be nothing less than a faithful proclamation of the gospel which he learned from St. Paul. St. Paul preached Christ crucified, "a stumbling block to Jews and folly to Gentiles" but "the power of God and the wisdom of God" to God's people (1 Corinthians 1:23-24). Luther sought to echo St. Paul's message. The gospel about the crucified Christ, about suffering, and about the cross remains a stumbling block and folly to theologians of glory, but it is radical good news to all theologians of the cross. Only theologians of the cross proclaim that gospel because they call the thing what it really is. Thus they call suffering, humiliation, death, and the resurrection good because these are God's ways through which God accomplishes humanity's salvation. At the same time, theologians of the cross call all human efforts to save themselves or at least to contribute to their salvation evil because they are human beings' attempts to reject God's ways, to usurp God's place, and to be their own redeemers. Luther's theology challenges theologians of every age to be theologians of the cross, theologians of justification by grace through faith for the sake of Christ apart from the works of the law—in short, theologians of the gospel.

2. The theology of the cross is a theology of revelation.

Luther's dialectical way of thinking is also operative in his doctrine of God, specifically as he explores God's self-revelation. The Reformer asserts that God is both hidden and revealed. He explores this notion particularly in the "Heidelberg Theses" and in "Bondage of the Will,"[10] his challenging response to the respected humanist scholar Desiderius Erasmus. Luther's doctrine of revelation is informed especially by Exodus 33:18-23 and by Romans 1:19-25.

a. *God hidden* (*deus absconditus*). Not only does Luther propose the dialectic of God hidden and revealed, but he also explains the hiddenness of God in two ways. In "Bondage of the Will" he asserts that there is much about God that remains hidden, for God has not even revealed it in God's Word.[11] Specifically, God's majesty and glory and God's inscrutable will are hidden beyond revelation. Human beings, even believers, dare not seek to explore the mystery of God's majesty because they need not and because God wills that they do not, for God's sake and for their sake. Rather, humans must be satisfied with and focus on how God chooses to be revealed. That revelation is sufficient because it is saving revelation. The story of the encounter of Moses and God recorded in Exodus 33 clearly impacts Luther's thinking. Moses, having been chosen as leader of the people and God's spokesperson, asks to see God's glory—to look into God's face. However, God refuses and indicates that Moses could not bear to see God's glory. God therefore covers Moses' face and passes by him. Only then is Moses allowed to see God, but only the back of God. God is thus gracious to Moses by allowing him to experience a theophany and yet saving him from harm. At the same time, God makes it clear that certain aspects of God's being and will, specifically, God's majesty, must and will remain hidden.

b. *God revealed* (*deus revelatus*). In the "Heidelberg Theses," Luther also speaks about the hidden and revealed God. However, here Luther stresses that even when God is revealed it is in hiddenness. Luther argues that theologians of the cross are not to focus on the invisible things of God revealed through God's mighty works of creation, those invisible things such as God's ". . . virtue, godliness, wisdom, justice, goodness, and so forth. The recognition of all these things does not make one worthy or wise."[12] The reason true theologians should not seek the invisible things of God revealed through God's mighty works of creation is explained by Paul in Romans 1. It is because humans have misinterpreted these natural revelations, have not honored God, have become fools while claiming to be wise, and have "exchanged the glory of the immortal God for images resembling mortal men or birds or animals or reptiles." Thus God gave them up to their sins "because they exchanged the truth about God for a lie and worshiped and served the creature rather than the Creator" (Romans 1: 21-25). St. Paul maintains, and Luther agrees, that although God is revealed in the wonders of creation, human beings have misinterpreted that revelation and have become idolaters, making God into their own image rather than recognizing God for who God is and confessing God to be God. For this reason, says Luther, God has chosen to reveal God's essence in a radically different and surprising way, in visible things, namely, in weakness, in folly, in human nature, in the incarnation and on the cross. The echoes of 1 Corinthians 1 are apparent in Luther's affirmations. The Reformer explains in his commentary on Thesis 20:

> Because men misused the knowledge of God through works, God wished again to be recognized in suffering, and to condemn wisdom concerning invisible things by means of wisdom concerning visible things, so that those who did not honor God as manifested in his works should honor him as he is hidden in his suffering. As he says in 1 Corinthians 1[:21], "For since, in the wisdom of God, the world did not know God through wisdom, it pleased God through the folly of what we preach to save those who believe." Now it is not sufficient for anyone, and it does him no good to recognize God in his glory and majesty, unless he recognizes him in the humility and shame of the cross.[13]

It is crucial to recognize Luther's emphases. God is revealed and wishes to be recognized in the suffering, humility, and shame of the cross. However, God is hidden in suffering. Hence God is revealed in hiddenness, and only this revelation is sufficient and redemptive. The theologian of glory seeks to know the invisible things of God, namely, God's glory and majesty, God's wisdom and justice, through the wisdom of natural revelation. However, such a theologian will never know God. The theologian of the cross focuses on the incarnate Christ suffering the shame and humiliation of the cross and in that hidden revelation recognizes God and God's will for humanity.

What kind of God is revealed in the hiddenness of the cross? In Christ theologians of the cross see a God whose divine majesty is clothed in human flesh, who exercises power in weakness, whose glory is shame and humiliation, who brings life by means of death, whose suffering leads to resurrection. It is no wonder that Luther maintains that God is hidden in God's ultimate self-revelation. Who is able to recognize God in the crucified Christ? And yet it is only in the Christ that God wishes to be revealed. It is only through the Christ that God can be known. Luther supports this assertion by recalling Philip's request to Jesus in John 14:8-9: "Lord, show us the Father, and we shall be satisfied." Jesus response was: "Have I been with you so long, and yet you do not know me, Philip? He who has seen me has seen the Father. . . ." Luther concludes, therefore: "For this reason true theology and recognition of God are in the crucified Christ. . . ."[14] The theology of the cross is a theology of revelation.

3. The theology of the cross is a theology of faith.

The theology of the cross is a theology of faith particularly for two reasons. The first has just been proposed and the second was explored in the first major section of this discussion. The theology of the cross is a theology of faith, first of all, because faith is necessary in order to see and recognize God in God's hidden revelation. Humans are able to recognize God in the incarnation, in suffering, in humility, in shame, in Christ on the cross only when they look with the eyes of faith. It is only through faith that they are able to see God's love and mercy, God's gracious will, and God's wondrous saving acts in Christ. Only faith enables them to recognize that what appears to be folly to humans is actually God's wondrous wisdom, that what is a stumbling block is actually God's message of life and freedom, that the One who appears to be an unfortunate victim is the victorious and living God. The theology of the cross is a theology of faith because it is revelatory.

Secondly, the theology of the cross is a theology of faith because it is a theology of justification and of the gospel. The theology of the cross rejects human works as salvific and confesses that God alone can and does redeem humanity and the whole creation. It is only faith which enables humans to affirm that this is so, to trust God's promises, to rely only on God for their life and salvation, to let God be God and to give God all honor and glory. It is only through faith that people are united with Christ and receive all the blessings he has won for them. That faith is created and nurtured by the Holy Spirit through the message of salvation which is the gospel and which is proclaimed by the theologian of the cross. Luther, who is such a theologian, asserts in Thesis 25: "He is not righteous who does much, but he who, without work, believes much in Christ."[15] Furthermore, in his explanation of Thesis 26 he maintains: "For through faith Christ is in us, indeed, one with us. Christ is just and has fulfilled all the commands of God, wherefore we also fulfill everything through him since he was made ours through faith."[16] The theology of the cross is a theology of faith because it is only through faith that human beings recognize God in the Christ, and it is only through faith that they are justified.

4. The theology of the cross is a theology of suffering.

It is this aspect of Luther's theology of the cross which has received particular attention in contemporary theological scholarship. Suffering is surely a crucial feature of Luther's theology of the cross, and it has both theocentric and anthropocentric, both divine and human, dimensions. Luther emphasizes in his theology of the cross that God suffers, no matter how scandalous or foolish that may seem. Of course, it was St. Paul who so powerfully impressed on Luther that God's saving acts required humility, emptying, shameful treatment, weakness, loneliness, physical and emotional suffering, and even death before resurrection and victory were possible. It was God in Christ who chose to suffer this way so that the power and punishment of sin might be overcome and the divine–human relationship might be restored. Suffering is, therefore, redemptive, and the theology of the cross is a theology of suffering because it proclaims God as the suffering Redeemer.

It is also a theology of suffering because it asserts that suffering is a reality, indeed, a necessity in the life of the believer. That should not be a surprise. If suffering is Christ's way it is also the Christian's way. There are a number of things that should be said about Luther's understanding of suffering.

a. *Luther was not a masochist.* He did not seek physical or spiritual suffering. He was, however, a person of profound faith who experienced a good deal of suffering—physical, emotional, and spiritual. *Anfechtungen,* spiritual struggles, were a persistent part of his life, and he expected that they would be of every Christian's life.

b. *Suffering is God's will, but it is not an indication of God's anger or rejection.* Instead, it is a sign of God's love and acceptance.

c. *God does not simply allow suffering and then watch from a distance.* Rather, God always stands with the one who suffers. Even Christ experienced forsakenness on the cross. The sense of being alone and forsaken while suffering is quite natural. However, God did not forsake Christ and does not forsake the believer. God knows what it means to suffer and suffers with God's people. God hangs on their crosses with them.

d. *Suffering is the lot of the individual but also of the whole community of faith.* Luther emphasized, therefore, that the cross is one of the marks of the church.[17]

e. *Suffering is redemptive.* This is not to say that their suffering redeems human beings and that they are saved through and because of their suffering. Rather, it is redemptive in this sense: Christians will suffer when they faithfully follow Christ and faithfully proclaim the gospel in word and in loving action.[18] That proclamation through word and deed will be used by the Holy Spirit to create and nurture faith in others and thereby to bring life and salvation. Suffering is redemptive also in a very practical sense. Luther maintains that people are able to hear the good and freeing news of the gospel only when they cease to be theologians of glory, become aware of their sinfulness and helplessness, and recognize and admit that they cannot be their own saviors. Theologically speaking, that happens when God confronts them with the law. Practically and experientially, it may well happen through suffering, suggests Luther, for suffering, perhaps as nothing else, makes people aware of their limitations, their weakness, their mortality, their dependence, their finiteness, their humanity.

Only then are they ready to hear and to recognize God's radical good news. Luther clarifies this point in his explanation of Thesis 24:

> . . . he who has not been brought low, reduced to nothing
> through the cross and suffering, takes credit for works and

wisdom and does not give credit to God. He thus misuses and defiles the gifts of God. He, however, who has been emptied [Cf. Phil 2:7] through suffering no longer does works but knows that God works and does all things in him. For this reason, whether man does works or not, it is all the same to him. He neither boasts if he does good works, nor is he disturbed if God does not do good works through him. He knows that it is sufficient if he suffers and is brought low by the cross in order to be annihilated all the more. It is this that Christ says in John 3[:7], "You must be born anew." To be born anew, one must consequently first die and then be raised up with the Son of Man.[19]

f. *As these words of Luther indicate, suffering is never the final experience of believers.* Resurrection, wholeness, and life are their final destiny, for if they suffer because they are people of faith who follow the way of Christ then they will also share in Christ's marvelous victory. The theology of the cross is a theology of suffering because it is a theology of life and salvation.

5. *The theology of the cross is a theology for the Christian life.*

The reasons for this assertion are diverse and may be summarized in the following way. The theology of the cross brings life because it is, in its essence, a proclamation of the gospel. It brings freedom, for it emancipates humans from their self-reliance and their self-preoccupation. It frees them from their efforts to earn salvation and to bargain with God. Only then are they able to do works which are truly good, that is, pleasing to God. These are the works of love inspired by faith and done to the glory of God and in the service of the neighbor. The theology of the cross lets God be God. Human beings do not have to rely on their own speculations about God and God's will for them, for the theology of the cross points them to Christ who is their Redeemer, who grants them his gifts freely and graciously, and who is God's ultimate self-revelation. When people are theologians of the cross they do not usurp God's place and do not make God into their own image. Rather, they recognize God's will and trust God's promises in and through the Christ. The theology of the cross provides perspective on the meaning and significance of suffering. It calls believers to a life of humility, of service, and of love, and it clarifies who people of faith are and whose they are.

Conclusion

The theology of the cross is not simply the central theme in the thought of a fascinating historical figure and a creative theologian of the church. It points to the very heart of the scriptural message and proclaims Christ crucified. This Christ is a stumbling block and folly to the theologian of glory, but to the theologian of the cross he is the living and incarnate God who brings life and salvation. Luther was a theologian of the cross because he had experienced the power of the gospel in his own life and because he firmly believed that the gospel was God's ultimate gracious word to humanity.

Whatever else it is and does, a theology for the twenty-first century must be realistic about the human condition, clarify the divine–human relationship, bring freedom, and be life-giving and life-sustaining. In short, it must be radical good news. If it is, then it will not be simply a theology for a specific historical moment. Rather, it will transcend and transform any particular time or place or human experience, and it will bring meaning, comfort, and hope. The theology of the cross is such a theology.

Endnotes

1 The "Heidelberg Theses" may be read in translation in Vol. 31 of Luther's Works, hereafter referred to as LW 31. In addition to the "Heidelberg Theses," Luther's lectures on Genesis and on the Psalms are further sources of his theology of the cross. The classical discussion of Luther's theology of the cross is Walther von Loewenich, *Luther's Theology of the Cross*, trans. Herbert J. A. Bouman (Minneapolis: Augsburg Publishing House, 1976). Other important studies are Alister E. McGrath, *Luther's Theology of the Cross: Martin Luther's Theological Breakthrough* (Oxford: B. Blackwell, 1985) and Hubertus Blaumeiser, *Martin Luthers Kreuzestheologie: Schlüssel zu seiner Deutung von Mensch und Wirklichkeit* (Paderborn: Bonifatius, 1995).

2 LW31:40.

3 LW 31:53.

4 LW 31:40.

5 Thesis 16, LW 31:40.

6 Thesis 21, LW 31:40.

7 LW 31:44.

8 LW 31:41.

9 LW 31:44.

10 This lengthy treatise, one of Luther's most significant and challenging writings, constitutes volume 33 of Luther's Works.

11 LW 33:140.

12 Commentary on Thesis 19, LW 31:52.

13 LW 31:52-53.

14 LW 31:53.

15 LW 31:41.

16 LW 31:56.

17 "On the Councils and the Church," LW 41:164-5.

18 LW 41:165.

19 LW 31:55.

Contributors

DEAN M. APEL has served as a student secretary for Sweden's Evangelical Student and High School Movement, as Academic Dean and Instructor in New Testament at Matongo Lutheran Theological College in Western Kenya, and as pastor of congregations in Kansas. His major academic interests include the New Testament, Martin Luther's theology, and African anthropology and religion. In addition to publishing several articles, he is the translator from Swedish of Ingemar Öberg's magisteral work *Luther and World Mission*. He currently works with unaccompanied refugee minors in northern Sweden and with EFS, a mission and revival movement within the Church of Sweden. His wife, Anki, and their four children are considering a move back to East Africa to continue their work in theological education.

MARK P. BANGERT is the John H. Tietjen Emeritus Professor of Pastoral Theology: Worship and Music at LSTC where he served as Dean of the chapel as well as teaching courses in worship, preaching, and church music. Bangert has tuned his knowledge of liturgical studies to include issues of culture and worship as well as the meaning of music. He served on the drafting committees for the *Lutheran Book of Worship*, chaired the task force that produced the 1982 *Occasional Services* book, and served as a consultant for *Evangelical Lutheran Worship*.

LU BETTISCH currently serves as pastor of Peace Lutheran Church in Morris, Illinois. She graduated in 2010 with a Master of Divinity from the Lutheran School of Theology at Chicago and was ordained on May 1, 2011. Prior to seminary, Lu served for seventeen years as a church musician in various churches in the suburbs of Chicago and has a bachelor's degree in vocal music from Eastern Illinois University. She currently lives in Channahon with her two cats. In her spare time Lu is an avid NASCAR fan, likes to read, and exhibits her purebred Maine Coon cats in shows.

DAVID D. DANIELS III is Henry Winters Luce Professor of World Christianity and Missions at McCormick Theological Seminary where he joined the faculty in 1987. David earned a Ph.D. degree from Union Theological Seminary in New York City. The author of over fifty scholarly book chapters, academic journal articles, and general essays, he has published on topics related to the history of African American Christianity, Global Pentecostalism, and World Christianity. David has delivered public lectures at over twenty colleges and seminaries in the United States and other countries along with presenting academic papers at conferences in over ten countries. He has served as a president of the Society for Pentecostal Studies and co-chair of the Reformed–Pentecostal International Dialogue. A bishop in the Church of God in Christ, he chairs the denomination's Board of Education.

RUBEN DOMINGUEZ graduated from Augsburg Lutheran Seminary in Mexico City. While preparing church workers in the Chicago area, he enrolled at LSTC from where he received the Th.M. degree in Church History. He currently is pastor at El Buen Pastor Lutheran Church in McAllen, Texas.

JOBEY HENDEL was born in Fort Wayne, Indiana, to Helen and Travis Disler, grew up there, and continued her education at a local school of nursing. She met Kurt at a Christmas party at Concordia Senior College. Following graduation from nursing school, she and Kurt married. She worked as a nurse in a variety of locations and areas from delivering babies to caring for the elderly. She enjoys spending time with her family and friends, working with children, attending adult education classes and church activities, traveling both in this country and abroad, and spending more time with Kurt.

ELIZABETH L. HILLER currently serves as associate pastor at Dilworth Lutheran Church, Dilworth, Minnesota. She has served also churches in Davenport, Iowa and Chicago, Illinois. She received a B.A. from Concordia College, Moorhead, Minnesota, a M.Div. from Yale Divinity School, New Haven, Connecticut, and completed her Lutheran ordination requirements through Luther Seminary, St. Paul, Minnesota. Elizabeth is married to Timothy Hiller, and shares life and faith with her children, who were baptized into God's family by Kurt K. Hendel.

TIMOTHY HILLER is a Ph.D. candidate in theology at the University of Chicago. His dissertation focuses on the role of creation, subjectivity, and ethics in the thought of Martin Luther. He has taught courses at the Lutheran School of Theology at Chicago, the University of Chicago, St. Xavier's University, and Concordia College in Moorhead, Minnesota. He currently lives with his wife, Rev. Elizabeth Hiller, and children in Moorhead.

KEITH KILLINGER retired from ELCA parish ministry in the fall of 2015 after serving congregations in New England and Illinois. Part of the second Seminex graduating class (1975), a course in medieval church history with Kurt Hendel added an interest in church history to his existing fascination with the Old Testament. At a summer session at Lake Geneva a decade later, Dr. Hendel encouraged him to consider graduate study, which he began in 1987, receiving his Th.D. in 1992. He and his wife, Pam, currently live in Monmouth, Illinois.

RALPH W. KLEIN is Christ Seminary-Seminex Professor of the Old Testament emeritus at the Lutheran School of Theology at Chicago. He is the author of the two volume commentary on 1 and 2 Chronicles in the Hermeneia Series. Curator of the Rare Books Collection at LSTC (http://collections.lstc.edu/), he also manages a website called The Old Testament and the Ancient Near East (ot-studies.com). In his retirement he has become a docent at the Oriental Institute of the University of Chicago.

CARRIE L. LEWIS LA PLANTE serves as Pastor at Redeemer Lutheran Church in Indianola, Iowa, where her primary profile is children, youth, and family ministry. She is married to Scott, and they have two young daughters, Abigail and Madelyn. Carrie graduated in 2004 from the Lutheran School of Theology at Chicago with her Master of Divinity with a biblical emphasis and again in 2015 with her Doctor of Ministry in Preaching. Her D.Min. thesis is entitled "Preaching with the Whole Congregation: Inviting Children and Youth without Losing the Adults." Carrie serves on the Candidacy Committee of the Southeastern Iowa Synod, ELCA. Beyond the church, she serves on the board of directors of the Indianola Hope Foundation, as the president of the PTA at her daughters' elementary school, and as a Girl Scout troop leader. Her previous publications include "Narrative Insights into the Crucifixion of Jesus in Luke," in *Currents in Theology and Mission*, October 2005, and several preaching helps in both *Currents in Theology and Mission* and *Homily Service*.

KEN SAWYER is Associate Professor of Church History and Associate Dean at McCormick Theological Seminary. He has been part of the LSTC and McCormick community since 1980 when he joined the JKM Library staff. He welcomed members of the Seminex community when they first arrived at LSTC. He completed doctoral studies at the Divinity School of the University of Chicago under prominent Lutheran scholars Jerald C. Brauer and Martin E. Marty. In 2008 he joined Kurt Hendel in leading a travel seminar to Reformation sites in Germany, Switzerland, and France.

ROBERT L. SHANER, an ELCA pastor, has served in the Chicago area for over forty years in a variety of ministries. He has been an adjunct professor/lecturer at the University of Illinois, Chicago (UIC) as well as the Lutheran School of Theology at Chicago (LSTC). In addition, he has served as campus pastor at UIC, was president and chief executive officer at Augustana Hospital, vice-president at Lutheran General Hospital, pastor at Grace Lutheran in LaGrange, Illinois, did visitation ministry at Redeemer Lutheran, Hinsdale, and served in interim ministries at Our Saviour's Lutheran Church, Naperville, and at Grace Lutheran Church and School, River Forest. He is a graduate of LSTC, Trinity Seminary, and Duke University.

JAMES A. SCHERER is a LSTC professor emeritus. He received an M. Div. (1952) and a Ph.D. Degree (1968) from Union Theological Seminary in New York City. He served as a Teaching Fellow for the Yale–China Association in Changsha, Hunan (1946-49) and later as an ordained missionary for the Lutheran Church (ULCA) in Southern Japan (1952-56). He was called to become the first dean of the Lutheran School of Missions and served in that capacity (1957-1971) and as Professor of World Mission and Church History until his retirement in 1992.

MARK N. SWANSON is (since 2006) the Harold S. Vogelaar Professor of Christian-Muslim Studies and Interfaith Relations at the Lutheran School of Theology at Chicago; his teaching ranges from inter-religious studies to global Christian studies to Christian history and historiography—in which areas he had the privilege of working with Prof. Kurt Hendel. Before coming to LSTC, Swanson taught at Luther Seminary (St. Paul, Minnesota) and the Evangelical Theological Seminary in Cairo (Egypt). His publications are in the areas of medieval Egyptian church history, the history of Arabic Christian literature, and the history of Christian-Muslim relations. He is the author of *The Coptic Papacy in Islamic Egypt (641-1517)* (AUC Press, 2010), and was the Christian Arabic section editor for *Christian-Muslim Relations: A Bibliographical History*, vols. 1-5. (Brill, 2009-2013).

ROGER E. TIMM retired in 2011 after serving as pastor of Ascension Lutheran Church, Riverside, and St. James Lutheran Church, Naperville, both in Illinois. Timm served in campus ministry positions from 1973 to 1992 at Carthage College, Kenosha, Wisconsin; Muhlenberg College, Allentown, Pennsylvania; University Lutheran Chapel at UCLA; and Concordia College, Bronxville, New York. Timm's first pastorate was at St. John–Concordia Lutheran Church in the Bronx, New York, from 1970-1973. He received his M.Div. degree from Concordia Seminary and an M.A.

SUBJECT TO NONE, SERVANT OF ALL

in philosophy from Washington University, both in St. Louis, Missouri, in 1970. Timm received a Ph.D. in religious studies from Union Theological Seminary and Columbia University, New York, in 1975. Pastor Timm and his wife, Marilyn, have two adult daughters and two grandchildren.

PETER VETHANAYAGAMONY is Associate Professor of Modern Church History at the Lutheran School of Theology at Chicago. Before joining LSTC, he taught Church History at HBI & College, Chennai, India, for sixteen years, where he also served as Academic Dean. He grew up and received his early education in India. He received his Th.M and Ph.D "with distinction" from Lutheran School of Theology at Chicago. His research interest includes early Indian Lutheranism and immigrant non-Western churches in the West. His publications include *It Began in Madras: The Eighteenth-Century Lutheran-Anglican Ecumenical Ventures in Mission* and *Benjamin Schultze* (New Delhi: ISPCK, 2010) and *Mission after Christendom: Emergent Themes in Contemporary Mission,* compiled and coedited (Louisville, Kentucky: Westminster John Knox Press, 2010). Dr. Hendel is his doctor father.

ANDREW F. WEISNER is the campus pastor and dean of university ministry at Lenoir-Rhyne University in Hickory, North Carolina, where he has served since 1995. He studied patristics at LSTC and the Association of Chicago Theological Schools, and completed a dissertation on John Gerhard under the direction of Dr. Kurt Hendel.

VÍTOR WESTHELLE is professor of Systematic Theology at the Lutheran School of Theology at Chicago and the chair of Luther Research at Faculdades EST, São Leopoldo, Brazil. Born in Brazil and ordained in the Lutheran church, he is adept at playing different keys of the theological ivories. Known as a Luther scholar, Westhelle is an author with thirteen books and over 150 articles. His writings on Luther, liberation, creation, the apocalyptic, postcolonialism, and eschatology are widely acclaimed.

JONATHAN M. WILSON graduated from LSTC in 2015. He is under orders and in pastoral call in the Evangelical Covenant Church, a denomination with its roots in Swedish Pietism as it gave form and later brought schism to the Lutheran Church Augustana Synod. An American citizen by birth, he has also been a legal resident of both Canada and Germany. A husband and father of two, Jonathan commuted to LSTC from his home and pulpit in Elgin, Illinois, where he continues to serve. He enjoys the academic life of publication and adjunct teaching roles.